献給
毛沢东阁下
及
中华人民共和国人民

尼克松总統
及
美利坚共和国人民贈

For the story of the Mute Swans of Peace see pages 45–46 and 50.

☆ ☆ ☆ ☆ ☆ ☆

THE WAR OF IDEAS

☆ ☆ ☆ ☆ ☆ ☆

THE WAR

America's
International
Identity
Crisis

OF IDEAS

BY

George N. Gordon and Irving A. Falk

COMMUNICATION ARTS BOOKS

HASTINGS HOUSE, PUBLISHERS
New York 10016

*In memory of Bill Hodapp,
wise collaborator and kind friend.*

Library of Congress Cataloging in Publication Data

Gordon, George N   The war of ideas.
  (Communication arts books)
  Bibliography: p.
  1. United States—Relations (general) with foreign
countries.   2. Propaganda, American.
I. Falk, Irving A., joint author.   II. Title.
E744.5.G63   301.29'73   73-10337
ISBN 0-8038-8064-2

Published simultaneously in Canada by
Saunders of Toronto, Ltd., Don Mills, Ontario

Designed by Al Lichtenberg
Printed in the United States of America

CONTENTS

Yielding to the forces of change, Radio Liberty and Radio Free Europe have a rendezvous with their long-term suicide pacts. RFE and RL must also look into the past of their own respective operations and ameliorate the onus of the well-meant deceptions that they have perpetrated with the help of the American Congress and the Executive branches of government.

Tapping the sources of human greed and institutionalizing them as a motivating force for the good of mankind in the world arena of multi-national corporations, foreign aid, trade and tourism is not as eccentric a scheme as it may appear at first encounter in the *War of Ideas*. Discussion is given to the complementary roles of the United Nations and other supranational bodies in dealing openly with idealism in human affairs.

PART THREE

The Only Thing We Have To Fear Is the Future

Dramatizing honestly and fully the discovery of ourselves for the rest of the world in a bicentennial celebration provides an agenda for the *War of Ideas*. The need for formulating a viable philosophy of public life in which mass communications play not a cosmetic role but one integral to a recommended reconstructed foreign policy, is indicated. Unheeded, America may be heading for its demise, brought about by the implosion of its own arrogances.

Comprising a list of recommendations and *caveats* for future conduct and dealings with other nations based upon a restructuring and reordering of US policies, priorities and values to achieve more ideal social intercourse among nations.

Contents

ACKNOWLEDGEMENTS

The *Mute Swans of Peace* photograph on the endpapers is by Charles P. Mills & Sons, 7th and Rand Streets, Philadelphia, Pa.

Chinese translation of The *Mute Swans of Peace* inscription is by Dr. James Hsiung, Professor of Chinese and Politics, New York University. Note that the spacing of the characters is according to Chinese custom and courtesy.

PREFACE

MEMO TO: Russell F. Neale, Publisher of *Communication Arts Books*, Hastings House

FROM: The Undersigned

RE: THE WAR OF IDEAS

When we lunched last year at the Harvard Club, seated (symbolically in the correct place) beneath an oil painting of that illustrious Crimson man, John Fitzgerald Kennedy, you suggested that we might be interested in bringing our now obsolete book *The Idea Invaders*, published by your firm more than a decade ago, up to date. Concerned as it was with American international persuasion and propaganda, you felt that an up-to-date revision (or possible rewrite) of this moderately successful volume was a viable publishing proposal. Considering the death of our former collaborator, the two of us, you thought, were the men to do the job. This was a good idea then, just as it is a good idea now. Its only drawback was that it turned out to be absolutely impossible.

When the former book was written (during the winter of 1962), we were all living in quite a different country in a different world. The President under whose portrait we sat that noon hour at the Harvard Club had not yet met his appointment in Dallas, and Vietnam was just a remote Asian troublespot stewing in a legacy of former French ineptitude, brewing what we believed was a religious war and serving as a feeble bastion—about which we cared little—against Red China, or so we thought. In our international thinking, we were as naive as children. Our concerns at that time centered upon a noisy but non-productive propaganda battle between the United States and the USSR that we called "The Cold War." A colorful Russian oligarch named Nikita Khrushchev had recently threatened to "bury us." How excited we were over his rhetoric. His words turned out to be as meaningful as the aforementioned Kennedy's observation that his father once told him that all businessmen were "s.o.bs!" We had also just discovered the James Bond novels. None of us knew what Beatles were, and Richard Nixon was a washed-up politician—a dead issue. Great days, huh?

The old book remains a souvenir of that period, and trying either to rewrite it or bring it up to date, we discovered, was as futile an endeavor as reactivating an old Sen Sen factory. True, we are now living in a period of cutely packaged and merchandised nostalgia, but we are certain that this is not the sort of thing you had in mind when you asked us for an up-date of *The Idea Invaders*.

Not only are we today living in a world where the very *concept* of international communications has changed almost beyond recognition, we are—all three of us—more than a decade older and (we hope) wiser in our experience and understanding of the cross-cultural information and propaganda issues that filled up the lion's share of our luncheon conversation.

Therefore this new *book*. A new book meant a new approach, the tortuous re-thinking of old ideas, new research, new interviews (some of them with the same people we talked to eleven years ago; they have changed too) and, worst of all, rubbing our noses in our own past errors, enthusiasms and misjudgments, admitting, when necessary, that we were pretty naive kids and often dead wrong. None of this was particularly pleasant work—although we *had* been prescient enough to keep our files up to date in the years between and we believe that it has been worth both the trouble and the pain. Mostly, we hope that it stimulates you, our first reader, to further speculation concerning a major contemporary problem (or bundle of problems) that often gets lost in the shuffle along with many of our other troubles, and that it serves the same function for others.

As a publisher, *you* are naturally most deeply concerned with sales, classroom adoptions and other schemes that, one way or another, induce people to separate themselves from their wealth in order to buy your books. So are we, of course. But we were unable to write *The War of Ideas* so as to adhere to any "time-tested" commercial format except the one we chose, simply because the issues of international communications with which it deals are of such general importance that *every* socially and politically alert American—not just to "target audiences of book consumers" like professors and students, foreign policy experts, communications scholars and other specialists—should, at least, be aware of them.

We have therefore tried to cover as wide a range of topics relevant to our theme in as lively a manner as possible, and to invent and use forms of discourse for them that are neither stuffy nor dull. Hence, our occasional "fun and games," monologues, dialogues and short-take vignettes, starting with the *Introduction* ahead. Your suggestion that we include "Topics for Further Discussion" sections at the end of each Chapter, we have discarded offhand as redundant. *The War of Ideas*, in fact, contains *nothing but* "Topics for Further Discussion."

You may also be somewhat unhappy with our occasional moods of levity, sarcasm and gropings after humor that pop up in grim contents that most people do not find suitable for laughter. Well, all we can say to any such criticism is that, after a certain point in life, some matters simply become *so* serious that the only reaction a sane person can have to them (and preserve his sanity) is to laugh. So it goes for many of the life-or-death considerations we raise in *The War of Ideas*. Contrary to most accepted beliefs, we do not believe that men laugh *best* at trivia, but rather at the ironic spectacle of the noblest mammal treating his most vital concerns as if they did *not* in the end control his fate, but were themselves trivia. Come to think of it, maybe this is what *The War of Ideas* is all about, in the final summing up.

One other matter: We did not write *The War of Ideas* from armchairs. Many people helped us along the way in many ways. A list of them would include not only those in the worlds of communication, politics, government and academia who have shared their time and thoughts with us, but countless others, both in the United States and overseas, whose words and special insights run throughout this book. Many of them are also the people with whom we have both worked and lived during the decade or so between the publication of *The Idea Invaders* and this book. We hereby extend our thanks to *all* of them. We cannot list them specifically, first, for reasons of confidentiality and also because of problems regarding ascription that will be clear to our readers. Second, there are just far too many of them! In instances where prominent (and obscure) living sources have given us permission to use both their names and their words, this fact will be clear in the text. And we hope we have spelled their names correctly.

We would also like to make specific our gratitude to the fine ladies who helped us so dilligently in the preparation of the manuscript itself. Mary Brophy typed the entire first draft. Anna Friedman, Elizabeth Marks and Rita Turner prepared the document that has now passed from our hands into yours. And thank *you*, too, for your encouragement and faith, neither of which was, we hope, misplaced.

We suspect that many of the issues raised in *The War of Ideas* will rub our readers the wrong way and stir a bit of controversy here and there. We make no claims that it is an objective book, untainted by prejudice or favor. Such volumes on international communications are a dime a dozen, and worth the price. We have written what we believe, based upon (we hope) realistic observation and responsible conviction. We have also attempted, whenever possible, to put our cards on the table face up and to warn the reader of our biases and idiosyncracies. In a book of this size, we have certainly committed errors of fact. These are our responsibility entirely. Also errors, no doubt, in judgment. Again, the reader should know that we alone are culpable.

New York, N.Y.   George N. Gordon
July, 1973   Irving A. Falk

☆　☆　☆　☆　☆　☆

THE WAR OF IDEAS

☆　☆　☆　☆　☆　☆

INTRODUCTION

International Dialogue Without Actors

The people of Warsaw literally cannot wait for spring.

When, in March or April, a little hiatus breaks out of the apparent eternity of winter in the form of some prematurely warm weather, they plant forced hothouse tulips in many of the parks and squares that make Warsaw an urban walker's dream city.

Yellow tulips seemed slightly anachronistic to the American visitor making his way, in the winter of 1972, towards Warsaw's most hated building, the Culture Palace, through the small park that surrounds the Moscow-modern skyscraper. The Culture Palace had been "given" to the people of ravaged Warsaw by the USSR after World War II, while the city was on the brink of starvation and housing was a luxury compared to food. The immense building with its theatres, museums, lecture halls and offices was therefore, to the citizens of Warsaw, an ironic joke—unfortunately a Russian joke and, at the time it was being built (so the American was told), the punch line to an enmity sunk like a shaft into time and place and still immovable.

This luncheon took place (no coincidental fictional incident) in one of the half dozen restaurants in and around the Culture Palace, probably the best of them. Called the *Troika* and blessed by a Soviet mural of this vehicle, the food was not, to the American's palate, as tasty as good Polish food. But the Colonel (his host) defended his preference for it, because it was "different" (which is was) and because Russian vodka was the reigning libation (as well as Russian wine) for which the Colonel, during the vaguely cohesive travels of his life, had acquired a taste either fighting for or with the USSR during World War II.

3

The American was, to the Colonel, just an American who liked *blini*, sour cream, American cigarettes (which the Colonel abhored) and did not drink alcohol, a clear sign either of insanity or perversity. The Colonel, who had known many Americans and spoke their language (and the British version of it) with a mere trace of an accent, accepted their eccentricities with neither comment nor surprise.

This Colonel was not a Colonel out of Werfel; and the American was no Jacobowsky. The former was fully a man of the twentieth century, a born survivor of the hell that Europe produced in the past half century, whose smooth skin, long white hair and continental élan smacked more of Paris or London (where he had lived at one time) than of East Europe's seventeenth-century heritage of grandeur.

The Colonel made his way about rapidly and efficiently with a cane. Was one leg false? Possibly. He had obviously used a cane for a long time, tirelessly and without strain, as if a young incubus inhabited a well-appointed but aged body. He smoked much, he ate lovingly and he drank—as Poles are inclined to—like a thirsty fish, but—also like many Poles—rarely showed in public overt signs of inebriation.

The American enjoyed the Colonel—enjoyed the inconsistent mystery of the man's past, his slight suspicion that the old man might be an agent of either his own country or of the USSR or, as often occurs, of both at once. And the auras of excitement, wisdom, compassion and haughty but sly amusement that survivors—*real* survivors at the life-and-death level—often cultivate interested him. Such a life-style, the American was convinced, included an entire vocabulary of vanity by which survivors signalled their functional superiority to nonsurvivors like himself. The main problem with such people, the American knew, grew out of meetings that included multiple survivors, and he had reaffirmed this wrinkle in Warsaw 1972, a city of survivors and their children.

This luncheon, however, was to be safe, since the Colonel and he sat at a table for two and were unlikely to be interrupted by anyone, much less a survivor, and possibly all too infrequently by a passing waiter, most of whom had cultivated Russian service habits (painfully slow) at the expense of Polish ones (efficiently fast).

The conversation took place mostly in English, a bit in French and, when necessary, in the American's weak Polish. The Colonel ordered the meal in Russian. The *Troika* was cavernous—as high in illusion, the American thought, as the Radio City Music Hall. Voices did not travel, and conversations were mercifully lost at their points of origin. This one has been remembered, not recorded or overheard:

COLONEL: And what is so strange about a love of flowers?
AMERICAN: Nothing. But why does everybody in Poland give everybody else flowers?
COLONEL: In Poland? No, not everywhere. Supplies vary. In Warsaw, almost yes. Would you be offended if I gave you a bouquet of flowers?
AMERICAN: Not particularly. In America, though, we give flowers on special occasions.
COLONEL: (Shrugs a Polish shrug) To live at all is a special occasion. Most Polish bouquets are small. We are not a rich nation. In America you give dozens of flowers at one time, no?
AMERICAN: Not always, but flowers are usually sold by the dozen.
COLONEL: Here the roses are often sold one at a time in cellophane. Less, but more frequently.
AMERICAN: Do you just give them—for no special reason?
COLONEL: There is always a reason of some sort. Do you need a birth, a death, a surgical operation, a wedding anniversary to give someone you like—or don't like—flowers?
AMERICAN: No. It's just that flowers seem to be more integrated here in Warsaw into people's lives than in any other city I've been in. In rural areas . . .

COLONEL: And how many cities of the world have you been in?

AMERICAN: Enough—East and West. And in the summer, too. The flowers I received here are hot-house flowers, grown in winter.

COLONEL: (Smiling) You received? I understand your problem. They were given you—*sent* perhaps—by a woman?

AMERICAN: Colonel, I am a married man with a wife in America and numerous children. I am also middle-aged, bald and not being paid by my present benefactors to get involved with women. Although I *have* noticed that the women of Warsaw . . .

COLONEL: Everybody notices that! Didn't your Rudolph Friml write in one of his operettas, in the chorus, that the women of Warsaw were the most beautiful in Europe?

AMERICAN: I wouldn't know.

COLONEL: I am sure he did. He was right, although he exaggerated. (Man to man) If you, like so many of your countrymen who come to Europe without their wives, are simply looking for sex, try Copenhagen—or Amsterdam or London. Stay out of Sweden; it is an imaginary country, and you would not like it. And I presume that you know about Paris, the erotic joke of the Western world.

AMERICAN: I know. I lived in Paris twenty some years ago. I met my wife there.

COLONEL: Sad—but fitting. A French girl who was happily tamed into American eccentricity and subsequently returned to Paris.

AMERICAN: An Australian—

COLONEL: Worse. Very sad.

AMERICAN: —who was tamed into nothing but an American citizen and returned nowhere.

COLONEL: Typically American. You are divorced, however, like most of your fellow countrymen.

AMERICAN: *Was* divorced. I married her again.

COLONEL: Not only are Americans sick, but are disturbed

in the way many non-Catholics today are sick. There is but one kind of slavery, and it is called misery. And only the benign liberal who thinks he is free can be deeply, truly miserable because, as Ortega said, "Wide is Castile." The man of independence—like you—thinks he can do anything and is therefore damned: a moral pervert. No, an *a*moral pervert. Do you understand my meaning?

AMERICAN: Yes. But I don't think it applies personally to me. It sounds bad. I *have* read the *Revolt of the Masses*, many times and for many years.

COLONEL: In Spanish?

AMERICAN: No, in English.

COLONEL: Neither did I. I read it mostly in German. It is not the same. Do you know Unamuno?

AMERICAN: I am re-reading *The Tragic Sense of Life*. I happen to have a copy in my suitcase at the hotel.

COLONEL: (Suspiciously) You *are* a Catholic or *were* a Catholic?

AMERICAN: Neither. I don't suppose—as a matter of fact —that, right now, I am much of anything, religiously speaking.

COLONEL: You *read* like a Catholic. Or do you just carry Unamuno with you when you take long trips on aircraft?

AMERICAN: Seriously, I don't give a damn what I do while flying. I survived a crash about twenty-five years ago, and I despise air travel. But, in fact, at this point, I don't care.

COLONEL: Even to be hijacked?

AMERICAN: Kismet.

COLONEL: How?

AMERICAN: Fate, I am a fatalist.

COLONEL: You are no such thing. In America, perhaps. Here you are living in a city of fatalists in a country of fatalists in a restaurant of fatalists, and you cannot pose.

AMERICAN: How do you know what I have lived through? The war, for instance—

COLONEL: War! To survive a war is nothing. To survive a thousand wars is nothing. Believe me, I know.

AMERICAN: I was born a Jew. I know something about survival.

COLONEL: (A little taken aback) Of course! In America that is nothing. If your grandparents—correct?—had remained in Poland, it would have been a different matter. (Pause) Am I right? Have I bit somewhere near the nerve? My ethnic speculation is correct?

AMERICAN: Too correct. My grandparents *were* Polish, all four of them. As a child I heard terrible stories of the pogroms, mostly second-hand.

COLONEL: All of them probably true, unfortunately. But matters are not so simple.

AMERICAN: And, if they had not come to America, I suppose I would have in my youth been incinerated at Auschwitz after a therapeutic shower of death gas—.

COLONEL: Standing naked next to my wife's brother—her politically-minded Catholic brother. But here we are reading ancient history that did *not* happen—to you. It *did* to my wife's brother. If memory serves correctly, he did not like Jews to live with, but I doubt if he was as selective about the company in which he was murdered.

AMERICAN: Is Poland still an anti-Semitic nation?

COLONEL: How you simplify. She was never an anti-Semitic nation, in the genuine meaning of the term. How long did your many ancestors live here? Or don't you know?

AMERICAN: It happens I do. For about two hundred and fifty or three hundred years.

COLONEL: Ah! Now, I ask you a question: Will your grandfather's progeny remain in the United States *as Jews* for an equal length of time?

AMERICAN: As Jews? I doubt it. I think time may have already run out for them.

COLONEL: Your Australian kangaroo, she is Jewish?

AMERICAN: Raised as a Methodist. And my children have just been raised.

COLONEL: (Shudders) You not only simplify rhetorically; you simplify, in fact. And simplisms are rarely correct. (He laughs.)

AMERICAN: And you dodge my question.

COLONEL: How? What question?

AMERICAN: (A smile) Is Poland still anti-Semitic?

COLONEL: Absurd! No more than five or ten thousand Jews remain here. Most are dead—at *Nazi* hands, my friend—or have migrated to Israel. Half of those who remain are like you, modern Marranos who have lost the skull caps in the wind and melted their Menorahs into door-knockers. Visit your synagogue in this city. I have. It is discouraging, and not the fault of the government. One man hits another in Poznan, or a fool writes a play in verse in Crakow, or an aged poet gets the hiccups in Lodz, and the newspapers prattle about pogroms. *Our* newspapers and *your* newspapers. If there are anti-Semites in our midst, my American friend, they will soon be forced to hire five hundred indigent Jews to live in Poland so that they keep their antique faith alive.

AMERICAN: The fact remains that the 1968 anti-Zionist purges—

COLONEL: The fact remains that I can embarrass you more than you can embarrass me in an absurd mythological discussion of this sort.

AMERICAN: How?

COLONEL: I'll ask you about how Jews in America feel about Negroes. About American anti-Semitism. About a hundred things. And you will not answer. You will equivocate like a sociologist. (Pause) I see the blood has gone from your eye. Good. It shows a residue of sanity in your head.

AMERICAN: And what *are* the Poles?

COLONEL: You mean who do we love and who do we hate?

AMERICAN: If such things make you what you are, yes.

COLONEL: I am an old man who knows only what he sees. Don't ask a defeated people if they are defeated. It is not worthy of that residue of sanity and wastes time.

AMERICAN: Defeated? Now that is a surprise, or is it a manner of speaking? You yourself certainly don't seem defeated by anyone in any way. And neither do the people of Warsaw as they look to me. They smile more than the people of New York or Washington.

COLONEL: Possibly so. (With sarcasm) It has taken *us* a mere twenty-five years to imitate the facial expressions and gestures that the Germans and Japanese mastered but *five* years after the war. *The* war, do you hear me?

AMERICAN: It was *my* war too.

COLONEL: Because you put on a soldier suit and fired a gun? I doubt it. But I find no pleasure in embarrassing you on that matter either. So I shall answer your question, both as a fair inquiry after knowledge and because I feel that, despite your surface stupidity, you have redeeming qualities—that bit of sanity I mentioned, and perhaps a good heart. What I judge that you are entirely incompetent to do, however, is to tell the difference between reality and illusion, like most Americans I know. So you will probably misunderstand everything I say anyway.

AMERICAN: You aren't the first person who has told me that. But, in some measure, we all live on illusions, don't we?

COLONEL: (Slapping the table) Agreed! Then add this to your collection of myths: Poland and her people are defeated and frightened, yes. No more thoroughly defeated nation exists, and yet, paradoxically, we are in some ways thriving, as you noted. We are Communists; we are Catholics; we are Capitalists; we are a nation of psychotics and alcoholics. *But* we have fully earned both our paranoia and our superb vodka, this Russian nitroglycerine notwithstanding. We are deeply frightened. To the East, we are frightened of the USSR for reasons you must comprehend. But it is impossible for you to feel and empathize with them. You do not know enough *fear*. To the West, we are frightened to the point of insanity of Germany: fragmented, at least; unified, to the point of hysteria. But again you cannot understand. You do not know enough *hate*. The rest of Europe is now a fairy-tale land except England, in which we once had great faith. You know the Polish Air Force flew with the RAF?

AMERICAN: Yes.

COLONEL: But the rigid British social order always destroys in time the faith that other nations have in her, and the United States is no exception, is it? We Poles, perhaps, expected too much. You Americans did not. But why should you have expected anything from such recent allies in the face of their long history as your enemies?

AMERICAN: What did *you* expect in Poland?

COLONEL: I do not precisely know. That peacetime Britain would produce a Winston Churchill, I imagine. This is simply a mystery. Period. We are and have been a police state, as you know. But you are aware only of the superficial trappings of the game. It is deep enough now to have become a way of life, and it is bad business to speculate on promises that capitalist democracies held out to us a generation ago. In this respect—and this one only—we have been drawn against our instincts into the Russo-Byzantine mystique. In Warsaw, don't trust anyone. Every word of this conversation may find its way into an official document or police *dossier*. Don't trust me!

AMERICAN: I don't.

COLONEL: Good. You are learning. We have come grudgingly also to admire the real Asian East—the very part you Americans have, until recently, refused to admit even exists. Admire, but not trust. You have seen the oriental young people around the city university and night clubs?

AMERICAN: "Seen," yes. But my Mandarin is rusty and my Cantonese is pure San Francisco.

COLONEL: It wouldn't do you any good for communication beyond amenities, because to you, as an American, the very existence of the real Eastern world is questionable. And, by force of habit, you have nothing to say to it. These children are North Koreans, Vietcong, mainland Chinese, Laotians, Cambodians—all Communists titularly.

AMERICAN: They seemed like nice youngsters, the way American kids were a generation ago on college campuses.

COLONEL: You are merely identifying their present youthfulness and idealism with the death of your own ideals and the passing of youth. Another illusion.

AMERICAN: Possibly. I notice that they seem more mature and serious and respectful to their elders than American college youngsters.

COLONEL: Than the ones you teach.

AMERICAN: The ones I *try* to teach. Last night at the Budapest they graciously applauded a singer who looked like Sinatra and who sang *Strangers in the Night* in Rumanian.

COLONEL: This to you is good manners? To encourage a Rumanian Sinatra?

AMERICAN: No. But there was something about the way they danced with each other that reminded me of the Hotel Pennsylvania in New York in the late 'thirties. You are familiar with this ambience?

COLONEL: Thank heaven, no. I have told you I have never been to America and never want to go. Our Polish youngsters are *not* like this in your estimation—only the Orientals?

AMERICAN: I can't judge. At the universities and other schools I have visited, the students appeared to be much like today's Americans. They are looking *West*, not *East*, for their styles of thought and life, it seems to me.

COLONEL: (contemplatively) So they are. So they are. You respond well to the obvious, although they may merely have been trying to please you, expecially because their apparent suspicion of Communist politics, even as it is played by the new regime. (Pause)

AMERICAN: Why wouldn't you *want* to visit the United States if you could?

COLONEL: Your cigarettes, for one thing, are abominable. So is your coffee. What you are drinking is real Java, not South American *erzatz*. That is why you drink so much of it, especially, I notice, because you use it in place of alcohol. American whiskey is poison. And I am too old to be attacked on the streets of New York by thugs and predatory whores.

AMERICAN: That case wasn't typical. Prostitution in America is a side product of the narcotics trade and therefore dangerous. Our legitimate call-girls are every bit as wholesome as those of London, Copenhagen—or Warsaw.

COLONEL: I also said I was too old to experiment. And, anyway, the Poles, like the Americans, have always adulterated prostitution—and possibly sex itself—with other things.

AMERICAN: Such as?

COLONEL: Not narcotics, certainly, but politics, espionage, money, power and the other fascinating vices that are worse than narcotics. No, I shall stay in Poland and study America at a safe distance, taking my chances with the familiar.

AMERICAN: All Poles do not feel that way.

COLONEL: I am not all Poles. I am simply a relic of East Europe who should have been dead long ago. But I am too obstinate to die, because the devil does not want my company.

AMERICAN: How do you live?

COLONEL: Ha! Like most Poles of education and aristocracy—real or imagined—I get by. I am clever with languages and am therefore useful. Simply that.

AMERICAN: How many?

COLONEL: Fifteen, including Polish. This is not a difficult accomplishment, when you have spent many years in places where all you could do was to study languages.

AMERICAN: Prison?

COLONEL: (Shrugs) Sometimes. Prison camps. Army barracks. Retreats to the hills, the country, the farms. You would be surprised at how many places there are in East Europe where there is nothing to do but contemplate or study.

AMERICAN: Everywhere, not just East Europe.

COLONEL: Granted, but especially before technology finds its way into a culture. It is for this reason, largely, that our young people admire you.

AMERICAN: Admire me?

COLONEL: Admire Americans.

AMERICAN: (Sourly) How dull—and how typical. They admire our technology, our standard of living, our car-washes, color television and our credit cards. Is this admiration or envy? Does it, in fact, mean a damn thing? And is it any different from all the other young people, in other countries almost everywhere, who envy and admire quiet Americans and ugly Americans, simply because they are well-fed specimens and so sophisticated in technological matters that they take them for granted?

COLONEL: I appreciate your references to the British writer Greene and the American actor Brando. But what are car-washes?

AMERICAN: Different things in different places at different prices. Mostly, they are semi-automated belt-line laundry assemblies for automobiles.

COLONEL: Before or after they are purchased?

AMERICAN: After. In the United States, when you car gets dirty, instead of washing it yourself, you bring it to a car-wash, and it gets scrubbed by machine. But human intervention is required for vacuuming, drying and polishing it.

COLONEL: (Quiet for a moment, wishing the subject had

not been brought up) Yes, I imagine it is this sort of thing
that makes people envious of the United States. Your technology has uncovered facets of human nature that no one
before knew existed. But I think your trips to the moon
are clearer examples than car-washes, however. I understand *them*, I think.

AMERICAN: The Russians are great technologists, too.

COLONEL: But their technology is of little interest to the
Polish youngster. He has seen too much at second hand
and lived with too little of it. It is the American's concern
with technology effecting the inner-psyche of the individual that he or she admires. Your neatly contrived
comedies, for instance, both on cinema film and, I'd conjecture, matters like car-washes and the automobiles they
wash.

AMERICAN: I wish I could say the same for myself.

COLONEL: You are feeling guilty because you also find
much in America and its technology that is irreverent and
sometimes vulgar?

AMERICAN: (Sighs) Irreverence is the price of freedom. In
America we are still free. For better or worse. I cannot defend vulgarity on a national scale.

COLONEL: (Smiles) Are you talking about car-washes and
space travel now? Or is your reference Women's Liberation, Black Moslems, everywhere pornography, television
advertisements and the cultivation from birth, in homes
and schools, of bad taste and futile life styles? You see, I
read your magazines: *Playboy, Time, Harper's* and other
legitimate ones. And once someone managed to get me a
few issues of *The Free Press* and something called *Screw*.
The name Charles Manson is quite meaningful to me—
partly, I suppose, because of his oblique connection with a
former Pole. So are the names George Jackson and, of
course, Angela Davis, on the other side of the coin, so to
speak. Does the freedom of your news establishment to
unload your national guilt for a Vietnam war upon the

head of a dolt like Lieutenant Calley produce in you a discomfort and distrust of what you *call* "freedom," a term that I am not certain you either understand or appreciate?
AMERICAN: Let us simply say that we are free to cultivate *both* irreverence and ignorance in the United States. And, as I get older, I am increasingly disturbed by the methods we have evolved to eliminate the past, as Ortega predicted. And I don't think your particular examples of irreverence or freedom are—
COLONEL: They were merely symbolic, some of the symptoms of pathology that I have noticed in white, middle-class, college educated—but not necessarily intelligent—Americans who find their way to East Europe to visit or live. Yourself excluded, naturally, because you obviously have no intention of remaining here longer than your work assignment requires, which is too short for a real education into the life of Poland.
AMERICAN: (Not listening) America is in trouble. I believe that.
COLONEL: When was she *not* in trouble? And *who* is not in trouble? And is life without trouble worth living? Remember your Aquinas, if you ever knew him in the first place.
AMERICAN: Aristotle: good and evil. Avererroes. I studied with Jesuits. I know too much Aquinas.
COLONEL: Would you believe that it is what you call "trouble" that the young people of Warsaw mostly find *attractive* about you Americans; why, as you have noticed, they are so friendly to you and solicitous of your welfare? Can you understand that what to you is bitter truth is to them honey, because they have been raised as mere marginal survivors of a war, a defeated race and as dull receptacles of Marxist propaganda so crude that even the stupidest political scientist or Kremlinologist in your country would laugh at it. Do you choke on the truth that the corollary to the freedom to discover refinement is the freedom to be vulgar—Aquinas again—and that if you ever wish truly to

discover your own country, you will not accomplish it by going to your movies, watching your television or treating the vapid nonsense of your hippies seriously—or by taking your other idealogues of the left, like Reich and Marcuse, as any more seriously as Marxists than the brothers in *A Night at the Opera?*

AMERICAN: Where *do* I look then?

COLONEL: I fear you will *never* discover it, because you are living in its medium—like the carp who never feels wet in an old European fairy tale. Ask the young people of Warsaw. They will respect the integrity of your naiveté and envy your truthfulness. This is entirely because they are deeply attracted to the *idea* of America. Oh, of course, they are entranced with your technology. But they are aware that in the next generation the Japanese will prove to be far, far better technologists than you are now. Or, God forbid, the Germans. Or the Russians, although I doubt it. (He savors his fifth glass of vodka with a preliminary sip, like a wine taster.)

AMERICAN: Will you answer one intimate question?

COLONEL: Anything.

AMERICAN: Which is *really* better—Russian or Polish vodka?

COLONEL: (Lightly lubricated) I shall tell you a secret. They are nearly the same: both are neutral spirits distilled from potatoes. Worse than this, your American Smirnoff is also much the same, although it is made from grain, not potatoes. Any differences result from filtration methods, of little importance either to ethyl alcohol or its taste. Weak and strong; these are the only differences in vodka. Otherwise, it is also all a matter of illusion.

AMERICAN: I thought so.

COLONEL: You see, *we* also feed and care for our illusions in this world of supposed dialectical materialism. And they are not all throwbacks to antique empires of church and state; nor are they simply matters of ideology. What a pity you do not drink! How do you maintain *your* illusions without alcohol?

AMERICAN: I travel, read the newspapers, teach children and read and write books.

COLONEL: Ah! I understand. Yes, then there is no valid reason for you to drink hard fluids. You also make love?

AMERICAN: Whenever possible—and with Puritan discretion. We have already discussed the issue. I have nothing to add.

COLONEL: Nevertheless, your life must be quite interesting. Like most of your countrymen you are therefore *happy* to be alive?

AMERICAN: I don't think I understand.

COLONEL: A semantic problem: "Happy" rather than "thankful?"

AMERICAN: A bit of both, I imagine. I *have* thought of suicide from time to time.

COLONEL: Who has not? (He drinks some of the vodka) And what do you prize most in life—beyond the mundane, domestic things?

AMERICAN: (Hesitating a moment) In my travels, I meet the damndest people!

COLONEL: (Finishing the vodka) Agreed, brother American; agreed! You *are* a Pole! You did not fool me for an instant!

Curtain

PART ONE

Yesterday Has Been Cancelled
Due to Circumstances
Beyond Our Anticipation

1

The Battle of the Birds

To put it in the simplest terms, in the age of lethal technology it takes much less time to kill a man than to change his mind, or your own.

RICHARD BARNET [1] *

Bird Brains in the Nest

Neither Poles nor Americans nor Army Colonels nor traveling gomerals of any nationality cosset memories or fears of warfare. They sit at little luncheon tables, weep for their dead and fear for their futures.

We, the present writers, have yet to meet a sane, rational man or woman who, on philosophical grounds, is willing to defend legalized murder as a viable instrument for nations—or any coalition people—to employ in order to settle their disputes. Inside madhouses, of course, such people exist, but even

* Footnotes are collected at the end of each chapter throughout this book.

their fellow patients usually keep a secure distance from them.

Certain political realists (and we shall meet some in the coming pages) solemnly accept warfare as inevitable and defend it on collective quasi-biological and ethnological grounds. Their sunlit day has probably passed as interesting, non-conformist freak sages, not so much because of the recent invention of so-called "doomsday" weapons but, as we shall see, of the now all-pervasive nature of common and not-so-common cultural artifacts that most people do not regard as weapons and do not relate to warfare.

In time of war, and if we are competent at rationalization, most of us will, however, defend as expedient necessity warfare, collective murder and genocide, particularly when our positions depend upon mysticism, personal spiritual matters and/or religion. The average American veteran, therefore, cannot be forced to regret his complicity in World War II. In his eyes, the carnage was a legitimate reaction to the murder of millions of innocent civilians in Nazi concentration camps, the clever Japanese attack on Pearl Harbor (on a Sunday) and such symbols of diabolism. So we pass over similar deviltry in our own collective and individual behavior—acts like the destruction of Cologne, the bombing of Nagasaki or beating our wives and children—as the work of angels (us) for super-political or transcendent causes.

Neither atom bombs nor anti-war movements nor the dissents of Quakers have modified this rationalizing tendency in world-wide private and public opinion, and, when desirable, behavior. Recently—quite recently—Americans of many faiths cheered the wholesale murder of Moslems in the Near East for good (and largely mystical) personal reasons as just retribution for these heathens' spiritual *hubris*. A fine motion picture, that, we have been told, was intended to characterize World War II General Patton as a psychopathic, eccentric murderer enmeshed in the uber-insanity of mechanized warfare, metamorphosed on the screen in a panegyric to a misunderstood but heroic American. And many of us fairly believe that our wives and children require a good beating occasionally to keep them in line.

So it goes. Examples are limitless, reaching the apex of absurdity a few years past, when young pacifists across the United States might be discovered committing gratuitous acts of violence and blowing each other into vapor in order to demonstrate for their elders their steely willingness to kill, die or risk their own and others' lives for the cause of peace, even if the "others" were passing strangers.

Since the preface of recorded history, men have been enthusiastically willing to kill one another for the cause of peace. Women, as Aristophanes was *not* the first to note, have also rarely hesitated to kill in order to eliminate warfare, even by nastily terminating means for the continuation of human reproduction. Women in the modern world possess powers far beyond those available in Periclean Greece to accomplish this latter end and may be counted upon to conjecture about the utilization, in fiction and fact, of the simple and lethal power that steroid chemistry has placed in their hands—with instructions to use at their discretion.

As time passes, most historical realities dissolve into myths and fantasies, but they eternally and eventually re-integrate into viable home truths as the pendulum of the life of our race moves in its great arc. Patton called the United States "a warlike nation." Closer to the truth would be the irrefutable fact that nearly all men and women everywhere are constituents of a war-like species most of the time. Little in history, social psychology or the abstruse meanderings of various social and behavioral sciences contravenes this record, too open and awe-inspiring for literate persons to read with rubicund tinted spectacles. Some modern psychologists and their camp followers and many, many modern politicians lay claim to the belief that this type of behavior *may,* by various means, be diverted into what they consider "harmless" pursuits, or may be eliminated by conditioning, chemicals or education with Lockean gentility. They attempt to sell to apathetic people, their bellies filled and thirsts slaked, a snake-oil anodyne that the label says will modify human behavior and curb primal blood lusts that probably do not exist anyway.

Neither author of the book you are holding is more than bemusedly committed to any notions in this key, regardless of their undulating fashionableness. They accept grimly the news that the history of mankind has been, indeed, a sorry record of institutional and free-lance bloodshed. They believe also (and at the same time) the apparent irony that this same history has been one of amazingly glorious and, at times, godlike moments of productive peace. The authors cannot admit, as well, anything at heart contradictory about this bifurcation of historical record, any more than they are able to deny the relevance to man's affairs of the best symbol of this irony in man's culture: the Sphynx, an animal with the face and brain of a majestic human and the body and hind quarters of a beast.

In this manner do we therefore approach the contemporary *War of Ideas:* disarmed (or unarmed) of illusion, but certainly blind neither to the historical realities nor to the contemporary impotence of both our best intellectuals and our wisest statesmen to make good the benign, but possibly necessary, hypocricies of the velvet gloves that both wear in line of duty. We wear them too.

Maturity on one hand (perhaps "early senility") and accident of training and interest on the other (perhaps "bad luck") permit us to offer a few prejudices and conceits early in this present volume, and we may as well produce them here. One's biases are a good place to start one's arguments and debates. Their honest statement, we have been told, sometimes even clears up subsequent misunderstandings, although not often.

Primarily, we believe that any and all war, properly so-called, involving bloodshed is absurd, entering a careful *caveat* that warfare is not the only, or possibly most ludicrous, absurdity mankind has long pursued in its long adventure on earth. Therefore, do we also, like other proper, civilized hypocrites, both despise warfare and cannot defend rationally its most noble and holy manifestations, granting that any other device or instrument may, in other ways, achieve a reasonable quantum of its practical objectives. We mean, of course, that we prefer absolutely the substitution of intelligence for brutality in any of its manifestations. And we believe *all* wars that men have fought have had open before their combatants such pragmatic alternatives.

The reasons that intelligence has so often been ignored in favor of brutality are not difficult to comprehend. They may simply be explained, as they are in most histories and psychologies, in biological, psychological, educational, economic, or other causal terms. Take your choice or combine your reasons. Such theorizing, in our opinion, *explains* a good deal but *excuses* nothing. Intellectual understanding, we maintain, cannot substitute for morality, ethics, or ideals. They are different classes of experience.

With the exception of the sometimes unfortunately civilized personal option of suicide (a modern illegality that is also an ancient human right, if efficiently accomplished), we firmly believe that murder or intent to kill, no matter how euphemized into collective mysticisms involving nations, races or religions, is one of the foulest immoralities of which man is capable. Thus is warfare, even and especially "good" warfare, untenable. Our faith applies equally to wars of independence, revolutions, revenge for carnage—or wars that last six minutes, six days, six months or sixty years.

We do not credit with much logic or reason the *deus ex machina*, past and present, who sanctifies the dirty work of a fighting army, especially since all armies exorcise their own true gods who specialize in this sort of magic. In this wild construction, therefore, wars may be transmuted into battles between gods, some of which end up, by virtue of certain men's technological and tactical zeal, better or truer than others. By all means, say we, let the gods pitch their battle tents at random—in the theatre of the heavens or mortal playhouses of stage, screen and television (a matter to which we shall subsequently return in some detail), but leave human beings out of the contests, if knives are sharp and weapons are loaded. Ironically, in the long run, none of mankind's war gods—or a single pacific, defensive god—has ever achieved an ultimate, universal victory and maintained his original earthly form for more than an instant of history. And the territory such gods have won in the minds of their constituents and adversaries is somehow lost with discouraging ease when men multiply in peacetime and forget their liturgies even while practicing them.

Heaven is, we think, a perfect battlefield. And so is hell. We cannot then justify the use of less adequate arenas like the globe that Barbara Ward has called "Spaceship Earth." In this prejudice we are firm.

We are just as firm, however, in the conviction that the present moment represents no great turning point for mankind in the pursuit of his classic habits, good and bad. We have both been fed—and fed up—with the pseudo-science of futurology and "future shock" treatments that promise to tranquilize, computerize, cauterize and/or educate our species into peace, whether we desire it or not. Technological geniuses who cannot run railroads that do not fall apart, who cannot stop threats of the moronic arrogance of psychopathic skyjackers, who cannot feed and house adequately their own citizens or cure their sniffles are certainly not equipped, in one's wildest dreams, to sprinkle their whoofle dust on competing armies and transform them into debating societies or contests of gamesmanship. We have been exposed to too much of this piffle in print and press either to take it seriously any longer or to wait for its wonderous alchemy. Having been involved ourselves in pandering to a now diminishing public appetite for comfortable illusions like these, we may, with some authority finally reject them here and now, for the time being at least. Let us hustle the over-publicized prophets of unreality back to their drawing-boards and listen to their perfumed vagaries only when they have, at the outset in their assumptions, theories and hypotheses, delineated clearly in their *own* minds the differences and purposes between science and science-fiction. Otherwise, they must be treated as the third-rate oracles and the quacks they are, until they have something to say or show for their smug gall. They belong in the world of Jules Verne and Mandrake, where they function best and amusingly, if taken with suitable salt. And *eramus culpa*, dear reader, no less gullible than you were during the passing (we hope) great decade of the futurological "put on."

We affirm also a hearty skepticism, still best characterized by Dr. Galbraith's rubric "the common wisdom," that "war is hell," because it is sometimes exciting and profitable to certain people, and Russell's pleas that modern war with nuclear weapons is *worse* than hell, merely because it may eliminate what is referred to as "civilization as we know it"—not so terrible an idea, we conjure, if one knows *all* civilization with enough intimacy. Nor are we so naive as to overlook history's message, clarified by realists from Machiavelli to Arthur Koestler, that the man or woman who cries, "Peace at any price!" is probably a killer in disguise, hiding a scimitar beneath an ersatz angel's robe. Nor are we saintly enough to deny, as the humanitarian Nobelized pacifist, Dr. Valkonen, in Robert Sherwood's play *There Shall Be No Night* recognizes on the brink of destruction by Russians in the first version of the drama, and by Germans in the second (it makes little difference), that a moment may come when the most gentle of men—if he is a man—may be hurled into the company with the giants of mysticism from Socrates to Christ to Lincoln. He will then tear off his visible icons of gentility (a Red Cross armband for Sherwood's hero) in grim exchange for a machine gun or other instrument by which to translate ideals into death for a purpose that transcends any human being's personal need for life.

No, we have no intentions of ensnaring ourselves in such obvious functional paradoxes of "the common wisdom." During our own lifetimes, we have seen great "peace candidates" like Italy's Mussolini, China's Mao and Chiang and Germany's Hitler (whose victory at the polls in 1933 shrewdly articulated with

his tearful pleas for plowshares, not swords) perform their de-
vinely inspired bloodshed on massive scales that history has
not known before. Mass murder belied their neat "peace"
shibboleths. And, ironically, we have lustily cheered and
served (in the name of "peace") the work of well-meant mass
killers like Wilson, Roosevelt, Truman, Churchill, Eisenhower,
MacArthur, and Marshall, to name but a few of the elite whom
"the common wisdom" has recently cannonized as saints of
peace (meaning winners of wars) in the modern world.

While neither of us, at the moment, is eager to re-arm our
rifles in order to defend a state we see—and shall show, we
hope—falling into such new depravities that it may hardly be
worth saving for posterity, we have not lately been tested either honestly or well. Nor do we incline to compose sonnets to
psychopaths or galled ignoramuses who might murder our families or plunder our homes, in the manner of the certified Con-
scientious Objector, or give up all our rights to revenge and
self-protection. Despite our beliefs and aging reflexes, one
cheek is sufficient to turn to brutes, whether they be sane
goons or, in modern parlance, "sick" ones. If the former, they
are worse and sillier hypocrites than we are; if the latter, they
have no business transacting business of any sort with the
healthy until the contagion of their illness has disappeared.

So delicate is this matter of the worship of peace that we
are even hesitant to swallow whole those obvious and crude
"wisdoms" spun during the past generation about nuclear
weapons, doomsday technology and the destruction of the
human race by means of its own weaponry. Most of us are
aware that "total destruction," as defined during various eras of
history has for millenia been possible, and mankind, in its curious way, has always stopped comfortably short of that total-
ity, even when plague and disease appeared to be controlling
his fate. Carthage *was* destroyed in as heinous a way as Hiroshima, perhaps more cruelly, if one can measure such matters.
The Inca of Peru fell victim to a devastation so complete and
efficient and fast that it remains, to this day, but superficially

explained. An incinerated victim of atomic radiation is neither more nor less dead in a Japanese grave than the unmarked victims of the White Man's Burden who fell in colonial massacres on African and Asian soil, or the dead hordes of once-proud American Indian nations that ruled our continent, and are presently kept as museum pieces in filthy zoos we call "reservations." These figurative piles of corpses serve to remind us that we in the West have long cherished the lie that we are destiny's children, suitably godlike to eliminate heathens, not only at the command of father and mother gods, but in consonance with solid Lockean philosophy varnishing our own cupidity.

We therefore choose to look at all varieties of atomic, biological, chemical and science-fiction warfare with respect, but through clenched teeth and with a cynical sneer, in the same way that we regard other and more primitive military devices that, if expertly used, may eliminate, indeed, our species just as thoroughly. Although we cannot argue that the first nation to place an atomic warhead installation on the moon may, for a time at least, not rule the world, such awesome power in the hands even of those whom we count as enemies may engender a *Pax Romana,* preventing a generation of wilder wars, bloodier battles, and crueler casualties than history has yet witnessed in a short period, saving mankind to greet the year 2000 A.D.

This century is, after all, not completed yet. Staring at an armed moonrise, ready at any moment to dispatch its lethal rockets to its host planet, philosophers, like our Joint Chiefs of Staff, may wish to study further that easy epithet, "Better Dead than Red" in the light of all new evidence, both tactical and semantic. And the fact that you, dear reader, are perusing this paragraph either a year or a decade after it was written, is empirical existential evidence that man, the peaceful truth-seeker, is much more difficult to eliminate *in toto* than man, the hostile political animal, bit by bit.

New Wings on the Horizon

In disposition (if not entirely in letter), we agree lustily with the thesis of Elizabeth M. Borgese who construes [2] *post-*nuclear warfare as a phenomenon which must function in quite a different setting, and with a different script, from the bloody gamesmanship that for thousands of years preceded it. (In our opinion, the atom, hydrogen and other fission and fusion weapons are but an ancillary culmination of two major military innovations of the present century, and that they followed in direction and spirit: first, the concept of "total warfare," engaging vast civil populations in battlements, and second, the displacement of the words "unconditional surrender" from the ambit of rhetoric to that of actual practice.)

As appalled as Borgese finds herself at new increments of deaths to non-combatant people (as opposed to professional soldiers) during the past generations, she views a future of *worse* multiple modern fanatic terrorist-type conflicts (like the various bloody wars of liberation and decolonization that followed World War II) as new and endless methods of preserving national bloodlusts. By means of repeated sequences of quasi-international civil conflicts of unspeakable guerilla brutality, due in part to over-population of the affected geographical areas, we face an era where such civilities as international law and rules of combat are sick jokes. We count conservatively that well over thirty-five such mini-wars have already been fought on our planet since V-J (Victory in Japan) Day. Most of them tend to exclude the large nuclear powers as direct, face-to-face participants, with few exceptions. These powers have not scrupled to provide men and material for the limited objectives of their overseas alliances, just as long as local antagonisms can be contained and limited, as in Algeria, Palestine, Biafra and, naturally, Korea and Vietnam, where major powers *did* participate within careful limits.

In every case, these blood baths are construed by diplomats and propagandists as civil insurrections or inevitable revolts, more political than military in thrust and importance.

Almost invariably they are blood-thirstier than larger ideological world-wide conflicts, thanks to man's proclivity to deal most insanely and cruelly with enemies he knows best. So it has recently occurred in Vietnam, as hordes of American witnesses will attest. And so it happened nearly two and a half decades ago, when one of the authors of this book departed Algiers shortly before its hour of unbelievable carnage with his tail-feathers slightly singed, anticipating, even in his youth, a note of truth concerning the bitter hatreds brewing about him in a colorful city that was once called "the little Paris."

We are not referring here to the so-called "domino theory" of imperialistic conquest engineered by major powers, although revolution *sans* dominos occasionally does spread from nations poised in civil conflict to similar and nearby nations like brush fire—if the climate is right and the flora and fauna are flammable enough. On the other hand, only one or two dominos fell after the Cuban revolt—and then apparently half-heartedly and temporarily—even when set up by as volatile and clever a revolutionist as the late Che Guevera. And sometimes there are simply no available dominos to fall: as in the Middle East, where competition for petroleum and other fiscal favors from the great powers calm, with the mystical power, the chain reactions that one might have expected after, for instance, the destruction of such modern dynasties as that presided over by the laughable King Farouk.

Domino explanations of spreading civil slaughter we must relegate, in large measure, to the realm of fantasy. They function mainly and primarily to interest wealthy, powerful nations arming and sustaining one or another hostile force against their enemies, in the fear that the enemy will allow itself to be conquered or subsumed into the bailiwick of another wealthy, powerful nation. And somewhere along the line raw materials, trade and/or cheap manpower will be lost to the latter. Because this rarely happens, or, as in the case of Cuba, happens sloppily, and with minor profit for the most part, domino rhetoric today serves best as persuasion to achieve public assent among the citizens of this or that wealthy nation (or coalition of nations) that may be called upon to sacrifice some portion of its own security and wealth in order to help its chosen ally in the civil holocaust. Sad to say (from the viewpoint of the propagandist), this perusal does not even seem to work well or for long, consigned to such a limited, short-term psychological stimulus.

The fact is—and has been, despite the impress of force by outside powers upon numerous factions in revolt during the past generation—that *all* parties involved in major civil upheavals usually do not enjoy the prospect of becoming fawning satellites to any major power and receiving largesse at the expense of economic dependence (not so bad) and political guidance (terrible). More often, civil terrorists (and sometimes factions of the old order) usually seek *three* objectives. And all of them are difficult to obtain in the context of limited guerilla warfare, depending upon many factors, including the complexity of various alliances with the rich and mighty:

First, most of the participants want what they construe as freedom in status—a new national state—even if this means freedom to follow Russia or China's brand of Communism *if they choose,* and, most important, the freedom to change their minds and paths, if they discover their choice was a poor one. This objective is almost impossible to reach and, simply, seeds new and more horrible revolutions and counter-revolutions, each yielding a progressively unstable utilization of governing political power. It has even failed in such "stable" nations as Israel, Yugoslavia and Turkey.

Second, they desire *instant* industrialization, modern technology, universal education and most of the amenities that are supposed to make the great powers great, and for which the latter had to suffer for generations to achieve at the less than perfect level they boast for them. No major power has the ability to wave a staff over a once-colonial pre-industrial society and turn it, *mutatis mutandis,* into a modern industrial paradise or anything approaching one. One reason is that industrial para-

dises do not exist; another is purely ethnocentric. Here is a
cold truth that certain great powers are learning slowly, the
United States no exception, both on an ideological plane and
in nuts-and-bolts matrices. An instance is the Peace Corps, one
of the United States' greatest impracticable ideas of the
century—and most well-intentioned. Some of its random disasters will haunt the USA for years.

Third, these hostile civil factions almost automatically
strive to attain loose and arbitrary borders of influence and hegemony. They aspire to the fact that some day, even if their
present insurrection is negotiated or compromised to death,
they *may* expand their influence to adjacent countries which,
almost invariably, possess natural resources they want or need
or who have evolved a way of life and set of alliances they
covet. Hence the variety of ceremonial meetings that continue
to this day with the formality of a Chinese opera at Panmunjon,
in order to keep open a final settlement of the Korean War because, as both sides to the conflict see it, the grass *is* just a bit
greener in the other fellow's yard. And, if a final peace settlement can be attenuated *ad infinitum,* soundings of corruption
and worse in each adversary's government and political structure (often quite authentic and promising) may just topple the
whole carefully designed stalemate (or conditions of non-hostility) to date, paying off in a quick, comparatively bloodless
and efficient victory. Intelligence reports usually predict such
possible victories, since they nearly always provide pelf for intelligence agents. This is a long-shot chance worth taking, less
applicable to Europe than Asia, Africa and the Near East, but
a testament to the longevity of human hope and avarice.

The apparent escalation of warfare—in terms of blood
and guts—on our planet rests, in each individual case, upon
defensible arguments pitting good gods against bad ones and
vice-versa. Wars involving Moslems and Hindus, Catholics and
Buddhists, Jews and Moslems, and Protestants and Catholics
are the clearest example of these wars and their propaganda
rationales—and the kinds of sanctions that inflame the means

of such conflicts. Most of the wars since World War II have, in traditional patterns, been propagandized as "holy wars." A colonial insurrection, revolt or revolution *must* at the outset be a mystical exercise, if only because "the common wisdom" regards nineteenth century political and economic colonialism as bad and evil *per se*. When the issues are almost entirely economic, as they are in parts of South America where certain nations are curiously and entirely dependent upon the United States, they are not esteemed as evil as the nineteenth century model—nor is the colonialism involved as benevolent, god-inspired and altruistic. And, as 1976 approaches, it is useful also to reconsider our own American Revolution as a spiritual revolt (or so the Declaration of Independence says) well-salted with economic realities. Nor should we overlook the equally mystical and pound-value motivations of the British to fight a foreign war in order to preserve the souls of wanderers of many nationalities who inhabited the thirteen colonies from the anarchy of competing national markets and England's avuncular acceptance of the tithe paid them, as well as the spiritual destiny of the Empire.

We are referring here to ends, some real and some fanciful, in a world that is presently war-torn but not "at war." To the hard analyst, these issues *must be ends* because the *raisons d'être* of contemporary civil hostilities do not appear to merit, on the part of the major powers involved, the use of nuclear, chemical (with exceptions) and bacterial (with possible exceptions) weapons, all of which have much the same potential for gross annihilation, although the latter two have hardly been given the field-testing that atomic warfare has. "The common wisdom" accepts this benign proposition, and the common propagandist, in the guise of the newspaper, television and radio newsman (a new costume for him), promulgates it. Whether military strategists and politicians high in the order of supposedly superior humans also swallow it, we cannot know, although we intuit that many of them whose superiority extends to trickiness but not intelligence manage to con themselves into accepting their own public relations gambits.

We are not the first writers to suggest in print that the highly touted "doomsday weapons" are *not,* in reality, the major instruments of modern warfare whose power is so great that it may eliminate life on earth. Notice, please, that other, more subtle weapons, *unlimited in any way by highly publicized agreements like the SALT talks or international treaties,* are quite freely available for military use by any technological nation, their effectiveness and power resting only upon the exponential function of that country's present technological genius. In fact, we are referring to instruments that may soon redefine the common (and possibly obsolete) notion of military weaponry. They are open secrets, and every bit as pan-deadly as the old weaponry of super-bombs and nuclear warfare that make such engaging feature stories in broadcasting, in newspapers, in magazines, and are so beloved by political speech writers.

Not being specialists in the technology and application of these new instruments of over-kill (nobody is, to our knowledge), there is little purpose in describing their lethal specifications as if we were experts. We prefer to leave explanations of this kind to specialists in the cold knowledge that they, too, do not yet understand the new weaponry much better than we do, because they have not yet been utilized properly as instruments of destruction. Their day will come, however, probably by accident.

Within the entire area of the earth's single great ocean, unbelievable mischief may be created by the employment of technology to change temperature patterns, and with this modification to re-arrange currents, streams, and marine life to such a degree that populations which depend upon oceanic stability for survival may be eliminated slowly and without much (or any) appreciation of what is happening to them. The vital bases of the support of their economies and ways of life will have been destroyed.

Broadcasting seers may look at the heavens instead of the oceans and conjecture about satellite systems that make good a McLuhanite vision of a worldwide village: actually sophisticated means of communication that it is said will bring enlightenment—if not a glass of milk—to every Hottentot. No type or manner of broadcasting sounds or pictures has yet succeeded in accomplishing anything resembling such civilized ends, even when limited to a small area of the earth. Borgese, therefore, is concerned about the hidden and absolutely lethal potentials of such a global communication system in much the same tenor that the British, quite realistically, are frightened of bridge or tunnel connecting Dover with Calais.

She writes:

> The "communications revolution" culminating in satellite technology with its tremendous potential for earth-resource monitoring and planning, the control of (redefined) "military" developments, and direct transnational television, etc., provides another example (of unconventional lethal power of global dimensions). This technology bestows on its "owner" an enormous and intolerable advantage. Without "war" or territorial conquest, the owners of such systems can set up a new type of functional world empire, inevitably reinforcing, in the twilight between war and peace, the trend toward the latest kind of guerrilla. Only rational international management can maximize the productive potential of this transnational technology.[3]

True enough is its final sentence, but do you place your odds (and ours) on "rational international management?" Outside of universal agreements concerning the size and direction of screw threads, internationalists have experienced little of it in the past century. What we see clearly is communication and propaganda used for expediency, a method less explicit than nuclear bombs as weapons, possibly, but entirely inadequate in the domain of ideation and no less deadly than yesterday's warfare.

Words and pictures are not extremely meaningful to some. Let us underscore their importance, then, with materialistic corollaries, more satisfactory to materialistic minds—and "the common wisdom." Large nations, dependent upon imports of fuel, will shortly be hurled—like it or not—into the use of fusion fuels to maintain their ways of life (and the United States will be among them) if, for purposes of undeclared warfare or subtle hostility, other nations one way or another, eliminate their supplies. Relatively *small* amounts of nuclear power probably produce radioactive by-products that will be assimilated into the biosphere harmlessly. There is no question, however, that increasingly massive amounts (as yet, at indeterminate levels) of these materials must create a "hot" environment (both in temperature and radioactivity) that will not sustain much of the life that presently lives in it, particularly as that life has developed in complexity. Again, the terror here lies in the almost unnoticeable increase of these slight hostile factors over relatively long periods of time, explained away by experts in "common wisdom" as temporary ways of meeting demonstrable emergencies while power requirements are diminished, for instance, by trading our automobiles for horses and buggies.

Other concrete and proven instruments of hostility also exist that may resist the inevitable counter-measures that clever technologists may bring to bear against the few (or many) new genera of weapon discussed above. They deserve mention, and the reader may imagine the consequences.

Meteorologists already have evolved devices and procedures for altering weather conditions in remote places, even to the extent, possibly, of activating volcanoes and pushing earth faults into earthquakes. Some of these procedures are quite complex and require advanced technology—for instance, the process of the creation of chronic conditions of relative deprivation of sunlight by means of stable mists. Some are as nearly as old and simple as the Indians' rain dance but are rarely used, because weathermen have not to date been considered front-line combatants by military strategists, except in local situations in the field.

The more familiar idea of introducing chemicals of various kinds into drinking water depends more upon the type of chemical employed than the source or amount of water supply, but someone other than Mother Nature has added the foul chlorine taste to the water one drinks in New York City and environs and the fluorine that supposedly hardens children's teeth to other reservoir systems. Psychotropic drugs (particularly those with metal compounds like lithium), slow acting poisons, and other cheap chemicals already exist for similar purposes. As long as their action is cumulative and slow enough to be generally unperceptible, neither laws nor executive ukases nor treaties will halt their use if they are needed by the new military establishment in any nation, large or small, that can afford them and use them for what they believe to be God's purposes. In fact, in some ways they even off the balance scale between the military potentials of big states and little states.

The most significant factor of the new weaponry—a most *partial* list of which we have noted above—is that, up to the present, both technological and military thinking has tended to be unilateral and progressive. That is, except for the hub-bub raised about atomic fallout, it tends to disregard one central principle of *all* technology, from mass-produced cat food to the discovery for a cure from cholera, namely that technological advance *invariably* produces side-effects, randomly destructive to the user, *of which he cannot possibly be fully aware until the technology has saturated the environment,* no matter how prescient or skilled in his specialty he is.[4]

The semantic of the word "weapon," we submit, is therefore rapidly changing, obviously for the worse. The word "warfare" has *not* been redefined, because it is presently enmeshed in procedures developed back in time and operates under the humanitarian guise of so-called "limited warfare" in the linguistic environment where its philological history began.

Flapping the Air

We also have entered, in our epoch, however (and we include this statement without sarcasm), a new era of peace as well. What remains to be discovered is whether the expedient and somewhat antiquated construction of non-hostility we call "peace" is an ultimate charade of devils or a plan of angels and benevolent gods who have tested us to what appears to be the limit. Regarding this puzzle, we offer no odds, merely prayers. The reasons will be obvious to all but those who—like professional futurologists—believe that globs of probability statistics, fed ingeniously to the proper computers, will lead mankind to deal with unknowable options in a rational manner, a high point, circa 1973, in multiple idiocies and a victory for the incredible gullibility for "the common wisdom."

One simple (too simple, we think) construction of this new kind of peace may with a straight face be called "coexistence," as if there were something modern about nations, tribes or families living together with respect and tranquility, although they despise each other at worst, and may learn to tolerate each other at best. Despite its astounding record of continual hostilities, this is precisely the manner in which Europe has survived (and at times flourished) for many, many centuries, either under the aegis of spiritual leadership, unilateral force of arms or, more lately, balances of power. The latter were often imaginary or sheer bluffs. But they served mass psychology well, because a working construct of a balance of power is one that never has to be tested in the field. When it is, it is no longer a balance factor, and it usually yields a short period of military hegemony leading to new alignments of nations, new treaties and other transitory documents—and a new balance.

Until the age of mass communications, it was of little or no importance whether or not the common man—including the members of the bourgeoisie—*believed* in the practical realism or potential of these alliances. If military leaders, politicians and the literate elite accepted them as a true reflection of the status quo, they were real enough to accomplish their ends of coexistence and maintain the peace out of prudence, fright or both.

The concept of coexistence has unhappily evolved, over the past century, as too worn, too inefficient and ineffective and too tenuous to substitute fully any longer for a genuine peace. Not only did it become impossible to fool the new breeds of social scientists towards the end of the last century with such hokum, schooled as they were in the razor-sharp analyses of scholars of the stripe of Gabriel Tarde,[5] the once impotent common man himself was learning (or had learned) to read. Newspapers and other instruments of political and military information were spread widely, and his opinions regarding policies of containment pressured the former ruling classes into reconsidering their attitudes and actions (or lack of them) towards national containment involving balances of power. Ask any German today, East or West. Progressive skepticism and dissatisfaction with theories of coexistence continue to the present. While most of us accept such rubrics and fictions as better than non-coexistence or hostility, few international scholars are reactionary enough to equate them for long with peace and keep up a straight face. Peaceful coexistence may be, accordingly, one of the saddest and fragile phrases in our contemporary lexicon.

But what are the alternatives? And are they not *worse* than *antique* coexistence, no matter how moth-chewed its fabric is?

Suffice it to note here that there *are* alternatives that (short of big power warfare), bleached of their sentimentalism, place their emphases not upon military strength or balances of power but rather on matters that are economic, historical, technological and psychological, none of them relatively new stabilizing factors in the game of nations but, at the moment, *more* up-to-date and *more* potentially effective than arms races, although less subtle than the other new weaponry we have described above.

The psychological aspects of these alternatives will be the major concern of this book—although their psychology is not a single subject of enterprise operating in any phase without continual interaction with economic, historical and technological factors of the most sophisticated and advanced sort. Older versions of so-called "international propaganda" and "psychological warfare" did not clearly recognize these interdependent factors that were critical to the successes and failures of propaganda or "psych-war," as it was called, except as side issues or gilt on lilies. Hoary reports of propaganda campaigns analyses of both American psych-war and that of her enemies (roughly from World War I to 1945) make harmless reading for those who want to quantify ostensible "successes" and "failures" unrelated to what we have learned since about group psychology. They are interesting but unenlightening for a rapid perusal of yesterday's trickery and attempts at mind-bending, in an era before such psychologically loaded terms as "brainwashing" became effective propaganda bullets themselves, and psychologists of language and persuasion related them to the dynamics of human dispositions.[6]

Coexistence is fundamentally and unfortunately a *military* notion that, variantly and at different times and places, offers opportunities for economic exchange, tourism, cultural exchange (a horrid term!), off-and-on official recognition of various nations via embassies and (often) consulates and, today, mutual recognition by peer nations in the United Nations. The latter factor, dramatized recently by a substitution of Red for Republican Chinese representation, is not tantamount to official diplomatic recognition, but we have seen the mechanism of its psychological power in the "ping-pong" gambits that preceded and followed recognition by the world forum of Red China.

Few—very few—historical paradigms demonstrate in the West that coexistence has energized a relatively productive and lasting period of peace. The East, with curious ways of combining coexistence, conquest and inter-breeding, has a more impressive record over the centuries.

Policies that effectively postponed in Europe the holocaust of World War I for about a generation are simply not adequate for the contemporary world of mass communication and complex technology. This fact is certainly not a secret to intellects as sophisticated in these matters as our President's official advisors and his foreign policy guru from Harvard. Both often appear, nevertheless, intent on sustaining them in, one imagines, the hope that they will provide a wedge or stalling time for a new construction of peace that our age of civil terrorism and undeclared wars demands, if the present era is to become a proper nexus between the old order and the next century with the world and its people more or less intact.

That these same statesmen (and others of equal ability we consider enemies) have not yet articulated between them a viable concept of international harmony that transcends yesterday's "peaceful coexistence" is equally as obvious. No doubt, many of them have cracked this atom individually and in their dreams, but the history of their goals and aims in print, gleaned from both governmental and non-governmental sources, indicates the glut of sweat and the shortage of brain power that the subject has been given in realistic terms since World War II.

Our thesis, the main (but not sole) one in this volume, is that such a construction of peace (if it is ever achieved) will be evolved, not from old-time notions like peaceful coexistence, but newer concepts derived in great measure from contemporary social psychological thinking. Naturally, it must pass in its development through a phase of coexistence and terminate its historical voyage with military considerations of yesterday: nuclear bombs, aircraft, destroyers, rifles and the ancient panoply of arms, until it undertakes to deal with those newer, more insidious and slower procedures for technological extermination and/or conquest we have discussed. But these practical matters in the hierarchy of today's international tensions may be of the *least* significance for the maintenance and insurance of contemporary peace, despite their fascination both for the general public, news reporters and governmental bureaus. The *possible* exception is the inevitably villified Central Intelligence Agency, whose considerations of both war and peace have, perforce, been channelled into psychological considerations as antecedent to the old-style diplomacy of the State Department and the antique gamesmanship of the Department of Defense particularly in the light of the CIA's role in the Watergate scandal of 1973.

Birds of a Different Feather

Precedent to all psychological matters, except for a small gaggle of academic die-hard behaviorists and the tick-tock speculations they have nerve enough to publish,[7] are the instruments that people use to express their covert feelings in those socially acceptable, but decorously ambiguous, communication devices we call "symbols." As individuals deal widely in symbols, so do political entities, nations and armies, the latter to an extraordinary extent, since pre-history. If guiding concepts for international life need to be changed, symbols and symbolism, the architects of this psychology, must first be changed, as A. N. Whitehead once noted with axiomatic zeal.

Since Noah's Ark, the dove has been western man's major symbol of peace, and the olive branch in the bird's beak a corollary symbol of life. We are dealing here, of course, with mysticism, not propaganda or diplomacy. But it has been (and possibly always will be) mysticisms of this sort that will serve as inevitable energizers of warfare, as well as crude abstractions of peace. This is because, as old G. B. Shaw maintained, men will fight best for their clear-cut symbols, and the word "peace" is difficult—if not impossible—to define in positive symbolic terms. As we have seen, peace means the *absence* of something (war), and the symbol of the dove has, if little more, served as a sentimental but positive symbol of a weak word with an ambiguous meaning.

Modern psychological warriors seized this classic opportunity for modest positivism for the hundredth time at the end of World War II. And the symbol of the dove has been revived by statesmen and artists, both benignly and invidiously, across the globe beyond Christendom. "Hawks" and "doves" became thumbnail symbols, verbal and pictorial, in the American political vocabulary during the Lyndon B. Johnson administration.

Each bird symbolized a "good" or "bad" orientation to the Vietnamese conflict, depending upon how one construed the simplistic polarities they bespoke, meaning so little that by the time Johnson went back to Texas almost every American considered himself a dove.

Most cleverly, the non-capitalist nations, the UN and leftist factions in the USA had already preempted the dove as almost private symbolic property, when the late Pablo Picasso, shortly after World War II, created a magnificent but simple dove symbol dedicated to the political left in Europe. At the time, multi-millionaire Picasso was suffering a perfectly justifiable reaction against reactionary forces in Spain that had supported the Axis during World War II. Since then, however, Picasso's dove (and imitations of it) has continued flying left, often providing symbolic cover for militarism, nationalism and the colonialism of communist states, big and small.

Despite his somewhat thin appreciation of the fine arts, President Nixon (or his cultural advisors) were aware in the early days of his administration that this sensitive issue was not to be belittled. Even before the 1968 elections, Nixon was apparently considering the matter, and immediately after, two unusual events in the history of American symbology occurred in less than two weeks.

Edward Marshall Boehm, considered by many America's most gifted porcelain sculptor, died, leaving, as a legacy to his wife, the Boehm porcelain factory in Trenton, New Jersey, replete with a staff of incomparable and specialized artists, skilled in the difficult medium of detailed porcelain statuary, many of whom were competent to duplicate their master's unbelievably life-like effects, particular in axian groups. According to Boehm's widow,[8] within ten days of her husband's death Nixon verbally requested (or commissioned) from Boehm, Incorporated, an enormous work of statuary that would, first, replace for the long or short run the symbol of the dove as *the* bird of peace and, second, indicate to the world the chauvinistic truth that American porcelain workers are equals of or superior to those of greater fame and tradition in England, Europe and the Orient. (Asia, incidentally, saw the original transmutation centuries ago of crude pottery into the more subtle and beautiful medium of "china," properly named.)

All participants in this interesting psychological venture agreed that a massive sculpture was in order, and the Boehm people suggested two life-sized swans. The Boehm craftsmen, however, faced the problems that all large porcelain sculpture is distressingly vulnerable to breakage from both internal and external stresses, and that the larger the object is, the more difficult it is to execute, right up to the point of impossibility. To their credit, these artists attempted the *near*-impossible, a breathtaking major hard porcelain group of two adult and two fledgling so-called "mute" swans almost exactly of life size, solid enough to be packed and transported around the world, if necessary.

The authors have discovered that many types of swans (including those called "mute" but which, in fact, communicate and vocalize "quietly and softly" in Mrs. Boehm's words) are often contentious, dangerous and ornery birds despite their beauty. However, these birds seemed to fill Nixon's bill exactly. Eventually, *three* of these spectacular groups were made. The approximate cost of the first one is said to have been a quarter of a million dollars. Upon receipt by the White House, it was displayed, for whatever psychological and artistic purposes it was intended, in the Executive Mansion itself and at other centers of diplomatic prestige in Washington and Western Europe. One of the groups is still traveling, and still another has been permanently installed in the White House. But it is the destiny of the third (actually the first one sculptured) reproduced on the endpapers of this book, that we find of greatest symbolic and psychological significance.

The masterpiece in china made its way to the land of its spiritual birth in the Spring of 1972 in the form of a gift from the United States to Red China, where it is displayed today bearing the legend: *To His Excellency Chairman Mao Tse-Tung and The People of the People's Republic of China from President Richard Nixon and the People of the United States of America.*

The distribution across national boundaries of such objects of art do not, *per se,* cause either lumps in the authors' throats or tears in their orbs. But, for many, these mute swans have taken more meaningful proportions than the usual artistic bric-a-brac that nations present to one another for protocol purposes. Partisans will see in these birds a measure of the kind of sleight-of-hand that the Nixon Doctrine and the President's bid for re-election signified. Were the birds *originally* designed for their journey to Communist China? Most likely, this question will never be answered, and most likely the answer is "yes." Nixon's peregrinations to the USSR and the Orient unquestionably carried enormous domestic political clout, no less than his nerve to accomplish what former Chief Executives had, in recent years, been afraid to do: namely, institute wage and price controls to salvage an economy that had nearly died of inflationary laughing gas. (The dirty work was left for a smart, at that time, Democratic, Secretary of Treasury to carry out, if *that* means anything.)

All things being equal (and they never are), President Nixon did not, however, require a highly visible *entente* in living color with Red China *from a strictly political perspective,* to assure his massive re-election victory the coming November, nor did he need the so-called "Watergate" caper. In fact, recognition of the "yellow communist devils" as authentic Chinese nationals in the UN without much American objection, and Nixon's chopstick banquets with Chou En-Lai and company, seem to have alienated to the point of non-support some influential and affluent conservatives in the Republican Party.

That what politicians call "deals" had been made during Nixon's meeting with Chou centered not only on economics and trade (the usual "cover" agenda items for much international diplomacy of a more sensitive nature) but concerned the

Vietnam War and ancillary matters including the continued presence of NATO and/or American force in Europe in order to keep the Soviets at bay, is unquestionable. It is difficult to estimate the abrasions many Americans felt as a result of these "deals," including scions of the powerful China Lobby (representing the large and frightened Taiwan government including the ancient Chiang Kai-shek) with a good deal of political and economic clout of its own. Nixon's decision to face at last the obvious was inevitable: Red China not only exists but, compared to its own past, is thriving in many ways under mish-mash mysticism and Marxism that bears a strong resemblance (in theory) to state communism regardless of what it is called.

Nixon's move was timed superbly and carried off with an élan unusual when state ministries meet at the summit. Like it or not, a milestone in contemporary international relations had been passed. From a psychological viewpoint, the gloss was superb, apparently as successful within China and other nations holding their collective breaths like the USA. The mute swans were icing on the cake—or monosodium glutamate in the shark fin soup—but they too accomplished their psychological ends, making them just about the most important porcelain work ever created by man, in, of all places, Trenton, New Jersey.

The dove, of course is not dead. But in the world of symbols he may be flying backwards into history. In all of their affairs, men deal largely in symbols, and there is little doubt that symbols are moving up the ladder of importance in international relationships. Older methods of discourse like weapons, trade agreements, treaties and other relics of yesterday remain potent, of course. But the psychological tide is turning.

Yesterday's so-called "propaganda" and "information" are also showing their ragged age in much the way that yesterday's so-called "intelligence" and "espionage" (fine-sounding words it will be a pity to lose) are turning moribund. Today, we live on an earth where there are few genuine secrets between or within nations that are worth keeping, and where spy networks lag behind conventional open press coverage and the instruments of still and motion photography and television. Advanced snooping devices are bringing senile spies in from the cold in droves and sinking them into bureaucracies as custodians of trivia files, where they belonged in the first place.

The pith of these changes, with emphasis upon the new age of international communications and its effects upon the minds of men—including those in executive mansions and palaces—is exactly what this book is all about. We have begun the examination of the passing of the dove in favor of a more majestic bird which, thank heaven, is also a formidable beast that speaks softly (but sweetly), and has not yet learned to carry concealed sticks. Welcome, therefore, to the era of the mute swan. Health and happiness to those fledglings too; the destiny of mankind will unfold, for better or worse, with their growth.

NOTES FOR CHAPTER 1

[1] "The Game of Nations," *Harper's Magazine*, November, 1971, p. 56.

[2] See Elisabeth Mann Borgese, "Between Peace and War" in *The Center For Democratic Institutions Magazine*, November/December, 1972, pp. 24–30.

[3] *Ibid.*, p. 29.

[4] Two volumes that treat this matter sensibly, the first in a gloomy mood, the second less alarmingly, are Jacques Ellul, *The Technological Society* (New York: Alfred A. Knopf, 1965), and Victor E. Ferkis, *Technological Man* (New York: George Braziller, 1969). Co-author Gordon has also sounded tocsins (less alarmed than those in this volume) in *Persuasion, The Theory and Practice of Manipulative Communication* (New

York: Hastings House, 1971). While they constitute a sub-theme of the entire books in the first two cases, Gordon's eclectic volume discusses them on pp. 87, 88, 130, 520 and 521, in the contexts of this chapter.

⁵ See the recently republished paperback by Gabriel Tarde, *Communication and Social Influence* (Chicago: University Press, 1969). These essays were originally published between 1880 and 1904. Tarde was the intellectual parent of the thinkers who followed him in the new discipline of social psychology, made up of men whose loyalties to former élites was displaced by faith in their new "science"—men like Gustave LeBon, Scipio Sighele, Sigmund Freud (in his sociological moods) and, with skeptical anti-scientism, José Ortega y Gasset, and many, many others in the Central European intellectual community.

⁶ *The Arno Press* of *The New York Times* has recently reprinted these reports, books and monographs at healthy prices considering their value. Titles and authors tell all to students of this historical period:

George G. Bruntz, *Allied Propaganda and The Collapse of the German Empire in 1918* (originally published in 1938).

Lawrence Harwood Childs, *Propaganda and Dictatorships: A Collection of Papers* (originally published in 1936).

Lawrence Harwood Childs and John Boardman Whitton, *Propaganda by Short Wave* including *The War on the Short Waves* (originally published in 1944).

George Arthur Codding, Jr., *The International Telecommunication Union: An Experiment in International Cooperation* (originally published in 1952).

George Creel, *How We Advertised America: The First Telling of the Amazing Story of the Committee on Public Information that Carried the Gospel of Americanism to Every Corner of the Globe* (originally published in 1920).

Robert W. Desmond, *The Press and World Affairs* (originally published in 1937).

Ladislas Farago (ed.), *German Psychological Warfare* (originally published in 1942).

Eugen Hadamovsky, *Propaganda and National Power. The Organization of Public Opinion for National Politics* (originally published in 1954).

Arno Hugh, *La Radiodiffusion Puissance Mondiale* (originally published in 1937).

International Press Institute, *The Flow of the News* (originally published in 1953).

Harold Lavine and James Wechsler, *War Propaganda and the United States* (originally published in 1940).

Daniel Lerner (ed.), *Propaganda in War and Crisis—Materials for American Policy* (originally published in 1951).

Paul M. A. Linebarger, *Psychological Warfare* (originally published in 1954).

Sir Robert H. Bruce Lockhart, *Comes the Reckoning* (originally published in 1947).

Sidney Rogerson, *Propaganda in the Next War* (originally published in 1938).

Robert E. Summers (ed.), *America's Weapons of Psychological Warfare* (originally published in 1951).

Fernand Terrou and Lucien Solal, *Legislation for Press, Film and Radio* (originally published in 1951).

Charles A. H. Thompson, *Overseas Information Service of the United States Government* (originally published in 1948).

Peter de Mendelssohn, *Japan's Political Warfare* (originally published in 1944).

Ralph O. Nafziger (ed.), *International News and the Press* (originally published in 1940).

James Morgan Read, *Atrocity Propaganda 1914–1919* (originally published in 1941).

Oscar W. Riegel, *Mobilizing for Chaos—The Story of the New Propaganda* (originally published in 1934).

Leslie Bennett Tribolet, *The International Aspects of Electrical Communications in the Pacific Area* (originally published in 1929).

Llewellyn White and Robert D. Leigh, *Peoples Speaking to Peoples —A Report on International Mass Communication from the Commission on Freedom of the Press* (originally published in 1946).

Francis Williams, *Transmitting World News—A Study of Telecommunications and the Press* (originally published in 1953).

Quincy Wright (ed.), *Public Opinion and World Politics* (originally published in 1933).

[7] See, for instance, B. F. Skinner, *Beyond Freedom and Dignity* (New York: A. Knopf, 1971), and/or the two intentionally conflicting reviews of this work by psychologist Robert Silverman and George N. Gordon in *Educational Technology Magazine*, January, 1972, pp. 2, 79–81.

[8] The story of the Boehm mute swans is told accurately in a promotion document by Mrs. Edward Marshall Boehm, a copy of which may be obtained by contacting Edward Marshall Boehm, Inc., either at 25 Fairfacts Street, Trenton, New Jersey 08638 in the U.S.A., or Tanhouse Lane, Malvern WR 141 LG, England. The British arm of the organization is an offspring of Boehm's original American studio.

2

It Only Hurts When You Laugh

. . . Listed below are 5 of the most pressing issues we face today. Please indicate on the reverse side the five issues you consider most crucial. Then return this entire form to us in the postage-free envelope enclosed. In this way, you help us keep our finger on the pulse of the country and to know which issues its citizens are most concerned about . . .

Brochure received in the mail [1]

Looking Backwards

During the late 'forties and early 'fifties, the city of London looked and felt like something out of Orwell. Gossip had it that his book title *1984* was simply an inversion of *1948*. And the traveler on a short budget—or no budget at all—had reason to believe that the gloomy futurist had played his numbers shrewdly, particularly after a sojourn through continental Western Europe which, particularly in Northern Italy and Germany, was brewing unmistakable portents of prosperity just around the corner.

The dominant mood of London, by contrast, was gray, dull, and dismal. Candy shop windows bursting with sweets displayed discrete signs, "For Export Only," reminding a war-weary people that their victory had merely led them to penury. A new government might, some thought, save the day with socialistic balm. The crowd in Picadilly on the brisk election evening in the winter of 1950, when the political trick to the left was finally turned, was both drunk and manic. Even the usually stern Bobbies recognized the uselessness of attempting to control the beggars' opera of assorted pickpockets, pimps and whores who more or less orchestrated the bedlam. They were only stealing from each other, like those legendary villagers who lived by taking in each other's wash. Few, if any, of the highly vocal mob really believed that a Clement Atlee (or any labor or liberal government) could or would solve the problems that had beaten their beloved Churchill, who, ironically, had recently been chosen by America's *Time* magazine as "The Man of the Half Century."

Daytime was worse than the smoggy nights in little ways that chilled an observer unused to galloping demoralization. Bombed-out areas punctuated the city. Signs warning of unexploded missiles had weathered and decayed into pulp that made them unsatisfactory even for childrens' games. Other notices announcing "Bombed Area, Will Rebuild Soon" had fallen from their rusty nails, but in the service of irony, neither were they replaced, repainted nor rehung. It was quite permissible to spit at them.

Should an American (or other millionaire by definition) want to import to a friend an illegal present from Paris or Madrid, a bunch of bananas was a perfect contraband gift. The day of the Hershey-bar nylon-stocking economy was over simply on principle, not that either were freely available—except for a price on the black market. But these commodities were reminders of that Great Conquering Army—particularly its Air Force—from the West that brought with its soldiers a fake boom in luxuries for a fortunate few, and that had, with its PX economy, long since departed. Bananas were neutral.

Candy dispensers in the Underground stood mutely empty

creating rust. Neither toffee nor chocolates had been near them for a decade. In the words of a man who had apparently lived in the subway since the war and had emerged only once a day for his bottle of gin, "Those machines will never go away and never be filled. They, m' laddie, are fitting tributes to the British talent for self-torture. Didn't G.B.S. say once that an Englishman thought he was being moral when he was only being uncomfortable, or words to that effect? You couldn't spare a quid, laddie, to keep a drunken philosopher alive, could you?"

Was it possible that the entire population had only memorized the lyrics to one song and the music to another? Indoors, it was the wordless "Harry Lime Theme," usually rendered on a zither. Out of doors, a conspiracy filled the streets of nearly every district in the city with radios blaring, voices singing and unconscious humming of the other ballad: "H'ive got a loverly bunch of coconuts./ There they are a-standing in a row./ Big ones, small ones/ Some as big as your 'ead./ You give 'em a twist—a flick a' the wrist/ Is what the showman said." [2] The latter composition more fully captured the irony of English life at the turn of the mid-century mark than the zither music: *nobody* had a "loverly bunch of coconuts," at least nobody you met in the street or drank with in a pub or struck up a conversation with on a park bench or even met at the theatre or cinema. It was a good time and a great place to lose weight, unless you bought a ration book on the "market," and, even then, there wasn't much to buy worth the money it commanded.

If you stopped at hotels like the Mayfair or the Cumberland, things were different. But an outsider didn't think it right to compare even these centers of comparative luxury with anonymous little hotels on the Left Bank in Paris, where even genteel poverty, rotten plumbing and intermittent bituminus heating (as well as general strikes in which even foreigners participated in order to enjoy their sheer lunacy) were colorful symbols of a city coming back to life, a somewhat tired but beautiful city where a bottle of the worst *vin ordinaire* ever made in France turned a working man's lunch into a social occasion. In London, no coconuts. In Paris, no Nazis. And somehow, economics notwithstanding, this made all the difference in the world between the two. The sages of the cafes in Paris agreed (forever on the lookout for a glimpse of Sartre or a disciple), that freedom tasted better than victory, and they were correct. Londoners were convinced that victory was a confidence scheme.

Of course, the Marshall Plan had something to do with all of this. But it was rarely discussed, either by London University scholars drinking cider with Americans (who paid for it), glibly venting angry (but well-earned) British hostility at American mass culture; or by the surprisingly international clutch of students who drank wine in the Paris *caves* (where everybody paid for himself) and misunderstood one another simultaneously in at least three languages. Neither did the Marshall Plan seem other than an abstract matter of policy for the Americanized so-called "newspapermen" (God knows *what* they really were) who lived at the *Scribe* and/or hung out at Harry's Bar down the street. Old Harry never gave a damn. He drank cold Danish beer while his customers played at being Hemingway or Fitzgerald, and Andy, his son, tended bar and constantly pruned his then magnificent RAF-style mustache. (Harry is dead today, but Andy is still behind the bar—*American.*)

Irwin Shaw wrote his last genuinely perceptive short stories about this time and these people. As he told it, they eventually realized how displaced they were and went home. He caught the causes of their disenchantment with literary sensitivity. The main problem for most of them, during those ambiguous years after the war, was that it was almost impossible for an American—even a broke American—in Orwell's words, to be authentically "Down and Out in Paris and London." And the "lost generation" for which they were unconsciously searching had been nothing but a conceit of the nineteen-twenties, published by Scribner's and eliminated by a war—

Europe's war, not theirs. The expatriate American syndrome had been blasted to hell by the insistent reality of atomic bombs in the Pacific and a new and greedy inchoate materialism in the West, yeastily spreading as far as the borders of West Germany and Austria. From the continentals, these Americans had learned nothing. From the British, they had learned only how to hate themselves. They then retreated to their native country (from which the economic revival of Europe was silently flowing in foreign aid) back home to American universities, to publishing and brokerage houses, to newspapers and broadcasting studios from which they have not yet emerged and probably will be dislocated only by death. In the time between then and now, they have rarely wondered why America participated in World War II and its aftermath. All that puzzles (and puzzled) them is the question of who won it.

Looking Sideways

How difficult, when returning to those parts of the world one once knew well—the new London for some, the new Paris for others, the new Tokyo for others and the new Hamburg for still others—to associate these modern centers of expanding enterprise and expansive aspirations with the world one remembers of the nineteen-forties, particularly if one is an American, and particularly if one has participated, in the years between, in what may unhappily be called the "American experience" of the past generation.

Certain Americans have avoided the problem by accident or intentionally—and they are exactly the ones who should have been facing it most directly over the years—by never coming home at all. An acquaintance of considerable experience and wide travel (who requests anonymity) calls these people "Mid-Atlantic" and "Mid-Pacific" Americans, referring specifically to those diplomats, reporters, broadcasters, columnists, writers, film-makers, military types and others who, for two or more decades, have been manning the bastions of negativism one finds in the so-called "American communities" that have popped up in almost every major city in the world, except in Red China. These individuals do not wear two hats; they simply carry two watches—one for local time and one for deadlines (real or imagined) back in Washington, New York or Los Angeles. Their reading matter consists mostly of *The New York Times*, possibly the *Paris Tribune* and *Time* or *Newsweek*, and runs through a few other exported American publications *comme il faut*. They are usually not particularly wild about Coca-Cola, do not consider themselves romantic expatriates and gab wistfully about a mother in Oregon or an apartment (in which someone else is living) in Manhattan. And usually—thanks to the remarkable speed of jet aircraft—they visit their mainlands with greater regularity and more often then any other colonials in all history.

Their great problem is that they do not, in most cases, when their airplane dispatches them at Kennedy or Dulles, stop traveling with their jets. They continue to fly at supersonic speeds to their old 'teenage haunts, rapidly shake a multitude of hands and sniff the American air superficially and quickly to "keep up with things." Unless they have raised families (a somewhat rare occurrence for them) and have children (who are rapidly driven to schizophrenia, attending "American" schools in Ankara, Milan, Copenhagen, Hiroshima, La Paz and other points around the globe), they are likely to be able to withstand no more than a single season of homeland life in the USA today. Then it gets "too hot" or "too cold," or allergies act up, or a tax problem arises that can only be solved by displacement to Vienna, Dakar or Mogadishu. And, once again, they are stretched out across oceans, seas and land masses, located as our acquaintance says, "somewhere approximately at a mid-point between here and there, but exactly nowhere."

For all their activity and travel and evenings studying light-weight editions of American paperback publications, they have succeeded in doing what most of us in the post-war generation have, like it or not, failed at. They have exempted themselves from the sore realities of the American scene for two and one-half decades either by mediating these realities, distorted into pat formulae, to populations overseas (like diplomats and information-cultural dispensers) and/or feeding back similar misconceptions to a homeland newsroom, a corporation board room, or a central office in the USA. They have marketed the kind of necessarily simple-minded viewpoints. press handout junk, and trite perceptions of the history they daily see unfolding in front of them. Most of them are both old and tired today. But they are raising a new generation of "Mid-Atlantics" and "Mid-Pacifics," who seem just as old and tired, despite their youth, as soon as they step on foreign soil.

What they have not experienced at first-hand is the enormous social-psychological-economic switch game that the flunk-out lost generation that could not lose itself overseas underwent when they came back home to sweat out America, along with war veterans who hung up their uniforms and swore never to travel again further than the corner cigar store. In a way, they are lucky, because they have not been called upon to survive one of the most disturbing periods of disillusionment that any modern nation—and certainly the USA—has had to survive for a long time, climaxed by the ten-year humiliation of the Vietnam War. This latter twisted mess of military misadventure was inherited from the last days of the French Foreign Legion. It is just too easy to repeat here the usual clichés describing it: a war we should not have been in in the first place, an unwinable-unlosable war, a conflict that threw us into unholy alliances with corrupt orientals, one that demoralized our armed forces, produced a hotbed of ground-level civil atrocities directed at poor, innocent peasants, and so forth, and so forth, *ad nauseam.*

From the perspective of today's displaced American ("expatriate" is now the wrong word), America's apparent decay (as diagnosed by its Jeremiahs) seems to them far less dramatic than the multiple miracles through which *they* were living. An all but forgotten Marshall Plan *did* work—in different ways in different places—and the cross-cultural demoralization in Europe (and, to a lesser degree, in the East) created a climate for the benign aspect of Parkinson's Law: the truth that institutions are most vigorous while they are growing, yielding eventually to stasis and decay when they finally succeed. Those candy dispensers in the London underground needed very little oil to start pouring forth their penny Cadburys' once again. By 1971, a revived host of World War II's belligerent nations (winners and losers seemed irrelevant to the issue) were finally facing Parkinson's ultimate twist: that the seeds of failure are planted in every success after its heady trip on the psychological roller coaster of recovery and its correlative economic and political game-playing.

Back in the United States, meanwhile, fantastic economic recovery alone, it seemed, produced no such psychological results, at least among the generation that accepted somewhat uncritically the idealism, patriotism and poetry of America's destiny that had energized her people during the Second World War. America's community of the concerned (not necessarily the various types called "intellectuals," either of the left or right) and their increasingly skeptical and critical offspring advertised their discontents in song and story, most of it noisy. Now, noise is one of the most bitter and confusing manifestation of social discontent, as the French social psychologists of the last century knew. (We count graffiti in the New York subways and mindless vandalism on a national scale as "noise" in a cybernetic sense.)

Some of us who had lived through these galloping disillusionments (for instance like London's in 1950, from which the British soon emerged) smelled early warning signs and tried to evaluate them as social history. The present authors have attempted just this (all too poorly) in their various books, including the spiritual parent of this one, written in 1962. After preparing that volume for publication more than a decade ago, at the last moment a man with a scissors and a blue pencil appeared, called our characterizations of and prognostications for American life "too gloomy," and he got to work cheering up the volume. One of the present authors feebly added a few paragraphs to a final manuscript lionizing the American image in a manner that would cheer a DAR cultural afternoon. Another optimist wrote an "upbeat" *Epilogue* to the opus. And the hand shakily wielding his pencil across this page today purged every paragraph of grit, cutting his own cynicisms and sweetening his vinegar. America's destiny, he was told (and he believed) could not *possibly* be as vulnerable to impending disillusionments as he predicted, nor could the black-to-gray picture he had painted of his native land *possibly* (in that era of ascending Dow-Jones averages) be as dour as he and his collaborators had painted it.

Their critics were right. The future was not as bad as they had anticipated. It turned out to be *far worse*.[3]

Looking Straight

We believed then, and we believe now, that the so-called foreign and/or diplomatic policies of any nation are, in large measure, usually reflective of national policies in action or—possibly more exactly—national attitudes. They do not merely follow political stances, simply because political rhetoric is so often fiercely larded with ambiguities and lies. National attitudes are indeed ephemera. But in subtle ways they appear in public discourse by means of assorted referenda (including opinions polls), the behavior of pressure groups and the visible fabric of culture at large spelled both with a small and capital "C." The writings of Walter Lippmann, from the publication of his classic *Public Opinion* in the nineteen-twenties to his present musings, have probably examined this phenomenon more completely than any literature in the West, covering almost the entire period from World War I to the present.[4] Without an appreciation of them—or without facing them directly—little that is said about international alliances, or the communications that accompany them, may be expected to make sense; one reason that we are, at the writing, so mystified by the People's Republic of China's international propaganda ploys: ping pong, acupuncture, Maoist mysticism, wrestling, dancing, and other curiosities. More will come as the gap between East and West closes.

If we are to understand our own foreign policy—or lack of it—during that great age of our disillusionment from the Marshall Plan years to the present, we must try to understand these attitudes *within* our own heterogeneous state, their political, social, economic and psychological by-play and, amidst the pull of fashion and competition for newspaper headlines and television coverage, the hierarchical significance of what these attitudes seem to be saying about the United States as a culture and Americans as a people.

For instance, during the final years of the nineteen-sixties, well-publicized, strange behavior of young people on and off of our college campuses baffled much of the public (the present writers naturally excepted; like most educators, we have faced young students daily and have learned the horrid truth about their apparent non-conformities: namely, that while they are often bizarre on face, down deep they are more illusory than real.) The communications industries made much hay out of this phenomenon for about two years. "The revolt of the young" (as scrutinized by psychiatrists, sociologists, physicians, ministers, philosophers and veterinarians) filled Sunday Supplements, television newscasts and panel shows, throwing plenty of heat, but little light, on the subject. Then, quite eerily, these soundings from our campuses began to die down. Now, conservative Al Capp and others discovered that the best way to get kids to adore you—particularly in quasi-political, sexual and hygenic matters—is to call them "slobs" to their faces. Thereafter, they are quiet. Except for a few quite sensible rhubarbs over race issues, all *was* quiet.

The election of 1972 followed, and the "young vote" showed its muscle. Surprise, surprise! It turned out to be an unexpected conservative muscle, as eighteen-year-old voters seemed to follow (as predicted by some conservatives in print) the path of the middle-America in which they were raised. This middle-road orientation simply provided for them a more satisfactory philosophy of politics and social programs than the moonshine of their political science, sociology and philosophy professors—young ones with unkempt beards and more neatly groomed older ones. The latter had been making polemical fools of themselves for so long that they could not (and do not) comprehend what comic figures they cut, or how quietly but devastatingly most of their students were (and are) laughing at them by parroting back their own inanities to them on term papers and "socialized" examinations.

The term papers were largely plagiarized, carefully pandering to the prejudices of pedagogues, and the exams were fabrics of lies. Exit the "youth problem," at least as a more significant problem in 1973 A.D. than it was in 1873 A.D., including the "drug issue" (always good, solid newspaper copy) that centers today mostly on the use of alcohol, just as it did a century ago. (Nor is *any* type of hallucinogenic medicine yet synthesized quite as devastating as the home-distilled Kentucky style "lightnin'" which was bootlegged to kids it blinded and killed in droves in great-grantfather's time.)

In short, one of the major questions of the day—and of this chapter—is what, if anything understandable, caused the "American temper," in Joseph Wood Krutch's old phrase, to modulate as it did during the years after World War II, and to continue to modulate, considering that foreign policy and/or international propaganda bounces back and resonates widely within American life itself? The Vietnam conflict was the best and worst example in recent history, but just one instance among many: the "Watergate" incident, the "spirit of Camp David," the Korean truce and the Israeli whiz-bang war, among others we may forget or de-emphasize in time.

One favorite way, accordingly, of taking the national temperature, is to turn the job over to foreigners who, in their favor, are at least not engaged themselves in our domestic messes. This tradition, started even before the American Revolution with St. John DeCrevecoeur, was sanctified spiritually by the over-quoted Alexis deTocqueville, and carried into modernity by the likes of Gunnar Myrdal, Dennis Brogan and a clutch of British anthropologists, too dreary a bunch to mention by name. True to their heritage, the American Academy of Arts and Sciences dedicated a recent issue of their "think" journal, *Daedalus,*[5] to this enterprise, gathering nearly a dozen observers of various foreign orientations to read us their riot acts or sonnets or both. The results are certainly amusing to anyone who has studied enough chemistry to know that bases plus acids yield neutrals. Some may find them enlightening.

The consensus—minus foreign policy issues, a limitation that cuts the material in half—ran this way: a Mexican intellectual and poet sees us as Puritans who like tasteless food. (Has he been to New York or San Francisco lately? And has he tried *British* food?) A French sociologist sees us as intellectually naive, a position popular and generally accepted by nearly all French sociologists, who, apparently, live on a diet of Durkheim, the only sophisticated (to them) sociologist who ever lived. (All French sociology is rewritten Durkheim.) Another, more journalistically-oriented Frenchman with much the same disciplinary leanings, sees us as increasingly isolated from the world community, given to contemplating our national navel. A native of Bombay (from an upper Indian caste, we assume), an economist, indicts us for disregarding "basic human values" in our national life. An Italian political scientist sees us as irresponsible in managing our own serious domestic affairs. An Algerian excoriates us for disregarding basic constitutional guarantees of equality. And a Brazilian lawyer comes down hard on American mass communication, the violence it supposedly teaches and its thrust towards cultural homogenization. From Britain, two voices are heard. One condemns the sloppy way we practice, teach and use science and technology. The other sees us as a culture of petty-minded bureaucrats. Two other observers, one Greek and one English, worry about the future of American cities and the decay into which they say they are, at present, falling.

This review above merely skims the surface of an enlightening anthology. The articles are neither uniformly critical nor uncritical, negatively nor positively hewed. No major aspect of our national life is overlooked, and quite a number of characteristics counted as virtues by a certain writer of one nationality are seen as vices by another from elsewhere. The total pith of the volume is, unfortunately, an exercise in futility: pots calling kettles black and replete with heuristically incompatible general orientations towards both cultural desiderata and the USA. (What particular USA? A different one, it appears, to the eye of each beholder, hard to deny in many instances, but difficult to affirm either as adequate or correct.)

The obvious moral drawn from these articles we knew all along: The USA is the most fiercely criticized nation in the world, both by its ostensible friends and enemies. This criticism has been developed and orchestrated like a fugue around the world since V-J Day and has, at present, reached into such hitherto virgin territory as our national aspirations, let alone our actual accomplishments. Such ferocity may be one of the many inevitable consequences of national wealth and power, for which historical precedents lead one back to the ancient Egyptians and Persians. But its insistence, growth and impact resemble the Chinese Water Torture, in the face of the apparent fact that, with some exceptions, we are not merely disliked or disdained overseas—as we have been, off and on since roughly the turn of the century—but quite roundly *hated* on what, to us, often seem irrelevant grounds or possible reasons for us to be admired.

Consonant with this near ubiquitous external hatred, we have also lived through many firecracker explosions of self-hate that flare up and quickly die, but have, in sum effect, so woven their way into American culture that they are, by most of us, these days taken for granted. Not so oddly as may seem at first glance, our paroxysms of masochism wax in periods of prosperity and relative peace, and wane in times of recession and conflict. Philosophers of revolution, from Suarez to Hannah Arendt and Chalmers Johnson, have made much of this historical principle: that revolts usually occur when things are getting *better* for the masses, not at times when they are stable or on the downgrade.

The general direction of cultural criticism of the United States in sensitive places on our home front, however, has recently turned increasingly ascerbic. We see it not only on the part of our "legitimate" pulse-takers in print and in broadcasting, but in such sensitive informal indices as entertainment films, the theatre off-Broadway (the one *on* Broadway once served a "nay-saying" function; today, it has quit saying anything), in our schools and universities, on our Public Television facilities (if you have tears, prepare to shed them when you watch "educational broadcasting"), by our few serious novelists (and their imitators)—and in our "alternate" media, like the colorful but sloppy newspapers that were first seen in general circulation during the early nineteen-sixties in Greenwich Village, New York and along the Sunset Strip in Los Angeles.

True, there are both money and popularity in this sort of breast-beating, if one's breast is beaten cleverly and with verve. Nor is it new. We also detect considerable cultural value in an on-going audit of *any* aspects of *any* society. The permissible latitude of critical thrust a nation can withstand defines, in some measure, the state of its freedoms and the health of the statutes which define them. We shall, we hope keep producing generations of new and vigorous iconoclasts (God willing) some as sombre and square as Ralph Nader and some as irreverently cuddly as Abbie Hoffman and his mirror image, William Buckley. They are all sure signs that the democratic ship of state is still sailing. Nor do the old-time malcontents give up with age. The press recently carried the follow-

ing electrifyingly timely story, delivered on the anniversary of
Pearl Harbor Day 1972:

U.S. Seen 'Raping World'

Dallas, Dec. 7 (UPI)—Margaret Mead says
the world cannot withstand the emergence of
another rich nation like the United States.
"We're simply raping the rest of the world
of its natural resources," the anthropologist said here last night.[6]

End of Story.

Dr. Mead, the living doyen of the many covens of cross-
cultural anthropologists across the land, is still at it, little diminished since such early efforts as her book *And Keep Your
Powder Dry.* How comfortable, in this regard, to remember
that it is practically impossible to be processed by an American university, and get a degree, without having been also exposed to Ruth Benedict's hoary and delightfully inaccurate
Patterns of Culture, just one of many quasi-anthropological-
psychoanalytic polemics (some written in younger days by the
aging lady from the American Museum of Natural History
herself) that add up, in the long run, to happy put-downs of
what Kaufman and Hart once called *The American Way!*
These put-downs usually drip loose notions of social amorality
("cultural relativism" in professor-talk) and almost invariably
compare American life invidiously to the folkways of people
who no longer exist, never existed, or exist in places so remote
that their life-styles cannot withstand closer scrutiny by methods of observation more rigorous than those loosely labeled
"anthropological."

Vigorous iconoclasism is one thing, of course, but explosions of nonsense, half-truths and sensationalized gossip are
others. What they have in common with one another in the

USA is, pure and simple, the same constitutional protection. And the day that our Constitution *stops* protecting the Buckleys, Rockwells, Hoffmans, Kunstlers, Rubins, Kahanes, Learys, Ginsbergs, and others, both lunatic and sane, is the day the authors will purchase one-way tickets to a remote culture that even Dr. Mead has not yet discovered. But, as old journalists rarely tire of repeating, exciting news fit to print is not alchemized from day-to-day events that go *right,* the doings of people who behave—the usual state of human affairs almost everywhere most of the time. An airplane that manages to get from New York to Florida in one piece *without* being skyjacked seems to the authors a formidable miracle (given the traffic patterns around most large airports.) But a safe journey is not news. It is the rare and occasional skyjacking that is provided cultural celebration in newspapers, novels, films, on the tube and in breakfast conversations.

How much national attention, therefore, is normally given those news events that result from break-downs in normal activities that usually run pretty well? The answer, in addition to commenting on the avidity and cupidity of professional exploiters of various kinds, is at any moment *reflective* of national attitudes—that is, something of an index of what people *want* to read, *want* to see in movies and *want* to watch on television. (Of course, up to a point people in a free market *must* read and watch what they are *given;* but in the long run they seem usually to *get* more or less what they *want,* because competition weeds out weak sisters in a dynamic society like ours.) One newspaper that bravely tried to print only good news recently failed. But the *New York Daily News,* a catastrophe-ridden periodical if ever there was one, thrives. And so do its imitators, if they imitate skillfully.

For a four-month period (September through December, 1972), the authors kept an informal record of major "fire alarm" stories in a wide-range of middle-road American periodicals: *The New York Times, The Wall Street Journal, The Reader's Digest, The Saturday Review, Life Magazine,* and various other publications that were found on subway and taxi seats, left outside with garbage,ˋ or stolen from the briefcases and desks of erstwhile colleagues and friends. Utilizing this *rigidly* scientific method of obtaining random data, these items (all of them in excess of roughly half-a-dozen paragraphs) were categorized according to the following *ironclad* criterion: the sensible ones were kept and the stupid ones were thrown away. A time control was also introduced into the study in order to insure an unbiased sample: namely, only that much of each periodical was scrutinized as the authors had time to read each day—enough time, that is, to interfere neither with business nor pleasure.

The results of this investigation, as anticipated, were something of a mess. The hypothesis, however, that the range and depth of American self-criticism conforms to no particular pattern, and emulates a shot-gun blast aimed at our own backsides, was confirmed at a level of statistical confidence impossible to apply to the data.

During the period of this investigatory breakthrough, the United States was undergoing the exuberant pressures of a presidential election, the Dow-Jones Industrial Average on the New York Stock Exchange finally (after many tries) broke the 1,000 level, unemployment figures were low, business was—modestly speaking—booming, and the war in Vietnam finally, after ten years, seemed to be winding down. A record number of American troops were sent home monthly, while the bombing increased to its highest level of ferocity over Hanoi and Haiphong. Our international trade problems, particularly with Japan and the Common Market nations, were apparently stabilizing, and we ended the period by sending mercy missions to the earthquake-stricken city of Managua, Nicaragua. We also showed a modest quantum of national grief at the death of Harry S Truman, our 33rd President.

The following issues, however, dominated the news in these journals to the degree that a foreigner might conclude that they were published in a nation on the brink of revolution. Because they were *all* handled with such monomaniacal intensity, they are listed below in no particular order. *Every* problem, *every* catastrophe or augury of one was, in most cases, treated as if it were *the one most serious problem* facing our nation on the day it was printed. The main issues were:

1. *Urban crime* was a winner on all counts—possibly because most of the publications we scrutinized were written or printed in large cities. The mechanics and nature of urban crime and its nuances seem to provide endless supplies of colorful news and feature copy, especially when the crime is supposedly "organized," a word the authors do not fully comprehend.

2. *Drugs and drug addiction* are apparently nearly ubiquitous today in the USA, although our various reference books calculate that, *including alcoholism,* no more than one in a dozen Americans is touched by an addiction to anything more serious than cigarettes and/or food. Drug addiction is, nevertheless, the stuff that front page news stories are made of both in sensational and in good, gray journals.

3. *Prisons and penology* seem to have attracted an inordinate number of self-made experts who write about their problems with deft certitude. As rarely as it has occurred, even in its most popular days, capital punishment also seems to have become a national issue of deep fascination, evoking major determinations of conscience from our citizenry and decision at the gut level. (Are the authors of this volume somehow subversive of the national welfare by *not caring much* whether the dozen or so men and women a year who are found guilty of planned murder in the USA are electrocuted, hung, incarcerated for life or, if they are crazy, sent to loony bins until they are either cured or die? Granted that capital punishment is a fascinating subject by virtue of its adventure-laden context, is it, at this time and in this place, an *important* issue for our society, especially when compared with others of wider effects and deeper pith—like the matter of equal educational opportunities for

twenty-two million Negro Americans, for instance? We think not!)

4. *The behavior of the young* is probably a corollary to our crime problems at large, but America's youth orientation seems to have created a climate in which the travails of growing up are, *per se*, a continent-wide area of national interest and discontent. Wayward children and their behavior seems to be an extremely "sexy" topic, in the *patois* of the public relations fraternity.

5. *Pollution and ecology* as *fashionable* issues of the moment seem to be losing ground in amount—but not intensity —of journalistic and periodical coverage. Writers these days seem to apologize to their readers before they bring up a pollution issue. And nobody mentions the death of Lake Erie any more, simply because it is not dead.

6. Balancing our scale of concern for the young is *concern for the aged*. There is general agreement that growing old in America is a pretty bad business, worse, we assume than growing old elsewhere, although aging is never a pleasure. *The Wall Street Journal* devoted a superbly researched series of articles to this problem, and other journals usually treat it at least once a week.

7. *The race issue* has been "cooled," perhaps from "benign neglect," as suggested some time ago by Dr. Moynihan during his sojourn into executive politics, but its ramifications live on in school problems, social problems, problems concerning black movies, black television performers and black radio (yes!). (Our purview, unfortunately, did not extend to articles in the Negro press itself. But a recent rough perusal of a number of Negro journals—pitched to a relatively affluent constituency—led us to conclude, roughly, that they display somewhat *less* strident alarm at the state of the nation than their white counterparts.)

8. *Sexual morality*, and particularly *our new apparent sexual permissiveness* in life, films, literature and almost every-

where else, seems to upset hard-boiled newspaper and magazine reporters and editorial writers considerably. Possibly, they mourn the passing of the New York Society for the Suppression of Vice. Possibly, they miss the old illegal "dirty pictures" and "stag films" the boys in the city room used to circulate and borrow from newspaper printers and engravers.[7] At any rate, modern America is endlessly compared to a declining and falling Rome in news stories and feature articles juicily concerned with "X" rated films, pornography in print, topless watering places, massage parlors and similar joyful enterprises. Oddly, few observers seem to take a stand in favor of *sexual permissiveness* (real and/or printed or photographed) or defend very convincingly our (now apparently selectively legal) pornographers, peep-show operators and producers of dirty feature films. Nor do they show admiration of or notice that new breed of actors (no worse as thespians than yesterday's Hollywood work-a-day movie performers) who seem to be able to indulge in sexual activity, recite their lines and remain "in character" —all at the same time.

9. A lot of people seem to be agitated to the point of mayhem about the *strains of violence* they detect in America's entertainments, occupations and daily affairs. The functional term is "the amount of violence in American life." According to them, we are, compared to others, a violent nation. Well, maybe; the issue is moot. And arguments here, pro or con, serve no end.

10. *Legalized abortion and birth control* are certainly hot issues, combining what is apparently an hypnotic fascination for the least attractive aspects of sexual behavior, popularized religious dogmatism and misunderstood public health problems. They are nibbled to the core, not only in articles and features written for women, but in news stories, feature stories for men and editorials as well.

11. *Conflicts between sub-cultures* and *the problems of the American "melting pot"* bring out the amateur sociological proclivities in the best and worst of writers. Overtones of C. P.

Snow's old warnings about England's "two cultures" (the scientific and the literary) weave in and out of these discussions, most of them as generally incomplete as Snow's original essay.

12. Something seemed to be percolating in or around the issue of *social and geographical mobility* in America. But we may just have been dealing here with advance soundings of publicity campaigns for Vance Packard's new book, *A Nation of Strangers*. Packard knows how to sell books, not the least of his virtues as man and writer, and, in his status as a literary celebrity, anything he says or does may well be construed by hungry journalists as "news."

13. *Busing* was a major subject of attention, but one too topical to mean much, we think, taken alone at the time of our experiment. The problem of racial equality is definitely *not* dead, Moynihan notwithstanding, but it is difficult to cleave any single aspect of it from its own causes, symptoms and results.

14. Despite our comments above, little more than elaborately detailed adventure stories seemed to center upon the pastime of *airplane hijacking*. Possibly, everything that can be said about this problem has already *been* said by novelists and script writers for television and films.

The "also rans" make up a strange group of ponies and old nags, but all of them are still serving as journalistic slap-sticks for beating heads and still make occasional loud noises. Noise itself, for instance, is a respectable feature story and editorialist's "ecological blight." It probably causes cancer. (Have those Americans who seem so concerned about urban noises ever tried to live in a French city or in an Italian town, where everybody is related to everybody else?) We are also apparently living through a period of revival of interest in Hitler and his Nazis and Il Duce in Italy, pitched mostly to a "It can happen here" theme. Health (declining, poor or worse), medical care (vile) and hospitals (foul) worry us considerably in print, as do a wide variety of consumer problems too dull to read or report in detail, along with the ancient issue of adver-

tising abuses, against which Americans supposedly are not
properly protected. (Who is?) Womens' Liberation—or more
precisely the illusion of female equality, in abstruse domains,
with the human male—seem to be heading hell-bent for the la-
cuna of public indifference. So is the shocking news that American education is, while it is universally applied and variently
free, pretty rotten nearly everywhere, from playschool to professional academy. Education, we are forever reminded, is also
financially deprived—a matter of poor priorities, says the official line. But possibly the public (or its information conduits)
are wising up to the fact that Americans pay more to receive
in toto poorer schooling than any other people in the world.
Civil rights, free speech, the threat of data banks to personal
privacy and similar other modest, but really serious issues, received more well-considered coverage than we had anticipated. But possibly this trend (if it is a trend) reflects the sensitivity of journalists to their *own* problems. The destinies and
caprices of both commercial and public broadcasters, giant
foundations and the state of televised news on commercial stations all pop up from time to time in a setting of *schmerz*. Little attention is paid any longer to nuclear warfare *per se*, or to
the effects of radioactive fallout. Recent epidemics of venereal
disease seem, in these selected publications, to pose greater
threats to the republic. For all we know, they may.

The reader, by now, may think that the authors, in their
jocular mood about the state of the nation, during the four-
month period they surveyed, have drawn a questionable pro-
file from the subway seat and from the newspaper-magazine
garbage cans that has doubtful value and validity. If the
reader will consider the combined circulation and total read-
ership of our research sources, which is in excess of fifteen million daily and weekly, the data culled therefrom becomes
significant. Contrast this with a forthcoming book (at this
writing) called *The State of the Nation*, edited by William
Watts and Floyd A. Free for Potomac Associates, Inc., which
labels itself as a nonpartisan, research and analysis organiza-

tion. Their study is based on "an exhaustive poll" (as *Time* Magazine tells it) of 1,806 Americans by the Gallup organization, wherein each subject was asked 87 questions regarding themselves and society.[8]

We do not know if the *interview technique* used by Gallup was structured or unstructured, if it was nondirective, focused, free-wheeling or non-wheeling; nor can we vouch for its *predictive validity*, its *concurrent validity*, or its *construct validity*. As for its *reliability* in regard to the test-retest method, the parallel-forms method, and the split-half method, no mention is made. Nor can we vouch for the scoring and the inventorying of the scales used by Gallup which may be nominal, ordinal, interval or ratio. Among the questions that come to our minds are: how "exhaustive" are 1,806 people who are asked 87 questions? Who are the 1,806 people? Are they the same that Nielsen uses in rating television broadcasts? If so, "Off with their heads!" Are any of these 1,806 people survivors of (or related to) the 1948 poll taken by Gallup and others who predicted the election of Thomas E. Dewey to the Presidency? We ask these questions both of Potomac Associates and of Gallup since their conclusions and ours seem akin. Where we differ (excluding the methodology; ours is more colorful than theirs) is upon the subject of pollution, which we put lower on the scale of the public's interest than they do. Perhaps it was because in our methodology there was a clearing-up fringe benefit that was not present in theirs.

For good reasons already noted, it is impossible for us to evaluate fairly or objectively these concerns, or to relate them accurately to the national mood today. The United States is a country extraordinarily prone to whims of fashion in important as well as in trivial matters. The ecology *cum* pollution issue seemed to burst suddenly upon us a few years ago, although early warnings had been issued years before by Rachel Carson. Crime has always been a popular issue in the American press, and so has sex. But *how* they manifest themselves as public concerns changes with the winds of fashion. Once upon a time, cigarettes caused cancer. Scare messages were printed on packages, and advertising on the air waves proscribed. Result: more of us are smoking more than ever, and carcinoma statistics remain fairly stable. Cyclamates were shown to cause cancer in mice and banned from the market, apparently, says logic, in an effort to protect the health of the average American mouse. Well, the mice did not care. They are not noticably healthier today than they were yesterday. And cyclamates will some day return.

Proving what? Not much, in truth, except that neither Americans (nor anyone else) are creatures of fashion by instinct but rather by training. Economists, for instance, will tell you that our "throw away" society demands this or that particular fashion, along with planned obsolescence and plastic gee-gaws that fall apart easily and thereby create employment. Possibly, whim and fashion are, under these circumstances, necessarily cultivated for the present in order to sustain our supermarket culture. But they cannot be cultivated in material or acquisitive aspects of life alone without producing side-effects in the daily psychological tonus of us all, including editors of newspapers and magazines and broadcasting executives. The indices above of our demoralization today *will not* be the symptoms of our disillusionments of tomorrow —as we move on to new fashions of "viewing with alarm," or as the pendulum swings, taking us back to old crises of spirit we thought were forgotten.

This instability, in and by itself, constitutes legitimate cause for concern—or so Packard and others are telling us today—although this same sort of instability and restlessness (we were once told by our grade school teachers) was the main aspect of human character that made our nation great in crossing the physical frontiers of yesterday. Does *this* change in attitude mean that Americans have given up their (once well-advertised) new adverturism in the domains of the frontiers-in-the-mind, in business, in technology and elsewhere? Evidence does not appear to sustain the claim, although in the period of psychological anti-climax following the decline of our moonshot space program, anything is possible.

Looking Around

Stretching our purview beyond the four-month survey mentioned above, we note that in the past decade, the United States has shown signs of panic at its own successes. Snatching defeat from the jaws of victory has become an American talent.

Motivated and incited as classical political gambits (in the best American traditions of dirty pool and venal manipulation) on the part of *both* Republican and Democratic partisans, the so-called "Watergate" scandal of 1973 possibly constituted an inevitable reaction to all the unexpected events that had so recently—and to many, intolerably—turned out right in an age of mythic doomsaying: American troop withdrawal from (and even tokens of military sagacity in) Vietnam, summitry and news of *detente* with Red China and the USSR, relative peace and quiet in our cities, a Dow-Jones Industrial Average that had popped the "1000 mark" and—most horrible to relate—a Presidential election in 1972 that sent back to the White House office one of the most skillful—and profoundly hated by his opponents—figures in recent political life in what appeared to be a national vote of confidence (everywhere but in Massachusetts).

The times were ripe for scandal!

In addition, Watergate also represented the apparent exfoliation of four stylistic evolutions in social and political American life that had been threatening to precipitate in rampant excess beginning with the Presidency of Franklin Delano Roosevelt.

First, considerable power from the Congressional and Judicial arms of government had, over the years, been flowing in the direction of the White House—to the Oval Room, in particular—at an ever-accelerating (and to some, alarming) rate, having gathered its greatest momentum during the Camelot-era of the short-lived Kennedy administration.

Second, tempered by extremism of left and right, a climate of "higher loyalty" had, by 1973, wedged its way into influential intellectual and political circles, whereby traditional restraints of law—almost as a matter of routine—were flouted in the name and service of causes seen by their proponents as "bigger" or "nobler" than law. Thus on one side, flowed an epidemic of leaks of confidences and secrets to newspaper gurus, columnists and broadcasters who, willy-nilly, spread them like apple seeds in the faith that they were serving the state, their readers, and viewers and listeners by dredging gossip, releasing for public view obtuse game- and contingency-plans and the texts of secret negotiations. In another part of the ball park, political motives impelled wily departments of "dirty tricks" into crude illegalisms such as amateur burglary, ad-lib wiretapping and political chicanery, as men of questionable and unquestionable repute came to the aid of their party—and most specifically, its leader. For the latter exercise in Republican party zealousness and "higher loyalty," the *buck* stopped on the Republican chief executive's desk. It had to!

Third, the growing excessive use of advertising, merchandising and selling techniques in the marketing of personalities for political office, from the lowliest of precinct titles to the Presidency of the USA, fell more and more into the hands of the management-merchandising-marketing experts of the advertising agencies in the country. Growing up in the nation, along with looser and easier-gotten money at higher political levels, was a plethora of techniques and technicians to establish political celebrity and a form of "stardom" akin to the Hollywood-television publicity industry. The ballot box was brought down to the level of the theatre box office.

The ballyhoo factories in America, incipiently peaking and spreading out with P. T. Barnum and incorporating such manifestations as the nineteenth century western-roaming patent medicine pitchman, the post-Civil War southern-roam-

ing carpetbagger and the Lydia E. Pinkham all-purpose panaceas were replaced by mass circulating newspapers, magazines and by such mass communicating devices as radio and
television (the telephone played no little part here) as conduits for the management-merchandising-advertising expert
and the efficiencies of this twentieth century manipulator-
salesman of fashions, fads and behavior. The mover of goods
and services now became pivotal as the mover of political
forces. At times, with excessive zeal, he has overstepped the
bounds of fair play; promised the voters more than he can
deliver; subliminally and insidiously manipulated the elector-
ate with questionable tactics to achieve (what we shall call
here) the successful exploitation of *the celebrity syndrome* to
which the American people are so readily susceptible.

Concomitant with this *celebrity syndrome* phenomenon
in American political life is the *spoils system* as first articulated by Andrew Jackson as a byproduct of the political wars.
This takes the form of handouts to the supporters of the winner. These handouts can be policymaking executive positions,
influence peddling, payments and repayments in cash or services for financial and other support, and the general fallout
of executive and legislative favors. The stage of political cam-
paigning in 1972 was a natural and inviting setting for such
over-zealous selling, payoffs and cover-ups in what sometimes has been called "a nation of salesmen."

Fourth, that relatively homogeneous and inbred institution loosely called "the American press" (including broadcast
journalists, and which represents the capital ownership of
less than a thousand powerful entrepreneurs, most of them
related to one another by blood and/or common interests),
had recently undergone real and imagined impositions to its
classical rights of freedom (or license) due to various pressures from executive and judicial sources motivated from
Washington and elsewhere. At the first sniff of scandal, the
press behaved like hungry cats in a salmon cannery. The
result was a particularly American orgy—self-praise and

sometimes pure bravado—in print and on the airwaves. Scandal in the form of Watergate, according to newspaper, magazine and broadcasting magnates somehow entirely vindicated an era past of sloppy (and often foolish) journalistic arrogance that had begun, roughly, two decades before, when reporters and editors hurled Senator Joseph McCarthy into national prominence and cut their careless paths in the high grass of American life ever since in search of headlines and "good copy." Faced by mounting criticism and even a specter of modest requests for performance accountability as professional men and women, their exploitation of Watergate (and particularly the ambiguous role of President Nixon in its shady dealings), vindicated, they were convinced, their stances as fearless journalists protecting, *pro bono publico,* American freedom, truth and law.

(If one doubted the proposition, it was confirmed *ad nauseum* in the newspapers, on radio and television and in news magazines which tirelessly explained the magnitude of their own heroism. "Higher loyalty" again, of course, because for all its righteous indignation at political snooping, the fraternity of journalists rarely—if ever—compared these acts to the bag of tricks, schemes, bribery and countless other quasi- and illegal devices that remain common journalistic practices, morally vindicated, as they see it, by the readers' and viewers' "right to know." Such is the orientation of the devout journalist that he cannot—or will not—relate his own "professional" sliding-scale of ethics to those of politicians, or anyone else, for that matter. And when the politician on the journalist's chopping block is a powerful, successful and tough-minded President of the USA, even Nixon's admirers in the nation's news rooms could not resist shooting from the hip—from behind their typewriters and microphones.)

America, in other words, was literally waiting for the Watergate scandals of 1973.

In West Europe, (and especially in Britain, where a sexier

scandal was mounting at the time), the episode seemed to many an incomprehensible American aberration. In East Europe, the intellectual grapevine had it that powerful anti-USSR forces in America were out to incinerate Nixon because he had eaten caviar with Politburo communists in Moscow. In Asia, much the same rumor persisted—but this time the China Lobby was the culprit out to discredit the man who had visited Mao and Chou and who had thumbed his nose at Formosa's Chinese Republic.

For America, Watergate symbolized a convergence, fusion and explosion of all these above-mentioned social and historical trends—as it lashed and backlashed in the maw of public opinion. A few sanguine souls thought that the experience might teach us some lessons about the abuses of power —all kinds of power—and the destructive potentials of unchecked authority in the hands of men propelled by godlike principles rather than by common horse sense. Some saw the efficacy of the American system to purge itself. Others extolled the press as the natural adversary of government authority. Still others condemned "trial by press" despite the public's "right to know." They cited the fact that the power of the press can at times paralyze the power of the courts as a setting for a fair advocacy trial. There were others who cited the gray line separating national security from domestic security. Secrecy in government was condemned and open administrations were extolled. Executive privilege, cabinet power, appointive power and subpoena power collided with low-key talk about Presidential resignation, impeachment, or impoundment.

Watergate sold newspapers (although it sometimes lowered television audience ratings). Watergate resonated on Wall Street. Watergate vibrated in the international money markets. Watergate threw a few old-time, long-standing (and young neophyte) politicians and their retinue into the public spotlight for an instant or two. Others, "all honorable men," were simply caught with their political plans down.

All in all, Watergate merely vindicated Lord Acton's dictum about the evils of absolute power. A page turned in an old history book.

Looking Ahead

A soft-spoken Negro in his late forties or early fifties, dressed neatly in the uniform of a private service organization, stood on a line in order to swear his allegiance to the United States, prior to finishing his application for a passport at a government office in New York's Rockefeller Center. (The oath is no longer delivered orally.) The year was 1971, and the season was fall.

"I've got to get it all figured out," he said in conversation with another applicant standing behind him. "And I'm not going to get it figured out *here;* I know that much."

As the queue moved desultorily towards the bureau window, he continued. "What I have in mind is to go back to the places in Europe I got to during the War. Places in France, Italy and Germany. I tried it once with my wife, but it didn't work. This time I'm going alone."

Another shuffle on the queue. A few moments' silence.

"Somehow, I've got to get it figured. Hell, I'm not going to solve any big problem; I'll leave that to the politicians. What I've got to figure out is myself. The way I see it, that's more of a job these days for a black man than it is for a white— although I can't say how mixed up you are, mister. Maybe worse than I am. Maybe much worse.

"It was different in the War. In that time, I understood where I was going. But when I got there, it wasn't the place, if you know what I mean. I'm not just talking about race stuff; I mean everything in this here country. Like you did, I guess, I really believed in President Roosevelt. Damn, I was just a kid, but he was a *great* man. And somehow everything was different here in this city in those days. You remember that time? You're about my age, aren't you? You from this city?

"Hell, nothing was perfect—maybe worse for black men

than white men, but it sure as hell didn't make the black man less American than any white. Not then. And if it did, you didn't know so badly as you do these days. What we been going through lately, seeing my own kids go to hell—one dead from drugs and the other in Vietnam doing God knows what —all this wasteful dissension among *my* people, black people wasteful, get it?—it seems we got off the track somewhere, whites *and* blacks, all of us, but sure as hell us blacks. Other Negroes get to call me down for what I think, but you have to believe what you see with your eyes, don't you?"

The line moved a little further.

"I've done pretty well for a poor Alabama sharecropper's kid—in money, I mean. Better than I ever thought I would— and better than plenty of white kids I went to DeWitt Clinton High School with. But that's not the answer. Maybe the answer is somewhere over at those places I went to in the War. Maybe I'll find them again, just being there and thinking from a distance. I've got this feeling to look back over the ocean and put it together. Talk a little bit to the people who lived in the middle of that damn war, people who were damn thankful to see any American G.I., black, white or purple, and, I want to see what *their* kids are like, and how they figure things. I guess I never met people like them before—or since. I wonder if I'll find somebody who remembers me?"

He had nearly reached the desk where the passports were being processed.

"I don't expect no miracles, and I don't think I'm very smart, so I'm not looking for revelations. Thinking isn't my business. And plenty of people as mixed up as I am have plenty more education than I do. But you don't need to be a genius to know that something is wrong in this place, dead wrong—and bad. I smell it, man. Maybe it's the Vietnam mess, but I don't personally count that for too much. The rottenness is inside here—with us, and there ain't laws or organizations or people that really seem to want to fix it. Well, I guess everybody will just have to fix it for himself! That's why I'm going back. Maybe I knew something when I was a kid that I've forgotten in the meantimes. Do you ever get that feeling that you've forgotten something real important that you knew once?"

At the passport officer's desk he handed his credential to a mustached drone, who scrutinized them, asked a few questions, made some changes, stamped them, took a fee and handed back change.

"You'll get your passport in about three weeks," said the officer. "Now raise your right hand and repeat after me, 'I solemnly swear to defend and support the Constitution of the United States against all enemies foreign and domestic, and I shall further promise to uphold. . . .'"

The black man repeated the oath carefully, listening with feeling to his own voice, almost as if he were someone else speaking these words for the first time in history.

The late Hamilton Fish Armstrong, an internationalist with decades of experience, shortly before his death, took a long, reflective look at his nation. His were the wise eyes of a man whose career in diplomacy stretches back to World War I. He wrote a retrospective article to terminate his many years as editor of one of our best professional journals on foreign policy. His attention, like the attention of many of us today, centers (in his ultimate considerations) upon the *malaise* of his country and the myriad discontents that so many Americans of all races, economic classes and educational backgrounds seem to be living with today. Our disillusionment is much like that of other war-weary nations in times past: like, for example, Great Britain in 1950, where this chapter began, in a period when the past hardly seems worth the effort to remember, and the future appeared to be problematical at best and catastrophic at worse—in short, wherever and whenever the spectre of demoralization casts its dim *umbra* over an entire nation, bleaching the color from its landscape from border to border.

Says elder statesman Armstrong:

> Our direction is not backward, in nostalgia, to the virtues of our forefathers, except that we will draw from them an adventurous spirit and in that spirit will answer the question, "What is wrong?" with the answer they gave, "Let's do something about it." The direction is forward, to recognize and accept the present ills of our society and to set about curing them—by rehumanizing ourselves, by readopting civility as a part of good behavior, by recognizing that history can inform the future, by encouraging the growth of elites in many fields, not in order to copy them snobbishly but to set intellectual standards to which everyone may in some degree aspire, by asserting that aesthetics is an essential element in art, by re-establishing learning as opening doors to choice, by leavening the mediocrity of our culture with snatches of unorthodoxy, by welcoming diversity of opinion as an essential element of strength in a democracy.[9]

As that wounded soldier in the old joke groaned, "It only hurts when I laugh."

NOTES TO CHAPTER 2

[1] The pitch here was for the *Common Cause Referendum*, seeking contributions from $15 to $100 in order to join "almost a quarter of a million other concerned Americans in this nation." The plea was from John Gardner, author of the breast-beating letter that accompanied it. Because the destruction of the Mount Rushmore memorial was not among the fifteen items, neither author contributed anything, and instead sent $5.00 each to the National Cat Protection Society, 2330 Maine Avenue, Long Beach, California, 90806.

² Known by the first line in the lyric quoted in the text, this song is sometimes incorrectly referred to as: "Roll-or-bowl a ball—a penny a pitch!" It was copyrighted in 1944 and 1948 by The Irwin Dash Music Co., Ltd., London. It was also copyrighted in 1949 by Warock Corp. by arrangement with Box & Cox (Publishers) Ltd., London. The above information was provided by the American Society of Composers, Authors and Publishers through the offices of Edward Collier.

³ We shall not verify or reincarnate the excised material, but note, in *The Idea Invaders,* the eleventh hour rescue given the chapter called "America the Not-So-Beautiful" (pp. 208–231), and the ambiguous (and possibly meaningless) "Postscript," p. 232.

⁴ See G. N. Gordon, *Persuasion,* pp. 142–143, for a reprise of Lippmann's shifting ideas, as well as bibliographical notations in the footnotes, etc. Clinton Rossiter and James Lare's, *The Essential Lippmann* (New York: Random House, 1963) is the variorium of his works for the non-political scientist. However, various noted social psychologists prefer their own recondite tradition of experiment and speculation into what they call "attitudes," many of whom are cited in the former volume by Gordon. While Lippmann's notion of "public opinion" is quite clear, the psychological fraternity rarely agrees on the nature of "attitudes" as opposed to "opinions," "beliefs," "dispositions" and other cognitive and affective states of mind. Nor do pollsters do much better. Taking advantage of this ambiguity in their so-called "attitude" studies, they frequently evaluate precisely any number of factors *except* "attitudes." A certain amount of ambiguity concerning what social psychologists try to define gives professional pollsters wide latitudes within which to do their polling.

⁵ See *Daedalus,* Fall 1972, sub-titled "How Others See the United States." Possibly the editors of the *National Lampoon* might find motivation in it to concoct an issue on "How the United States See Everybody Else." The present authors volunteer to compose a free article (worth the price) on the *true* American perspective of life in Liechtenstein. Neither author has, of course, ever been there or intends to go.

⁶ *The New York Times,* December 8, 1972, p. 11. The authors have not requested permission from the *Times* to reprint verbatim any of the considerable amount of their copyrighted material used in this book. (Other sources have been directly quoted only *with* permission.) Applying the same *philosophical* principle under which the *Times* printed the Pentagon Papers, we believe that we have the *right* to use freely anything that appears in the *Times,* because (1) the *Times* is a national institution whose output is culturally significant (an issue proved when the *Times* prints daily issues that are never intended to be sold or circulated during labor strikes) in keeping the national record and in informing the public of the news they have a *right to know,* and (2) this latter need falls into the philosophical and juridical area of public domain, as the *Times* itself

interprets it, one far more important to the welfare of our nation than, say a trove of prolix, obsolete "Top Secret" contingency war plans prepared for the use of diplomats and military specialists. Copyrights given to *Times* articles and stories by means of statute and other irrelevancies (like "fair play," for instance) are accordingly and logically subsumed to *our* rights as authors to spread the wisdom of the *Times* abroad sans permission, notification or payment of fees *as a public service*, identical in motive and process to the *Times'* treatment of the Pentagon Papers. (In this matter, our publisher presumably agrees.)

We are, Mr. Sultzberger, simply testing a matter of principle. What, if anything, happens next? From ignoring the issue (a classic *Times* method of handling sticky matters in its own house) to legal proceedings that, hopefully, will end in court, our own selfish purposes will inevitably be well served. In other words, at worst we shall not be forced to bother seeking your leave (which you would probably grant) to reprint *Times* material. At best, we may receive a good deal of free publicity which, these days, is about the only inexpensive way for a relatively small publisher to compete successfully with giants in the glutted book market. Let us add that this decision was also taken partly on behalf of the hundreds of school teachers who, every day, feel like criminals when they duplicate by photocopy various *Times'* articles for the use of their students, despite the solemn ukase, glued to many public photocopiers, that the *Times* prohibits such reproduction of its materials. Does the *Times* (or any major newspaper) have the *right* (or gall) to prohibit such behavior, in the light of its own assumptions defending its own decision to reproduce the Pentagon Papers in print, our hazy copyright laws notwithstanding? Because this move is also motivated by self-interest in the desire to publicize this book, in the words of Nathan Detroit in *Guys and Dolls*, "Sue me!"

(Details of the main issues involved in the Pentagon Papers incident may be found neatly summarized in the Twentieth Century Fund Task Force report, *Press Freedoms Under Pressure*, New York: The Twentieth Century Fund, 1972, pp. 37–48. Relevant Supreme Court decisions and dissents are reprinted in full in Appendix 3, pp. 133–193.)

[7] According to one of its ex-cultural editors, the press room of the now defunct *New York Herald-Tribune* was a virtual hotbed for the production, distribution and circulation of pornographic photographs and films, a fitting side enterprise, we think, for one of the last journalistic bastions of genteel conservatism in this country.

[8] *Time Magazine*, December 25, 1972, pp. 12–13.

[9] Hamilton Fish Armstrong, "Isolated America" in *Foreign Affairs*, October, 1972, pp. 9–10.

3

In God We Trusted

> *The possibilities of American diplomacy are not limited, therefore, to the correction of past mistakes, or the overcoming of the instabilities resulting from the heritage of the past war and the great process of decolonization. There are other possibilities: ones that have wider and more promising horizons— ones for the solution of which American strength is needed and the American genuis is peculiarly suited.*
>
> GEORGE F. KENNAN [1]

Yesterday's Magic

While the non-event that follows hardly ranks in the an-nals of idiocy besides Tennyson's Balaclava (because of ca-prices of fate and the frailities of men), we shall begin this chapter with a footnote to an obscurity of history. Possibly it is a trivial one, but it is illustrative of non-trivial consequences when discussing American foreign policy.

For most of us who lived through 1945 (in our adult life) the intense drama of that year has never since been equalled in pith, moment or machine-gun rapidity of critical events around the world. Newspaper headlines, taken alone, capture the incredible sequence of shock waves surrounding the end of World War II. And if ever there was one in our history, this is the single most fervid time of multiple climaxes through which we have (yet) lived. That numerous pieces of the historical record were, in those days, lost in the shuffle was, we imagine, inevitable. All the world *was* a stage that year, but the play was a living reprise of the ancient "Crazy House" sketch on the burlesque stage, and the actors of history were truely improvising.

The philosophy of our foreign policy that year was the same as the one that guides us at present: to muddle through the challenge of today and see what happens tomorrow—not bad practically, but shot through with hidden drawbacks. Men who dealt in the futures market of philosophy with long-term theories (like Henry Morgenthau, who wanted to turn the defeated German nation into a society limited by international law to peaceful pursuits, mostly agrarian) were considered slightly addelpated or hopelessly unrealistic. Peace would take care of itself, if its administration was applied in small daily doses—or so the best opinion avered.

As the war in the Pacific was dying down, a message was relayed to President Roosevelt via the United States Embassy in Chungking that two Chinese communist revolutionaries desired to visit the President in Washington in order to discuss the future of mainland China after the end of hostilities. Such an obscure message, naturally, means nothing taken alone; there are always foreign leaders who would enjoy a trip to, and a free meal at, the White House.

These two particular gentlemen, however, were Mao Tsetung and Chou En-lai, names not particularly familiar in those days to the American public, but figures of considerable importance to old "China hands" who had weathered the war in the Orient, to the hierarchy of the Kuomintang, to our (then) military ally Chiang Kai-shek and his lovely wife. (The latter lady, in her way and day, did more to fog eyes in our Executive Mansion and on Congressional Hill about political realities in the mysterious East than the high-powered and high-priced China Lobby.)

The request, or plea, for a visit to our shores by Mao and Chou (and let the reader chew his toenails as he considers what *might* have resulted from it) was accompanied (recently declassified World War II documents are purported to say) by *another* message of affirmation signed by the *entire staff* of the American Chungking Embassy, who could not help but antici- pate what was brewing in China, heartily urging Roosevelt to provide an audience in Washington for the two Red Chinese leaders. Everybody on the American staff, that is, except Ambassador Patrick J. Hurley, an enthusiast of the Chiang regime. Hurley, first delayed transmission of the request it- self to Washington, and finally accompanied it with an ascer- bic note to his boss, urging succinctly that the team of peti- tioners be ignored.

Roosevelt died shortly afterwards without responding to the request. It is problematic that he would have answered it affirmatively, Hurley's advice aside. Wartime allies like Chiang were, after all, considered brothers under the skin. The time was 1945, and the task of the moment was to get from today to tomorrow, regardless of what the actual political and military position of Chiang (and his family) was, in a nation we now know was teetering on the brink of revolution. Whatever the reasons, the request by Chou and Mao ended in the circular file, despite the importance that our Embassy people *knew* it clearly portended for the future.

President Truman, forgivably we think, did not heed this and similar pleas that an *entente* be arranged with the Red Chinese, even at the behest of more impressive figures than Hurley, both civilian and high military. Truman was smoothly gulled by Stalin's promises at Potsdam to support with arms the Nationalist Chinese against the Reds, as slickly as Roose- velt was taken in by the same tactic at Yalta. To his credit, General George C. Marshall, who had been Secretary of State in 1947 and Secretary of Defense in 1950 under President Tru- man, after a first-hand assessment of the situation in China, had concluded that the China regime on the mainland was both corrupt and inept.

The rest is grim history that will never be erased and cannot be rewritten. For a quarter of a century, the United States was forced into both public and diplomatic attitudes, of denying recognition to the existence of the sovereign government of a large portion of the earth's population, while supporting in various ways old Chiang's Formosan pipe-dreams of extending his island empire from Quemoy and Matsu to the Chinese mainland. This uncomfortable position meant exerting our influence to keep Red China out of the United Nations for the first quarter century of the world body's history, another long-term catastrophe that will not be reversed by recent changes. Nor will the countless people sacrificed to the consequences of this missed opportunity—or non-event—be revivified to laugh at it as a quirk of historical irony.

Proving what? That the trivia of yesterday become the crises of tomorrow? That American intelligence should have provided more realistic data to our executive arm concerning, *first*, the significance of the broad-based popular support of the Communists in China, *second*, the degree of dissension and ideological confusion—to say nothing of downright corruption —among the followers of Chiang, and/or, *third*, signalled anticipation of the bloody events that soon were to begin with Chiang's loss of Manchuria and end, in 1949, with the establishment of the People's Republic? Intelligence reports, unfortunately, provided *much* (often too much) such specific information of this type, we have discovered since, gleaned from highly reliable sources, covert and overt. And a lot of it may be found competently reported in American newspapers, as those who have carefully scrutinized this period of blunders will testify.

Proving nothing—and this is precisely our point! When policy is governed entirely by expediency, or does not exist at all as *policy* but merely as conditioned reflex, *history teaches no lessons*, except to note that, if a situation of this sort ever faces us again, our reactions are likely once again to be equally injudicious. And so it *has* happened, not only involving our relationships with revolutionary governments in Europe and Africa, but with those in our own hemisphere as well. Only one question seems relevant when our policy people make decisions such as these. Considering political pressure inside our nation, must we *approve* or *disapprove* of various insurgent governments merely, and entirely, because of our (inevitably) temporary moral stance of the moment? And, if the former, are we likely to offer them aid regardless of the pragmatic consequences of the issues involved? If we disapprove of them morally, do we simply disregard realistic political, social, economic upheavals abroad until it is too late or—as we saw at the nervous moment of the Cuban missile crisis—*almost* too late? (As we read the past and define "almost," no substantial nation in history has survived more than nine major "almosts." We are using up our quota quickly.)

No wonder, therefore, that the United States is so often accused by wise observers of not possessing a foreign policy at all (or stuck by one that has lived longer than Wilson's fleeting dreams for a democratic world) since the Monroe Doctrine. (And even the latter policy will fall under heavy questions if its implementation is studied carefully in—mostly—economic terms.) We are consequently often accused of ensnarement in a neat tautology: our foreign policy is a policy to sustain no consistent policy. Instead, we have consistent *morals*—that is, we always set out to do what is "right." What is "right" is, of course, a function of immediate political, military and economic expediency.

We are then inevitably forced to repeat the truism offered in the previous chapter. Our foreign policy is, when all columns are added, but *one* function of national policy, just as it is for most other nations. And our national policy, at any time, reflects a temporary fusion of highly volatile political, economic and military constituencies, all in states of cooperation one with the other at one moment and in combustion at another. Hence, the significance of President Eisenhower's warning to us (from his historical position as the *one* American President since 1928 who has *not* earned a place in history as a chronic victim of our vapidity in extra-national matters) to keep careful eyes on these particular domestic alliances. Hence also, the inherent common sense in the sociological work of the late C. Wright Mills' apparently paranoid extenuations of these domestic matters into world-wide predictions of an Armageddon, simply because he believed he smelled the odor of conspiracy at home. Eisenhower, in this regard, was peculiarly sage; just as was Mills (who pursued his science with the methodological rigor and mania of a football tackle) peculiarly correct, and—worse—prophetic!

A correct observation that may be offered safely even to high school students concerning America's foreign policy over the years is that it is titularly "bi-partisan." In this era of strange bedfellows, this rubric says precisely and exactly nothing about our conduct overseas, except that we *should* be in an unlikely position to make critical international decisions in haste. Somebody, on purely political grounds, is likely, at all times, to oppose any particular international improvisation, and, true to theory, most of the *unimportant* ones that have emerged from Washington have been filtered through protectively contentious committees where bi-partisanship is a working weapon of principle. On the other hand, such old bi-partisan notions do not seem to apply to *important* matters for two reasons that the authors would not like to be forced to explain to a Martian:

First, we are still subject today to arbitrary and "emergency" suspensions of our classical system of checks and balances that were freely ceded to the executive arm of government (and its various staffs, bureaus, councils and offices) in the early nineteen-forties, because the *original* emergency of thirty years ago, proclaimed by President Roosevelt during World War II, apparently has not yet terminated.

Second, from the era of Roosevelt to the present, that same executive arm has assumed, by Congressional default and other means, enormous powers regarding international affairs that at present seem to function as a reflection of the personality who happens to occupy the White House at the moment— his advice and advisors (a Schlesinger? a Kissinger? a Dulles?), his personal political style, his degree of popularity, the attractiveness of his wife and family, his love of animals and the way he employs mass communications (particularly television) to gain public assent for whatever he and his staff construe as moral. The Russians cutely call this phenomenon the "cult of personality." So it is, but in the United States of America it is limited now by an eight-year parameter, thank heaven, and, noticeably during the Johnson era, by the occasional unwillingness of the communications establishment(and, through them, the public) to encourage the policies (or the public's assenting reactions) of the executive at stage center.

Now, presidents are not, almost by definition, more than occasionally and half-heartedly bi-partisan animals. They are, after all, elected to serve as chief executives, not as gods, what ever they may think in the privacy of their bathtubs. To expect that such figures turn off their political glands in international matters and "put the country's welfare ahead of political considerations" (one favorite presidential phrase) is absurd, especially since top-drawer political animals are invariably convinced that the welfare of their particular political constituency *is synonomyous* with the national welfare. Eight years may be, however, particularly in an "era of challenge" (another presidential chestnut), a long time in which to brew mischief under these circumstances. As author, historian, presidential advisor and professor, Arthur Schlesinger Jr. has written: "'Allow the President to invade a neighboring nation, whenever he shall deem it necessary to repel an invasion, and you allow him to do so, whenever he may choose to say he deems it necessary for such purpose—and you allow him to make war at pleasure. Study to see if you can fix any limit to his power in this respect . . . If, today, he should choose to say he thinks it necessary to invade Canada to prevent the British from invading us, how could you stop him?' You may say to him, 'I see no probability of the British invading us,' but he will say to you 'Be silent; I see it; if you don't.' "

Here, Schlesinger is quoting from a letter that Abraham Lincoln, who was then a Congressman, sent to his friend, W. H. Herndon, on February 15, 1848, in regard to President Polk and the Mexican War. Schlesinger, making a parallel comparison to today's Executive power emanating from the White House in Washington, concludes that, "The President has become, on issues of war and peace, the most absolute monarch among the great powers—with the possible exception of China's Mao Tse-tung." [2]

Dredged from the gossip and breast-beating during the "Watergate" investigations of 1973, the extent, nature and peril of this executive power in its most partisan aspects emerged as a national issue of frightening potentials. Not only are presidents victims of personality cults, they appear also to live in the White House as virtual prisoners of the bureaucracies that they are forced to create to carry the burdens of office. This "insularity of power" is not new in history, and it has destroyed more than one great and powerful figure in the past. Possibly, there is no solution to the dilemma of the executive whose best and closest aides serve him poorly by insulating him from the world around him, but such a fate for the American Presidency was certainly not envisioned by the men who framed the US Constitution. It is however a harsh condition of modern complex government, apparently. And the dirty works that Watergate exposed to the public, one can be certain, are but the tip of a deep iceberg that ramifies from domestic to international matters, no matter how titularly "bi-partisan" they appear on official records.

Footprints in the Wind

How refreshing, therefore, whenever we expose ourselves, in this context, to the experienced, the brave and/or the gutsy, especially if their observations agree with our prejudices. Auditors of American foreign policy, it seems, often experience the feeling that they are slowly going mad, all the moreso when they are forced by profession or accident to take a part in actually applying that policy to matters abroad. Feeling frequently like characters out of *Catch-22*, they often prefer not to comprehend what they are about, rather than cultivate guilt at having to reverse their stands suddenly and announce their sleights-of-hand by attempts at simulated high drama and breast-beating.

Senator Fulbright, for instance, the great internationalist, whose bill implementing international scholar-exchange programs (the grants themselves are usually called "Fulbrights" on American campuses) made history by almost personally engineering the Gulf of Tonkin Resolution through Congress in the early 'sixties for his fellow party-member president. Shortly afterward, he was hoisted—as many were—in the rear flank by the petard of history, when it finally became clear that the Vietnam conflict was not to be the simple matter it appeared at first blush.[3] The result was Fulbright's rush into print by means of a prodigious output of books, which, their repetitions and contradictions aside, provide clear evidence that the Arkansas Senator is better at reading history after the fact than he is either at trouble-shooting it or distinguishing its mountains from molehills. The books, a psychologist might guess, represent guilt writ large—possibly to the extent of overkill— as did the Senator's painful dialogue in open committee hearings with then Secretary of Defense Clifford a few years ago.[4] Fulbright apparently sees himself as a hoaxed victim of America's foreign policy vacuum, and, in a curious way, he is pathetic because he broadcasts so loudly the courage of his convictions no matter how fast they oscillate. Protesting too much is suspicious behavior. And protesting while revising one's protests is worse.

Daniel Ellsberg (as close as Harvard University had yet come to producing a public figure with the insouciance of the creative biographer, Clifford Irving) fell into the same trap, unloading *his* peculiar type of guilt in helping to prepare the massive—and occasionally illuminating—Vietnam analyses, military options, contingency plans and just plain old plans by presenting copies of them to a couple of major newspapers. The journalists subsequently gave them the somewhat opprobrious name, *The Pentagon Papers,* and printed them; the rest is history. Professor Ellsberg presumably has found the martyrdom he sought in his curious act. The real beneficiaries of the Ellsberg exculpation, strangely, were probably the newspapers involved which—if inside stories are correct—lacked adequate policy guidance at the time (in much the same way that our State Department often does), or, at any rate, *an* operative policy guideline more specific than a single sentence in the Bill of Rights. As a result, they have been forced to face these problems squarely in the judicial arena and reconsider the consequences of the *obligations* this sentence in the First Amendment entails——as well as its clearly stated *license.*

So it seems to go, also, for men in the field—those old-time American career diplomats who are shifted around the globe from time to time, and have given their lives to the implementation of foreign policy that they suspect does not exist. Upon making the latter discovery, at some point in their early years of service, they then have three options: (1) to quit government service and return home and seek honorable employment; (2) to continue their careers in the belief that United States' policy *does* in some secret archive exist and that, in time of crisis, it will miraculously emerge like Browning's *Dark Tower;* or (3) to continue their careers as a kind of game, cultivating cynicism and playing the Mid-Atlantic (or Mid-Pacific) roles described in the previous chapter.

Each road produces its own built-in hazards. Those strewn in path (1) are obvious. Path (2) leads to chronic schizophrenia, possibly one of the most difficult psychotic ailments for clinicians to detect. Path (3) leads to demoralization, nail-biting, infidelity, ulcers, alcoholism and eternally glazed eyes, combined with a strange aphasia that appears whenever the word "retirement" is mentioned.

What diplomat Ambassador J. Robert Schaetzel, terminating a thirty-year career in the US Foreign Service, recently told an interviewer before he left Brussels for home is enlightening, not because he revealed anything not generally known about the *modi operandorum* of our international policies, but that he said what he said *at all*.[5] Schaetzel, a diplomat of the type (2) variety who has, for the past half-dozen years been involved in keeping the State Department's official eye on the Common Market, at the age of 55 now wants out, in the (slightly naive) belief that a career as a lecturer, teacher and writer will not, like diplomacy, require that he gush over the embroidery on some emperor s invisible new clothes. How many career diplomats at his level of attainment, even those on the way out of their careers, would have nerve enough to sum up our international policy by remarking for ascription, "There is no strategy. I know it isn't there!"?

Schaetzel's barbs at present policy vacuums are well-larded with anti-Nixon innuendo, a gambit we consider fair enough in the light of what we have noted above about the role of the Chief Executive in foreign affairs during recent history. Schaetzel firmly believes that once-upon-a-time (not so long ago) American power, in Europe at any rate, *was* directed by some guidelines more consistent than a mere moral stance, as it is today.

This is how Ambassador Schaetzel sees the past quarter century:

> We came out of World War II with a foreign policy strategy which both Americans and Europeans understood and on which they came to depend.

These changes demand a new conceptual framework so that people can know what to expect now. But it isn't there. The United States was central to the old framework, and the world depended on it. Now the United States has moved unilaterally in ways that have shaken and almost destroyed these understandings . . .

There was a crisis in the West in the 'forties and 'fifties, and it produced people who worked together to make decisions. When you look now, you can't help but be terribly sad.

The simplicity is gone and the new complexity cries out for leadership, for some person who can honestly synthesize the problems and the policy.

True enough, probably, in Western Europe and Japan (to which Schaetzel also refers), where "recovery" was defined mostly in economic and political terms. The NATO army (and American Navy and SEATO in Japan's case) provided a field of relative tranquility and peace for two decades to permit literal miracles to develop. The result was the growth of the affluent and stable societies abroad that some Americans envy enough these days to expatriate themselves to or want to retire in. Schaetzel seems to be—like many others —quite unprepared for the left-hand vamp and the right-hand ad-lib that has served us adequately in post-war Western Europe and Japan and so poorly in so-called "third-world" nations and other areas.

Schaetzel's criticism of America's recent tendency to act unilaterally in foreign affairs is not new or startling. American unilateralism, a tendency we have indulged in increasingly ever since Woodrow Wilson was pressured at home into pulling us out of the League of Nations, is an on-going issue. We question it mainly when unilateral action is irresponsibly detached from consistent, long-range goals and taken capriciously, contrary to the welfare of friendly nations. Schaetzel's critisism then is correctly placed.

The good Ambassador, his foot practically on the 'plane to his homeland, fired three shots into a vacuum, meticulously citing them as vulnerable areas of America's foreign policy.

Schaetzel centers his *first* shot upon our chronic confusion, in this advanced period of the nuclear age, regarding when and where we may or may not justifiably and/or judiciously exercise military force, or the threat of it. This deep confusion has produced, since Vietnam particularly, a form of strategic paralysis that has probably reduced our pragmatic potential to the power of threats alone. We are left fighting psychological warfare that will become more and more ineffective every time our bluff is called in the future, and we are forced to reconsider honestly our new military dilemma: non-nuclear containment that *cannot* work, as one option, or the use of a Brobdingagian arsenal of horror tools *we dare not* use, as the one possible alternative.

Schaetzel levels his *second* volley of criticism at the much-advertised speed-up of global communications and transportation which some believe will alleviate diplomatic troubles. We are in a world in which it is difficult to take *time* to consider the subtle ramifications of international intercourse. Some optimists have faith that electronic computers may be employed to solve this problem. But it is a faith comparable only to ancient Attic commitments to the *deus ex machina* that solves all problems, or to a child's belief in a conjurer. In recent history, the mindless use of information theory, cybernetics, games theory, decision theory and computerized wisdom, has produced in its wake more goof-ups, domestic and national, per square inch of protoplasm on our continent, than the damn foolery of any period of misadventure we have yet survived. But this is the subject of another (and funnier) book. Suffice it to say that a computer, for instance, is as good as the information it is fed; or as programmers put it, GIGO (translation: "Garbage In, Garbage Out.")

The *third* critical area that Schaetzel brings up is that of decreasing foreign aid—an issue to which we shall return when appropriate—and its curious effects on impoverished nations to the advantage of those nations with whom we merely "trade" to mutual advantage. He cites the old saw that "the rich get richer and the poor get babies," a notion to consider the next time we settle in our Danish armchairs, look at our Swiss watches and drive our Volkswagens (or Mercedes) to a dinner of continental repasts served on British bone china and eaten with Norweigen or West German cutlery. How well we remember Madame Luce's satire (directed, in another era, at Henry Wallace) to the effect that the objective of giving "a bottle of milk to every Hottentot" is a slightly ludicrous manifestation of American generosity she called "globaloney". But it is no more insane than pursuing an enormous program of foreign aid without clear and consistent political and humanitarian policy guidelines. And this is *exactly* what we have been up to since the Marshall Plan ended.

Our criteria for overseas aid seems to hinge (roughly) upon three factors: *one* ostensibly related to need; the *other* to our economic disposition at the time; and the *third,* whether we are helping people we consider at the instant (often incorrectly) friends or foes.

Schaetzel is, of course, merely *one* disappointed and bitter diplomat, expressing his particular opinions with more than a pinch of *pique* at his boss on Pennsylvania Avenue. He is by no means typical of his breed. The garden-variety foreign policy expert (unless he is a Kennan, Lippmann or Hans Morgenthau), is either less honest or less prescient than the most disillusioned of ambassadors. Some of them merely develop expertise in "nuts and bolts." Some actually attempt to carry out difficult concrete tasks for Uncle Sam overseas in the absence of genuine long-range policy. Those poor souls are often forced to work where explosions in their back yards reward their pains.

(Anyone, naturally, may be a foreign policy expert simply by saying he is, in much the same way Harry Houdini became known as the World's Greatest Magician: as the world's greatest self-styled authority on magic, he pronounced himself the master of masters. Neither history nor myth has, to date, seriously questioned his dictum, although it is wide open for both qualification and question. Psychiatrists, for instance, like Erich Fromm, may try their hand at the game, and someone may take them seriously. Nor does current legislation prevent pediatricians like Dr. Spock and linguists like Noam Chomsky from firmly and conspicuously allying themselves with the causes of virtue—and usually fashion. Actors and actresses of the stature of Bob Hope and Jane Fonda may also play the game in their own specialized, peripheral way. Folk singers, almost by definition, are foreign policy kibitzers these days. To their credit, they do not claim much expertise—contrary to the general practice of other professionals in irrelevant fields. Hence our own disclaimer: neither author of this book is an expert at foreign policy. Our interests in it are merely background prerequisites to what we *do* know—we think—something about: namely, communications and persuasion, necessary sub-components for understanding the issues that today face diplomats, political scientists and statesmen, the men and women who must grapple with the real knots of steel.)

Voices in the Sand

Both at home and abroad, many observers find it difficult to believe that American foreign policy (however they define it) is neither a set of divine instructions from Sinai nor a diabolitcal plot brewed by conspiracies either of Communists or super-militaristic capitalists. Nor is it a reasoned distillation of the best thoughts of the likes of Jefferson, Washington, Lincoln, Roosevelt and Roosevelt. The tenuousness of the thread upon which it has hung for more than one-hundred years seems an incredible feat of legerdemain (talk about Houdini!), and, in the acid test of experience—up to Vietnam, at least—the US seems to have passed the main pragmatic qualifications, not only of survival, but of growth and influence. Legend tells us that we have never lost a war, Vietnam notwithstanding (untrue: check the War of 1812). And we have, in this century alone, celebrated a good share of the world's military victories, from Admiral Dewey's homecoming from Manila to General MacArthur's sentimental return to the US at the behest of the late President Truman. Through it all, we have prospered. The "American Way" still lives in the hearts and minds of the majority of our people, meaning that our bellies are fairly filled and we have not yet hatched enough malcontents —even during the demoralizing depression of the nineteen-thirties—to mount a respectable revolution against the established order.

What we often tend to forget, however, is that, from Appomatox to the present, our foreign relations have indeed been *foreign*—that is, they have involved alliances and antagonisms (Pearl Harbor excepted) removed physically from our soil. Our wars have been fought mostly by blowing up other people's cities and fighting on other people's earth, usually as late entries into on-going conflicts. In a like manner, our various *en tentes* have usually accented the "American Presence" and "American Influence" here or there around the globe, rarely involving (and then mostly in economic matters) the "British Presence," "German Presence," or "French Presence" right here in America. The only foreigners Americans have had to deal with extensively on United States' soil have been either immigrants, who shortly bred and/or educated themselves into Americans (a classical Chinese method of conquest, incidentally) or American Indians. The latter, in spite of our unforgivable treatment of them as pariahs, are not exactly foreigners. They were here before Vespucci, although you would never know it from the way we regard them both in life and in fiction.

For many, even people occupying august chairs at our best institutions of higher learning, American foreign policy occupies the same class of events as much history that never happened: the infanticides of Richard III, the capture and death of John Wilkes Booth, the legend of Jesse James and Hitler's career as a paper-hanger. In the long-term record of history, only one postulate is certain enough to be a candidate for translation into a "law": namely, that if an event did not occur that should have, the record will someday affirm that it did. Horace Walpole made this discovery before 1768. And nothing we know of in man's adventures since then seems to us to deny the integrity of his wisdom.

As difficult as it may seem to solemnize non-events as facts, it is equally as hard to turn vapidity into strategy. But the trick *can* be accomplished. One standard method in the world of foreign affairs is purely semantic, and is limited to on-going events, but it works. This is the device of labeling whatever is being extemporized and/or reacted to in our relations with other nations at any given time as a "doctrine," a word lexicographers tell us is a "principle being taught," a hedge worthy of the Kansas City Commodities Exchange. The simple word "doctrine," of course, goes back in American international rhetoric to the era of Monroe (when it held religious connotations since lost in the expansion of our language.) Its timeliness is self-evident, and we are assured today that we are living in the era of the "Nixon Doctrine." The hasty improvisations and various inevitabilities that followed World War II are clearly recorded as the "Truman Doctrine." Memory does not recall whether we also lived through an "Eisenhower Doctrine," a "Kennedy Doctrine" and a "Johnson Doctrine," but the words sound familiar. And we probably did. Proprietorship of a "doctrine" implies, *ipso facto*, possession also of a consistent, meaningful set of policy principles upon which it must be based. But amplification is not affirmation, and there the semantic device fast fizzles out.

Another common device employed by foreign affairs experts is to read the record backwards and justify it *post hoc* by weaving its bits and pieces into a credible fabric that somehow justifies as solid strategy what happened mostly by accident, and actually resulted from unexpected reactions to surprises. (In this regard, the *Pentagon Papers* served a valid end by exposing the distance between planning and reality—in the light of a few years' history—of the Vietnam war during the period between the original preparation of the studies and their sub-sequent publication. But other similar depth studies of any issue facing the Defense Department since its creation—and the War Department before that—would have exposed the same sort of inevitable dissonance.)

Psychiatrists call this tendency to explain in logical terms what actually occurred as the result of uncontrollable or un-conscious forces "rationalization." While we are incompetent to pass judgment upon the adequacy of this bit of Freudian razzle-dazzle, "rationalization" seems to us, in its proper context of *individual* behavior, a fairer evaluation of motives than reading an historical record inside-out, in the not-so-proper context of *national* behavior. Let us remember that, if an indi-vidual is discovered rationalizing too much, a shrink is quite likely to commit him to a funny-farm for a long rest. But much behavior considered psychotic in people's personal life is re-garded as sane and even admirable by professors, politicians and soldiers alike, if it is pursued by enough people, sanctified by the rubric "collective behavior" and given the blessings of God and State. Murder is but a minor and obvious example.

In order to achieve parsimony, one may examine (even cursorily) the recent output, for instance, of the Rostow broth-ers, Professors Eugene V. and Walter W. One discovers in the musings of both that the recent history of international affairs (in which both men participated) is held together by *post hoc* historical threads that certainly qualify as "doctrines" and smell to the unsuspecting reader mighty like foreign policy.

Of the two, W. W. Rostow's reconstruction of such events during the past decade as American intervention in the Do-minican Republic's revolutionary mess, the Bay of Pigs inva-sion and America's mercurial (and inconsistent) attitudes to-wards various Central and South American governments and insurgents are all explained philosophically with considerable vigor but little strategic cement, in this experienced diplomat's recently published memoir.[6] In fact, Rostow—clever observer that he is—manages somehow to use his own presence at the side of many of our decision-makers as a unifying device to produce the *illusion* of consistency in America's official conduct of these and similar affairs where little (if any) really existed. Such hindsight bespeaks a mighty testament of faith—the same sort of faith by which a ground soldier operates during a battle he can neither observe with perspective nor comprehend clearly from his own particular foxhole. Later, the pieces will be pushed into a pattern. And, in such a manner, have disorganized debacles been turned into glorious victories and vice-versa. Rostow is familiar with this ancient military gambit.

The other Rostow, Eugene V., is somewhat more ideologically inclined than his brother, Walter. But ideology is not policy, although, in the words of the song, "You can't have one without the other." In his latest volume, E. V. Rostow uses still another classical device for spreading the patina of order and logic over clay that is essentially formless and abstract: a thick wipe of a theory (or a combination of theories) that artfully squeezes history into a series of cycles or set of opposing vectors, all so highly abstract as to be functions, mainly, of their teller's rhetorical abilities.[7] (Hegel, Marx, Carlyle and Toynbee immediately tumble out of the paperback racks at this point, along with other, less familiar, but more exciting out-of-print historical theorists like Johan Huizinga and—horrors!—Houston Chamberlain.)

One discovers little original in Rostow's manipulation of "balance of power" theories that explain why the United States has operated as it has in the international theatre, nor in his employment of them to make predictions and suggestions for the future. His advice boils down to the admonition to keep our eye on the "balances." Now, "balances of power" probably exist—and have for eons. Nor does it actually matter much how well-rooted in reality they are, as long as men *think* they exist, at least *until* the moment they are tested. But rewriting history in terms of a hoary theory drawn from arithmetic (and given a measure of credence by the manipulations of men like

Metternich) is far too easy to apply to *any* international check-erboard in history with adequate results. One must, however, construe the actions of states as no more complex or any less removed from human life than is a game of checkers.

Possibly, Rostow is correct in implying our foreign policy has *always* been directed by this simplistic notion that a "bal-ance" must be maintained somewhere and somehow, in the an-tagonisms and interests of the various powers in the world, in-cluding our own. In times of relative peace, such a balance operates satisfactorily, much as it did in Metternich's early nineteenth-century Europe. But if the pursuit of an abstract bal-ance of factors, impossible to measure, observe or describe, that, at their best, only add up to a fuzzy notion of *power* (in a world where psychological *power*, economic *power* and mili-tary *power* alone are neither clear, coeval nor stable from day to day) is the bedrock upon which American foreign policy has been (or should be) built, we had better immediately burn in-cense to the muse of history and pray damn hard and quickly for divine intervention tomorrow.

E. V. Rostow, however, is a good rhetorican. His checker-men, as he describes them, are awesome. And he endows both past and future with a frightening formidableness that disillu-sioningly dissolves after a few moments' conjecture concerning such matters as the force of ideological and cultural alliances, starving hordes in much of the world, revolutionary lightning rapidly spreading here and there, and the nuclear stalemate. The latter is possibly the neatest "balance" of them all, as we have seen, and possibly also the most invidious.

Policy? Well, Rostow explains honestly and clearly the best we have done along these lines to date with our giant na-tional intelligence. He does not travel, unfortunately, far be-yond the intellectual elegance of President Washington's self-evident, archaic dictum that we will not get hurt if we mind our own business—another vapid theory that (we thought) bit the dust years ago. Our best, if he is right, is execrable. The main peril of explaining history by means of theory is simply that the theory often remains logical and consistent, while the actions of men do not.

Certain aspects of history *do* indeed appear often to repeat themselves. Such accidents are coincidences and prove nothing whatsoever about "balances of power," cycles, great men, national destinies, the minds of the gods, the conflicts of class interest or economic inevitabilities, and particularly are they unreliable guides for soothsaying. They reflect merely the degree that men in most times and places in the history of our species have been more similar, one to the other, in the *important* matters of living (those having to do with birth, death, self-preservation, pleasure, pain and fear) than they have differed. Whether these multiple and baffling similarities may properly be termed "human nature," we leave to arguments of sociologists and psychologists deep in their concerns with how much "nature" can perform statistical minuets with "nurture" on the head of a pin.

Perils and Other Consequences

Since the era of deep disillusionment with foreign alliances that destroyed Woodrow Wilson at the end of World War I (the ironies that the idealistic college president from Princeton, New Jersey understood clearly but could not manage), one of the greatest burdens that the United States has been forced to shoulder is the uncomplicated, clear *contradiction* that neither common citizens, diplomats nor foreign policy gurus often permit themselves to face either squarely or simply. Wilson's broken blood vessel; the ghost of Secretary Forrestal, deep in paranoia, stalking the corridor of Walter Reed Hospital; Adlai Stevenson's final, futile mission, and the virtual incineration of Robert McNamara and Lyndon Johnson for the uses of posterity are—like other consummations of men of talent and good intent—too numerous to detail here, and too bitter for most human taste buds.

The ingredients of this contradiction are two undeniable sets of circumstances that have increasingly beleaguered the

USA since the turn of the century. Neither grew into a competing Titan until about 1919. But both have been growing ever since.

On one side of the Olympian empire of global politics, America has, for reasons that fill volumes, been thrust not merely into the cliché, stock role of a nation with profound international obligations, but one of the two or three genuine empires of multi-faceted force that (like it or not) has within its power the ability to return our planet to Neanderthal times, if its blunders are severe enough. And, as we have been careful to point out (possibly *ad nauseam*), we are not referring here merely to our much-touted nuclear arsenal alone. We are referring to the *entire thrust* of our technological culture—no matter how well it may be apparently oriented at the moment to peaceful pursuits—including our present and fantastic progress in the fields of genetics and neuropathy, right through a spectrum of psychological sophistications that ends with such apparently petty matters as building Disneylands. In between these extremes, our enormous national wealth, corporate structures, competitive zeal and national *chutzspah* have entwined our destiny, one way or another, with *every other* nation on earth—some to a greater degree than others, and each in quite different ways—to such measure that what was once the so-called "free world's" *quasi-dependence* upon a benevolent Uncle Sam (we liked to think) has now become an *interdependence* that has dropped its benevolent aura and is frankly and openly self-serving for all concerned. Nor does the American Empire of power end any longer at Iron Curtains, at Bamboo Curtains or at once formidable natural and national borders, any more than the power of either the USSR and Red China are contained in their influence, concrete or psychological, by impotent echelons of immigration officers and complicated lexicons of visa regulations.

Here we stand, face-to-face with the single most difficult set of facts, apparently, for both the common men and the elite intelligences that govern these great powers, either to appreciate or comprehend in nearly their full ramifications. We are *not* referring to defunct, archaic concepts of isolationism and interventionism, but to the situational state of the world right now that—again like it or not—has changed John Donne's tolling bell from a poetic conceit into irrefutable audible evidence of an impending worldwide funeral. And whether or not, and when, the ceremony will be held is an issue of responsibility that the USA may no more avoid facing squarely than can any other major power today and tomorrow.

All of this on one hand—a prospect literally too awesome to contemplate except when laughed away as "science fiction" or sent to oblivion by the double-talk of our so-called "futurologists", *all* of whom are so bent in their biases that they are literally blind to the immensity of potentialities in the "future" about which they so glibly prattle. (A. N. Whitehead once warned us to handle each new discovery made by man so gently as to leave the darkness surrounding it undisturbed. Whitehead also knew that as knowledge increases arithmetically, so ignorance inevitably increases geometrically. He understood that every problem that is solved by man must create its own heuristic universe of new problems yet to be solved. Of this intellectual humility, our futurologists know—and care—nothing. Their "predictive options" are therefore worthy of their flashy but shallow intellects.) To the authors' eyes, our science-fiction writers have served us better than our pseudo-scientific geographers of "Tomorrowland" in that, being creative critters, they have some wry appreciation of the dramatic twists of human history and comprehend the one and only serviceable axiom for augery: that the unexpected and unpredictable will probably happen.

But wait, our troubles are not yet competently described; irony displays two hands. We must face other complicated, but equally bitter, circumstances. Once again, we put the problem squarely: Not only do many of us still deny that empires of such mighty power really exist, let alone attempt to describe their constituent elements, but a discouraging quota of the supposedly wisest among us, first, refuse to believe that the United States is the master of such an empire, and, second, will not or cannot recognize that the exercise of this power to date has largely occurred in a policy vacuum and been played like a game of black-jack.

Nor has the United States, to the authors' best knowledge, turned the attention of its governmental conscience, except in the vaguest ghost-written euphemisms, to the strategy by which this power may sanely be exercised in all its breadth *tomorrow*. Nor do we know in what document to look, or what oracle of government to ask, in order to determine the specific ends we may or may not realistically pursue as a civilization, as we exercise the impress of our might upon the world. (Whether such clear objectives have been articulated by other major powers is not relevant to the problem, except to give it urgency. We suspect that the USSR apparently sees as its destiny a more sophisticated objective than Khrushchev's threat merely to "bury us." And behind that Red Chinese inscrutability, a generation of ideologists is being raised who think they understand *exactly* the role of their enormous population is in the world of tomorrow.)

The present writers once, years ago, laughed in print at the apparent insouciance of the late Henry Luce's post-World War II, *Time*-style much-publicized concept of "The American Century." We are not laughing today. As old-fashioned and naive a program as it was (born in the heady atmosphere of our recent military victory), it contained, at least, more than the mere jetstream of vague moral conceptualization that seems to propel us at present. It paid heed to the *obligations* that our power a generation ago—a fraction of our power today—demanded then of those who possessed and exercised it, and still demands. Foreign policy did not propell us into the Vietnam debacle, for instance; the jet-stream did, (energized by our relative success in Korea and elsewhere.) It encouraged us to impose our peculiar version of political and economic morality upon a people we neither appraised properly nor whose history (an open book, written mostly in French) we had studied, but were incompetent to relate imaginatively to our own international interests. We stood up to a rapid roster of loose commitments in order (we thought) to protect the weak against aggression, with little consideration, if any, of our own aggressive blunders around the globe in matters not only military but educational, cultural, economic and humanitarian. And should we continue our vapor-trail policy, Vietnam may be one of the *cosier* national adventures to which we shall be exposed before we die.

That we tend to recoil from so strong a dose of reality as this insistent irony fiercely undergirding both American political and social life today, may be natural, if not inevitable. Even so mild and generally conventional a diplomat as the Austrian Kurt Waldheim sympathetically recognizes the symptoms of psychological retreat in his homey, world-weary fashion. Referring to America's present disenchantment with the United Nations (because our moral aspirations for the world body did not—and could not—keep in step with its actual function as an open forum of national states, yielding to it not one iota of their own individual and jealously guarded sovereignty) Waldheim reflects:

> In 1945, Americans thought the United Nations would solve all the problems of the future. They had not gone through the sad experiences of war like the Europeans and others. The Europeans suffered their great disillusionment with the League of Nations and World War Two. They had no illusions left. So their disappointment was not as great. They wanted international cooperation, but they recognized its limitations. Americans now find that the United Nations is different from their expectations. They've had a hard time with reality. . . . I think there is much more confidence in the U.N. in other parts of the world.[8]

The disenchantment to which Waldheim refers—bound to increase as we are dosed daily with more "reality"—is but a tiny symptom of the United States' present battle with the inconsistent roles we are playing, both private and public, in our position as a "superpower."

Are we implying that our State Department and foreign policy geniuses have been standing idly by while the ship of state has floated in euphoria? Quite the contrary, and here we may discover one major cause of the debacle itself, if we read Hannah Arendt's recent stilletto-like evaluations of contemporary world attitudes correctly.[9] She notes often and well that Americans rarely pause, especially at high levels of so-called "decision making" both within and outside of government, to doubt for an instant that their country's technological genius, "know how" and instinct for quantification and data-gathering cannot "solve" any and all individual or collective problems (even philosophical ones), if they are given sufficient reams of accurate "information" and exposed to a mighty quanta of "brains."

To Arendt's perceptions, such *hubris* displays only stupidity. We agree, except that we shall coin the phrase, "the higher stupidity" to describe the exquisite foolishness of the medieval (but nevertheless modern) tendency to delegate freely sensitive matters requiring historical and political wisdom (as opposed to rote fact-piling of so-called "knowledge") to "think tanks," "task forces," and "investigating committees," as well as to individual contractors of "know how" (of which the Rand Corporation is but one—often, incidentally, unjustly blamed for the mistakes of others who conveniently misconstrue the clearly stated limitations of many of Rand's well-delimited investigations.)

These forays into the application of supposedly scientific thought to the delicate business of developing adequate philosophies and strategies of international policy are, of course, scientific only in the broadest sense. They do utilize the forms and methods of science, mainly the precisions of its quantifying power, but in much the way that computerized astrological forecasts cast one's horoscope. Problems which are simply not amenable either to pedantic or formal analysis and scholastic, Aquinian argument, and/or counter-argument by the numbers (like chess games), are therefore investigated beyond reasonable saturation by obscurantists and pseudo-scientists into tortured and detailed complexity. Worst of all, they are subsequently grabbed by crude but avid hands from computers in the form of complex inter-relationships, and are then simplified into nonsense readouts, published, and acted upon.

Such faith, as Arendt and others suggest, in the mere trappings of objectivity is possibly the inevitable result of a national compulsion to *avoid* making genuine decisions. Rather than facing hard problems squarely, our practice is now, all too often, to turn them over to preformulated arcane schemes for prediction, based upon misnamed "facts" that have been spuriously translated into languages of numeration and mathematical formulae. We then consign them to the comfortable determinations of committees, whereby their consequences will be shared by a non-committal group rather than one brave man. (In no manner are these modern procedures consonant with the careful and humane application of the social sciences to the affairs of men, as the pioneers in these fields once aspired for them and—mostly too quietly—still understand them today.)

The articulation of a viable national policy of foreign (and domestic) affairs has, since the dawn of civilization, required the total commitment, to death if necessary, of men and women of self-reliance, imagination, humility and vision— most especially of fully mature individuals of personal wisdom (rare birds in any culture) who are not easily frightened at being proved wrong, either by a turn of events or by their own carefully self-appraised limitations of insight. Nor do they fear the terrors—among the most severe in contemporary society— of losing face and swallowing both private and public disapprobation or ridicule, if they determine to stick to their guns despite derision and ridicule, in the manner of a Winston Churchill during the nineteen-thirties, for instance.

Neither scientific formulae nor committees generally distinguish themselves even faintly in this manner. Nor do most of our professional policy-brewing drones. They react like twitchy mice to the siren-call of each moment's hysterical need for improvisation. What our foreign policy therefore requires (if so respectable a name may be applied to the Gestalt of America's reciprocal and multi-faceted relations with non-Americans) is *brave* men. They need not necessarily be philosopher-kings, but experienced, clever statesmen who think for themselves, write their own speeches, trust their own ideals and keep active their glands of skepticism. Out of such material may a science of international politics one day emerge that will justify the cumbersome bureaucracies which at present merely worship form without content, to which diplomacy descends when diplomats yield their rights as men in order to become mere loyal purveyors of "output."

Years ago, Vernon Duke composed a lovely popular ballad he called "Words Without Music." We hope his shade will not be offended if we borrow his title for our ultimate description of American foreign policy during the past half century. We pray that we shall stand to be corrected in the future.

NOTES TO CHAPTER 3

[1] "After the Cold War", in *Foreign Affairs*, October, 1972, p. 227.

[2] Quoted from an article by Arthur Schlesinger, Jr. in *The New York Times Magazine*, Section 6, January 7, 1973, pp. 12–13, 26, 28, 30, 32.

[3] See the *Columbia Journalism Review*, Winter 1970–71 (sub-titled "Vietnam—What Lessons?") for a reprise of this entire mess and the role of the press in its unwinding. Consult particularly the disturbing article by Don Stillman, "Tonkin: What Should Have Been Asked," pp. 21–25,

in which part this comedy of errors is discussed curtly but clearly. Fulbright's role is accurately recorded here.

⁴ Where author Fulbright's published material comes from is difficult to guess; stylistic differences within and between his published output is ripe for literary detective work. Note especially, Senator J. William Fulbright. (This is the author's full name as printed on the cover and to the page of the paperback editions. Do many mothers, we wonder, name their sons "Senator"?) *Old Myths and New Realities, The Arrogance of Power, The Pentagon Propaganda Machine, The Crippled Giant* (All, New York: Vintage Books, 1964, 1966, 1971, 1972.)

⁵ *The New York Times,* October 27, 1972, p. 2. Direct and indirect quotes are taken from this article.

⁶ See W. W. Rostow, *The Diffusion of Power* (New York: The Macmillan Company, 1972,) a long but interesting autobiographical journey in company with an interesting and astute man, containing many colorful historical details that keep an honest record of *temps perdu* in a tortured era.

⁷ See Eugene V. Rostow, *Peace in Balance* (New York: Simon and Schuster, 1972), or, for a shorter sample of this technique, Rostow's slim summary of his position in "Triangular Power", an opinion piece in *The New York Times,* December 6, 1972, p. 47.

⁸ Quoted in Milton Viorst, "Kurt Waldheim: Embattled Peacemaker," in *The Saturday Review,* September 23, 1972, pp. 43–44.

⁹ See any and all of Hannah Arendt's superb analyses of politics, and, most recently, the collection of essays, *Crises of the Republic* (New York: Harcourt, Brace Jovanovich, 1972.) Political philsophers like Arendt —and observers like the authors of this book—may, with some justice, be accused of damning methods of science and analysis that they do not understand—the old alchemist's dodge. Such criticism directed at Arendt is irrelevant to her erudition. In our case, we understand *precisely* the methods of quantification employed in probability theory, information theory, games theory and communication theory. And, in concept, we comprehend clearly the supposedly scientific machinations of the analytic instruments applied to them. Because we *do* possess considerable knowledge both of the mathematical and statistical devices that are employed —as well as methods of eliciting and quantifying such data—we are, frankly, *frightened stiff* of any "decision-making" based upon such advice, not only in foreign affairs, but in all of the social sciences and even for such quasi-sciences as medicine and dentistry, mostly because we have agonized their outcomes often and deeply in our personal and professional experiences.

4

And the Devil Did Grin

> We are living in conditions of an unabating ideological
> war that imperialist propaganda is waging against our country
> and against the Socialist world, using the most refined methods
> and technical means. All the tools of influencing people's minds
> that the burgeoisie possesses—the press, motion pictures, radio—
> have been mobilized to delude people, to install in them the
> idea that their life under capitalism is virtually a paradise and
> to slander Socialism. The airways are literally saturated with all
> kinds of fabrications about life in our country and the fraternal
> Socialist countries.
>
> It is the duty of our workers on the propaganda and mass-
> agitation front to administer a timely, resolute and effective re-
> buff to these ideological attacks and to convey to hundreds of
> millions of people the truth about the Socialist society, about
> the Soviet way of life and about the construction of Commu-
> nism in our country. This must be done with conviction, persua-
> sively, intelligibly and vividly.
>
> LEONID I. BREZHNEV (1971) [1]

TAPE RECORDINGS REVISITED

Soviet UN Information Offices (*1962*): Why, I am more American than the Americans you meet at the United Nations. I
have been even to Miami Beach—difficult to do because *your*
government restricts the travel, even of the Soviet Legation. I
wish I were there now; New York is as cold in the winter as
Moscow, which nobody believes. And the girls in Miami? I tell

you, fantastic! Better than the French Riviera. I have been *there* too—in season, naturally. America is no mystery to me. It is fantastic. Take the shopgirls on Fifth Avenue. I even walk in the cold ice and snow to look at them. But I only look, because I must be careful, just as you would, professor, if you represented your government anywhere. You surely have nice looking girls in your class, too. These are graduate students, no? They certainly are attractive students—and intelligent too, I'll bet. To teach girls like this, it is a pleasure, huh? Perhaps I should have been a teacher . . .

You are surprised to find yourself here, hey professor? To teach your class in the Soviet Legation building under a painting of Lenin? Well, you wanted to see the film, *Friends From America,* so what else could we do? The sprocket holes of the film do not fit your projectors, so it is our pleasure that you should meet *here* this evening! I could not arrange the weather; there will be much snow by morning. You teach what you wish, professor. The sound-track of the film is an English version. You will not mind if I sit in with your class; and anyone can ask questions afterwards if they wish. The film is documentary. Of course, you call it "propaganda," but it is, as your people say, "white" propaganda. All of it is true. Everything you hear the Americans say about the USSR is true. Nobody was trained; no acting parts.

You will have trouble for people to believe you, no? All you do is call up on the telephone to the big-bad USSR Legation, and you are invited to our house—our home—with thirty-two of your men and women students—one, two, three. Everybody is reading too many spy stories. And they believe the lies your press prints about us. We have nothing to hide. Do you see any guns, bombs anywhere? Always, there is a New York policeman on the corner, but that is to protect *us,* not *you.* This is "Soviet soil," you know, and you are welcome guests. Would your students enjoy to try a box of Soviet candies or some Ukranian cigarettes? Do you permit them to smoke in graduate classes in America? This I do not know.

Smoking is permitted in our screening room. We have sufficient ashtrays, all products of the USSR. But no souvenirs,
please, professor.

**Bureau Director of Private American International Radio Ser-
vice (*later identified as covert arm of the United States Central
Intelligence Agency*) 1962:** Hard facts are hard facts. Propaganda is propaganda—theirs—I mean the other side's—and
ours. I suppose it's better than war with guns. But the strategy
is more difficult, like sculpturing something out of clouds. You
listen to so much of their stuff that, after a while, you get to
thinking the way they do. Do you listen to Radio Moscow?
Good. Then you know. They're getting a little sophisticated
these days, even imitating American radio formats. And the
voices are good, damn good. Some from here, and some trained
entirely in the USSR. But it's the velvet glove over the fist of
mail.

The temptation to answer back in kind is terrible, but
over there they get confused. In Poland, Hungary and so forth,
they don't catch the difference between private American
broadcasters like us and the official "Voice." That's a helluva
line to tread, and it's one that Moscow—or international services in any of the Red bloc, including China—don't have to
worry about. They know where they stand. We know where
they stand. And they know we know. So the sledge-hammer
comes down hard. Truth and lies and all that other idealistic
crap in the textbooks have nothing to do with it. Real hard
propaganda must live according to some higher morality than
abstract definitions of truth. And what *is* truth anyway? Simply
a clever way of *using* reality to prove your point or get your
hard-sell across. Some days I wish we could pull the stopper
on this end, without the inevitable accusation that we're incit-
ing the peasants and students to revolution, and *really* let
loose. But, you know, they blamed the Hungarian uprisings six
years ago on *us*. What a laugh!

Hey! Did you know that *both* Hitler and Stalin kept copies of Le Bon's *The Crowd* on their night tables to read before they went to sleep? I can't prove it, but I kid you not. Some day America is going to wake up to a swift boot in the ass, when the high brass discovers that propaganda is as much a weapon of warfare as an army of soldiers or an atomic bomb. Tell them you heard it *here,* kid.

Voice of America Bureau Director (1963): As an old-time broadcaster, I can tell you that it's like talking into a wind tunnel. All we really possess to guide us are our own directives and the knowledge that we represent the USA. So we try to tell the truth as accurately as we can, and leave it at that. But the joke is that, as far as we can tell, they think we're lying anyway—at least, in the Soviet Union and the Iron Curtain countries. The BBC's Overseas Service has the record for credibility. Everybody over there believes every word that the British say even when they *are* lying. We've made content analysis studies of their broadcasts and ours. Sometimes *we* are much more accurate than the BBC—give fuller, better and more concrete coverage to objective events than they do, even when the news might endanger the interests of the United States. But they still believe the damn British and think we're a batch of liars—or don't think *anything* about us, which is worse.

So we try new formats and knock ourselves out, and the only programs we *know* are popular, and maybe effective, are mostly music: jazz and now rock. That says a heck of a lot for the United States, I'll tell you. We get together a batch of American plays, or programs on life in the USA, and who listens? We don't know, but I'm here to tell you that if that kind of cultural stuff was doing its job, we'd know it. And we don't know anything.

Of course, we don't broadcast only to the Commies. But even our friends think we're up to tricks. They'd rather listen to the BBC for news and commentary broadcasts. And that's where the biggest payoff is in terms of international understanding—or propaganda, if we want to call it that, but we'd better not go too far out on the limb. We are, after all, under the Department of State. Do you know, now it looks as if they've even stopped jamming our broadcasts with phony static? Is that good or bad? You tell *me*, Doc, because I don't know, Washington doesn't know and *you* don't know. The only people who *do* know are in Moscow and Peking, and they're not talking. Not to us, anyway. Not now!

Bureau Chief of Another Private (CIA) Broadcasting Organization, (1965): (This nameless man did not equivocate about his real occupation: an Eastern European expert for the CIA, recently returned from the "field" in Europe. The "cover" of these broadcasting services—that is, Radio Free Europe and Radio Liberty—had not yet been "blown" in the press. But even a fool was able, by 1964, to figure out that the United States Government was paying for these radio services, and that the only closed budget-line passed through Congress that could cover their costs was the CIA's. Being a realist and a comparatively young man, this particular talented foreign service hand did not play the games of his older colleagues in mouthing fairy tales about the anti-communist altruism of "interested Americans" who supposedly supported Radio Free Europe and/or Radio Liberty in those days, or the benevolence of the motives of the CIA in keeping what it believed—and probably still believes—are potent psychological warfare assets on the air. For details, see Chapter 7. In other words, he did not want to insult the intelligence of his audience this evening as he addressed a graduate class in International Propaganda at a major university. He has just been introduced by the professor as a "professional propagandist," a title most propagandists deny immediately—which was exactly why the professor invariably used the term to introduce guest speakers. This man's reaction was atypical. He has, incidentally and apparently, in recent years, vanished entirely from the face of the earth.)

Well, thank you. I don't think I've ever been introduced like that before. Sort of takes you off balance, doesn't it? I suppose I wasn't thinking in quite those terms, although this *is* a lecture in *persuasion,* isn't it? When one has a job to do, one does it to the best of his ability, I suppose. And I had lately begun to think of myself as a writer or broadcaster or program director or something of the sort.

But yes, I imagine I *am* a propagandist, although the semantic connotations aren't very nice. Yes *indeed,* I am!

If you mean, professor, to put your introduction in the form of a question, you might ask, "Would you lie to save your country?" My answer, of course, would unhesitatingly be "Yes!" Men do far worse things, morally speaking, for their country, and—what's his name: Lord Haw-Haw Joyce notwithstanding—the issue seems fairly clear-cut to me on the moral scale, occupational scale, diplomatic scale, or what have you. Yes indeed, I *am* a propagandist, because everything I do, I hope, is directed towards the welfare, as I see it, of the United States of America. My mother didn't raise her boy to be a propagandist. And I'd rather be called a brilliant, young expert in international affairs. But that wouldn't be quite accurate, would it? Nor would *you* say it, professor. By all means —I *am* a propagandist!

More Words, Less Music

The voices above are replayed from an era of extensive self-deception, one not confined to the United States alone, and one that has not yet terminated, although the miasma in which it was entrapped is mercifully clearing.

The antecedents to the era may be located in the nineteen-fifties, a period when a massive studious assault on many levels was made upon certain cultural phenomena that had recently passed. To be specific, they were:

1. The apparent success of Hitler's propaganda machine in turning, some believed, the German people from a nation of

musicians and intellectuals into a nation of anti-Semites and barbarians.

2. Various claims, documented for the most part poorly and differentially, of psychological warfare victories during World War II, including Germany's international broadcasts (which, as a matter of record, accomplished little or nothing), the popularity of Tokyo Rose in the Pacific among American troops (again nothing; Rose played records of good American jazz,[2]) the supposed success of BBC and American propagandists upon both the German military and civil populations in contributing to a general demoralization during the period when the war was all but over anyway.

3. Myths and nonsense disseminated, mostly by woolly-headed psychiatrists and psychologists in England and the USA, about the so-called (and non-existent) techniques of Communist "brainwashing," and the apparent success of the Communist-line in spreading the belief that America had employed "bacteriological warfare" in Korea. The latter was yet another fantasy, and, like "brainwashing" in the West, is still, to this day, regarded as *fact* by many people who should know better.

(This last theme was picked-up, as all exciting cultural myths eventually are in modern society, by popular novelists and dramatists. After a certain amount of pickling in dramatic brine, they appeared in such fanciful stories in print and on the screen as *The Manchurian Candidate*, *The Prisoner* (film only), *The Clockwork Orange*, *Mad in the Streets* (film) and the masterfully performed British movie, *Privilege*. That these fanciful conceits, and many others like them, were mostly good fun—and satisfactory entertainments—is irrelevant to their influence upon attitudes—public and private, lay and professional—concerning the power, both of individual and mass hypnotism, the main topic of this "line" of literature and drama.)

4. A "media mystique" which crept into American and Ca-

nadian life, holding roughly, that the "peculiar powers" of electronic communications work high voodoo, not only in selling gullible consumers things they do not need, but also function convincingly in matters of ideology and public pressure upon international events. These flames were fired by the peculiar rise to popularity (or notoriety) of the Canadian futurist, Marshall McLuhan, whose popular thesis, while often obscured by the wit and confusion of his rhetoric, was fundamentally clear: Not only do electronic devices of mass communications influence people by means of their inherent nature *and* what is transmitted by them, but they also work a new black magic calling forth a whole strange pantheon of minor devils (succubuses, we assume) into public discourse and hence into contemporary culture. So charming an exponent of this witchcraft was (and is) Dr. McLuhan himself (nicer men with better motives are rare), that the public (especially the young and gullible) in North America bit and swallowed his strangely baited hook more profoundly than even he had anticipated, mainly because both McLuhan and his mentor, Harold Innis, had been publishing these soundings for two decades before they were caught in the maw of North American mass culture.

During this period, every American university of respectable size started offering courses on "International Communications" (sometimes euphemized into "Understandings") that dealt heavily upon the free flow of information around the world, information dissemination ("information" being the currently chic word for the hated term "propaganda"), and a new area of scholarship was constructed full-grown, like Karloff's lovable monster. Justifications and rationales ran the gamut of "hip" faddism. On the political left, the rather foolish notion prevailed that global-mindedness, cross-cultural and information and cultural intense intercourse between nations, might somehow prevent warfare (a feat never having been accomplished in man's history.) On the right, it was assumed that international mass communication was *per se* a class of human activity that might somehow be severed from *all other* international matters (diplomacy, economics, military strategy etc.) and taught to obey various abstract sociological and/or psychological principles, both for purposes of study and policy articulation, and that these notions may apply to *nothing else* in the world but international propaganda.[3]

Much was also made, during this period, of the slim idea that the "American Way," or America's international goals and aims, might be *sold* in much the same way that commercial advertising has been employed to influence so visibly and effectively the American consumer market. Talk was in the air, in those days, about "selling America the way you sell soap." Most of it was critical talk, directed against programs and policies that had never been seriously considered in the first place by our public or semi-private overseas information agencies. True enough, broadcasters, newspaper men and some advertising agency and show-business types had, over the years, been assimilated into the various agencies involved with American information (or propaganda). And a number of government projects had been "contracted out" to private advertisers and communicators, but usually and only when their special carnival talents were needed—as in the instance of an American campaign in Western Europe to stimulate tourism to the USA; or in the actual production of as skillfully made a documentary film as Bruce Herschensohn's *Years of Lightning, Day of Drums*, a smooth panegyric to the late President Kennedy.

For the most part, talk about using the "hard sell" and "America's advertising know-how(!)" in the delicate area of international communications (however defined) *was* just talk, in classrooms, among foreign service personnel and in print.[4] The fact that commercial advertising and international persuasion have little, if anything, in common was simply so obvious that a few simple experiments (and failures) quieted most discussion of the matter. The matter now remains almost beyond dispute.[5]

(In the broader international arena, the subject is far from dead or moribund, however. *Reductio ad absurdum,* while we no longer feel the fingers of the public relations community messing around directly with America's *own* international persuasion, the past generation has witnessed the introduction of Public Relations firms and personnel into *foreign* political and military conflicts, apparently following the lead of Dominican dictator Trujillo, who probably started the gambit in the nineteen-fifties. The more recent Nigerian-Biafran conflict, as an example, has utilized the following firms of private PR hucksters to publicize sordid revolts and their fallout in the interests of partisans on one or another side, in order to gain sympathies from American and European publics—sympathies that might hopefully be turned into money, material and military machines: Patric Dolan and Associates; Barnet and Reef; the British PR firm, Galitzine and Partners; Ruder and Finn—a firm that seems to specialize in revolutionary and counter-revolutionary publicity packaging; London's External Development Services; Dumbarton Associates; Robert S. Goldstein Associates in California; the Geneva-based firm, Markpress; and Burson-Marsteller in Washington D.C. In the light of this trend, the main theme of Woody Allen's farce film, *Bananas*, was not nearly as crazy as most of us supposed. Allen's most amusing premise was the concept of a South American assassination and revolution covered as a sporting event by US television cameras and reporters. Audiences laughed. But would they laugh as heartily at the PR battles, American-style, that color and distort the coverage they receive from insurgent nations on television and in the press, not only in South America but in Africa and Asia as well? Not likely, except that most of the PR gambits by the high-powered firms listed above have failed to accomplish much except to inflate the egos of their clients.)

So much, then, for the main (but not all) of the recent precedents, theories, delusions, myths and premises that have served as causes for the self-deceptions of America's thrust into international public opinion over the past generation. The delusions are, of course, both of a piece with and a function of

our foreign policy—or lack of it because nothing may be accomplished with words and pictures, even employing the over-
touted powers of electronic communications, that has been left
*un*done or done *wrong* in the real-life arena of international
diplomacy, another self-evident fact that has frequently been
blown up to recondite theory by academics.

The latter, operating on their fat campuses, traditionally
more slowly than the rest of society, are still teaching many of
these antecedents as cold facts and wandering about in the defunct era of self-deception past. Taking one of their courses in
"International Understanding" (or some similar name) at
nearly any American university will hurl the auditor into the
museum of yesterday, where he or she will not only be exposed
to a lexicon of these fantasies but will likely find him or her
selves studying some sort of list of "basic methods of persuasion," thrown loosely together by a group of curiously partisan
political scientists in the nineteen-thirties who once called
themselves the *Institute for Propaganda Analysis.*

(We know now, in this present great age of enlightenment,
that, whenever people *get together* to analyze propaganda,
their motives invariably are at best didactic and at worst manipulative. The particular social scientists who made up the institute were, in their time, entirely on the side of virtue, just as
most social scientists still are. Their policies and motives were
properly anti-Hitler, anti-anti-Semitic, anti-isolationist, anti-
racist etc. But they served the gods of intellect poorly, in that
their efforts bespoke one *hell-of-a-way to conduct a science,
even a social science.* Their motives and speculative meanderings served the pressures of the moment—namely, neutralizing
pro-Nazi and anti-liberal propaganda creeping around America
in the depression—but nothing scientific or of value for gener-
alizing or articulating principles of propaganda emerged from
their ambitious enterprises. Their output is, nevertheless, still
treated seriously by some retarded scholars of persuasion.) [6]

What, then, was (and is) the actual content and nature of
this self-bamboozlement; and why did it happen? Answers to

the latter question help to clarify the first, so we shall take
them up briefly and with Ciceronian locution. There is no
need to dwell here upon the general contempt for the discipline of history that pragmatic Americans often show. They
tend, instead, to bask in the radiance of their immediate successes at the art of innovation, their strongest cultural asset.
The importance of Henry Ford's claim, "History is bunk," lies
in the enormous success that Ford had achieved pragmatically
by adhering to his own dictum and ignoring the historical wisdom which told him that what he was accomplishing magnifi-
cently absolutely could not be done. Ford was the typical
pragmatist—moreso than philosophers like James, Dewey and
others—usually associated with the term. He was also a typical
American, insofar as most Americans are concerned more with
results than *processes,* and *material* rather than *ethereal* things.
Despite wails to the contrary, this stance is not easily criticized in our modern age, in that it has been imitated most as-
siduously by those, at home and abroad, who we hear damn it
most loudly.

Now, *nothing*—in song, story, legend and fact—is more
practical in its function than political life in the USA, at least
as we have experienced it since Andrew Jackson. And no aspect of culture plays more loose and deceptive games with history than politics and politicians. The latter constitute the men
and women who, when all is said and done, *set* public policies
and manipulate our multifarious relations with other sovereign
states.

At root, accordingly, of the failure of the United States,
during the period we loosely call the "Cold War," (speaking
bluntly) to score many brownie points in influencing the attitudes of friendly and non-friendly nations towards America
stands one obvious fact. It is *extremely difficult*—if not impossible—to articulate clearly or precisely by means of *any*
communications device (film, television, radio or print) a
vague and vacillating foreign policy based upon the ethereal
moral reactions of chief executives (mainly) to world events,

immediately as they unfold in the headlines. The main delusion, therefore, under which America's propagandists of the past two decades operated was, in retrospect, that they could not accomplish ends which circumstance may well have made impossible in the first place. A little study of the history of propaganda would have enlightened them. Some communicators saw this rock in the path of destiny quite clearly; but nobody listened.

Another factor should also be taken into consideration here: When, during World War II, the Office of War Information was organized, it functioned in the "psych-war" field much as an arm of the total hot-war effort against Germany, Italy and Japan. In many ways, it assisted the soldier in the field and the allied "fifth columns" of fighters behind the enemy lines. Its targets and methods were well defined and clearly articulated. When World War II ended, the giant American Army of fifteen million men were practically demobilized. The OWI, however, continued, though it changed its name to the United States Information Agency. But its objectives and targets and methods were not updated and remained stagnant. The "old-time" hot-war techniques did not work during the cold-war period of the 'fifties that did not demand "psyche-war" battlefield techniques.

Granting the premise, however, that to try and fail is better than not to try at all—an attitude endemic to this day among much of most of our international information personnel—one also discovers other causes for the path of self-deception that we have followed. None of them is as formerly stated as the simple-minded myth still sometimes heard on Madison Avenue, New York, that we failed because we did not choose to "sell America the way we sell hair oil" or words to this effect. With the exception of some low-ranking writers and other functionaries who were (or are) politically astute *emigrés* (or refugees) from the countries to which we sent our messages for twenty-five years, the propaganda policy, aims, goals and methods of the United States have been set and implemented by people woefully ignorant—and frequently contemptuous—of both the history of effective uses of communications of all types in extra-national matters and with the dynamics of the *art* of persuasion, as it has been carried on in the East and West since antiquity.

Where, in sum, social psychologists (or people who know what social psychologists are supposed to know) were needed at the helm, an apparently perfectly competent echelon of professionals from disciplines related, but in many ways antagonistic to, modern, viable social psychological study were called to Washington, New York, Munich and Vienna in order to make the relatively, few but really important, implementing decisions in our propaganda policies. They came, by and large, from "other worlds" in an intellectual sense—either from the ranks of foreign service personnel and diplomacy (the better choice of two bad ones) or from the ranks of our domestic communications industries, mostly journalism and broadcasting.

To be specific—possibly, too brutally specific—there is, for instance, nothing intrinsically *wrong* with the notion of an Edward R. Murrow, Carl Rowan or Frank Shakespeare (or, on different levels, clever documentary film-makers and noted news-analysts) delineating and activating America's propaganda policies, except that professionals of their calibre in their respective fields *cannot be expected to know much* about the history and psychology of mass persuasion, which is precisely what their game is all about. The right men, in other words, have for years been doing the wrong jobs at nearly every *important* point both of policy-making and policy-implementing.

The results are what one would expect. As worldly-wise communication expert and consultant, Bertram Cowlan, has recently observed correctly,[7] a major symptom of this problem is that we have, in effect, been sending abroad to certain nations (particularly those we call "underdeveloped") barrages of sophisticated communications software—books, films, radio and television programs, and all the impedimenta that our policy gurus have used so successfully from their executive suites in New York and Hollywood for *domestic* communications—into societies and cultural situations where, in Cowlan's words, "pen, pencils and paper . . . and chalk and blackboards . . . some few books and typewriters . . ." handled by individuals wise in the ways of human attitude-stroking, are really the instruments required to achieve whatever objectives we ask of our information people in the field.

The trouble with "high-powered" experts is endemic to their status: their power expresses itself in thinking and acting on simplistic but gigantic scales. And their expertise is most often intensively limited, as an old saying goes, to the *one* "for instance" that adds up to their particular spectacular career. Neither in depth nor breadth are our most successful and expert American broadcasters, journalists, diplomats and film-makers up to the sophisticated job of cross-cultural attitude manipulation—with some exceptions, of course. But the exceptions have been notable by their absence from the roster of "star quality names" upon whom responsibility for disseminating the "American image" (or whatever you call it) to our friends and foes has fallen during the, we hope, late Cold War era.

This situation is not so obviously a scandal at most of the lower echelons of our government's propaganda arms, nor, in general, among the information services of the CIA. The latter, however,—particularly at the operational level—frequently give the impression of feeling uneasy, because they have *not* been given communications celebrities to direct their destinies but rather CIA old-timers and foreign area specialists who may or may not (and differentially between them) *think* they are communications celebrities. When the wash is hung to dry, however, the clearest insights, we judge, belongs to the cloak-and-dagger craftsmen of the CIA, whose failures have been rarely (but once) the result of over-kill, and whose successes (mostly modest and sometimes accidental) appear to result from proper knowledge at the operational level of the psychology of their (wisely) segmented foreign target audiences. They, nevertheless, apparently feel diminished by the spectacular presence of front-office executives writing at other international persuasion factories memoranda on world-wide satellite television communications etc., in the face of their rather simple but realistic day-to-day policy directives concerned, quite correctly, with the content of news broadcasts, lectures and sermons.

The ghost of Cicero may now retire to its tomb.

We have no intention of reprising the history of international persuasion, the semantics of the word "propaganda" or of teaching the complex findings and hypotheses of modern social psychology, sociology and other fields of inquiry concerning persuasive communications. In the first place, we have already done the job in print almost to the point of redundancy.[8] And, second, we would be forced to fill this book with abstruse and specialized matters that require specialized training, extensive treatment and considerable study. The issue therefore closes with our flat pronouncement that propagandists and information specialists must, in the modern state, qualify as experts at *everything* modern science and first-rate responsible speculation have entered into the record concerning the dynamics of propaganda and information dissemination, no matter how difficult or incomplete this history is at the moment. What they know, or whatever their skills in running American television networks, making entertainment or documentary television programs, movies, book publishing, editing newspapers and magazines, and/or selling corn flakes or institutional philosophy to the American public are, these matters are, for the most part, unfortunately irrelevant to this ukase. To ask any less is—as has been demonstrated in practice—absurd.

In spite of the homespun admonition above, here are some minor "for instances" to ponder: Paul Joseph Goebbels, Ph.D., understood clearly everything that history could tell him in the nineteen-thirties about mass persuasion, particularly French social psychology and Italian and Spanish philosophy and political sociology of the past century. And he used what he knew, with results that naive political scientists and psychologists are (unnecessarily) still, to this day, trying to explain.[9] Today's Soviet propagandists are also schooled intensively and realistically in everything, in this respect, that Soviet psychology admits as tenable intellectually, *as well as* that body of theory and experiment that it rejects, ideologically Marxist "truths" notwithstanding.[10] The same may probably be said of Red China's information specialists, although we know of no reliable non-speculative data on the subject available at present in the West.[11]

Love Lyrics

As we listen to these old tape recordings, another ghostly aspect of America's international information delusion rises from the resulting nostalgic gloom, all the sadder because we find ourselves observing this poltergeist from the perspective of a period in which the United States' authority and prestige has, in the wake of the crazy-quilt events surrounding the painful termination of the Vietnam war, never been lower in the market of international opinion—starting at our own borders of Canada and Mexico. One is almost ready to posit that, peering from the present and into tomorrow, there is "nowhere to go but up." Our futile policies and efforts during the worst years of the Cold War, more than a decade ago, recall an enviable idealism now vanished under the pressure of insistent events lately blown in from Southeast Asia. Under such circumstances, even yesterday's chronic galloping stupidity and self-deceit may take on a momentary nostalgic warmth and a cozy glow. One may indeed detect, in some circles of propagandists, a sentimental hankering for the past when (as it almost always does) yesterday seems more comfortable than it was, particularly because these functionaries knew—or thought they knew—our allies from our antagonists and how to talk to them.

This feeling—by no means a literary whim on the part of the writers—is also vestigial manifestation of one of the major weaknesses of our role in the *War of Ideas* during that Cold War period and up to the present. To be precise, we confused (and still confuse) our *intentions* with our *objectives*. The very use of the word "understanding" placed so freely in our literature next to the word "international" is a clean symbol of this deception and the *blatantly incorrect* assumption it implies—namely, that "international understanding" is an anodyne for anything, particularly intercultural conflicts, with or without swords and guns.

Possibly Freudian psychologists and Lasswellian sociologists have, by now, hammered our collective brains into instant pudding, but we *know* that, despite what we may *like* to believe, the intention or motive or accomplishment of understanding between national states in the modern world means *nothing* of and by itself. The most brutal wars in history, including World War II, were fought by antagonistic nations that "understood" each other distressingly well. On the other side of the coin, the United States is at present unlikely to declare war upon Communist Tibet (and vice-versa), despite the fact our degree of reciprocal understanding with her is quite low. *Non-understanding* and, frequently, *misunderstanding* may function as a diplomatic buffer that keeps sharp blades at bay, just as the extraordinary and keen *understanding* of Red China by Nationalist China keep them continually slashing one at the other.

This observation, of course is no secret. But it remains, at the moment, as much a delusion in the USSR as it is in the USA —if that is any comfort. (Freud therefore, may have nothing to do with the issue.) In the USSR, however, the situation is reversed: cross-cultural understandings are generally suspect, lest they somehow incite the Russian citizenry to dissatisfaction with life in their socialist paradise and lead to rebellion.[12] We suspect that both views (in their pure forms) of the same issue are equally unrealistic, based, as they are, upon transparently spurious premises. How the Red Chinese political establishment feels about the subject, we have yet to discover.

The fact remains, however, that Americans tend to believe what their behavioral science textbooks tell them, a tendency that may prove more deadly for the USA than the Punic wars were for Carthage. (There are many paths to extermination.) Nearly all "mental" therapy, personal and social, is launched on a bedrock assumption that "understanding all" is more or less tantamount to "forgiving all," and that two-way communication is therefore both a moral and strategic societal virtue. Such communication—or "dialogue," in the current *patois*—is therefore seen as an objective to which individuals, differing socio-cultural factions—and even nations—must strive to achieve *as an end in itself, and regardless of the content of the dialogue.* One immediately perceives, therefore, how goals in many areas of national endeavor are deeply influenced by this arbitrary assumption, but nowhere more clearly and directly than in international affairs.

"Dialogue" (or whatever you want to call international reciprocity of arts, science, culture and so forth) is, on its face, *neither* an end nor a policy: It is just a *means* to certain policy objectives that may succeed or fail, depending upon many, many factors. These objectives cannot be undertaken, of course, unless this dialogue is achieved in the first place. But the dialogue usually means precisely as much, taken alone, as an international ping-pong tournament, a chess game between an American and a Russian or an exchange of ballet dancers between New York and Moscow—simply what they imply about the values of ping-pong, chess and ballet—and not one jot or iota more. (Let us recall that the Japanese were playing professional American-style baseball on the day of the Pearl Harbor attack, and that American children frolicked in Germanic *kindergartens* all the while our own "strategic" bombers pounded the Hamburg waterfront to rubble.)

This simple fact of cross-cultural life seems somehow too deep, dense or realistic for most American propagandists and information personnel to maintain in their cerebella for a second longer than it takes to tell it. To a lesser degree, the same principle applies as well to World's Fairs, Trade Fairs, International Exhibits and other attempts at overseas hand-grasping—less *once in a while,* because *some* ideational content invariably travels along with these occasions. And, as slight as it may be, this content is invariably *the* crucial element *in* the event that either creates (usually) small currents of *rapprochement* or overt hostility between the publics to whom they are exposed—marching pickets, public-relations flacks and other molehill expanders that they attract notwithstanding.

The practical propagandist is not, however, fundamentally interested in side-effects, "scratches on the brain" (as these vague impressions have been called in the literature of overseas persuasion) of love and hate—unless through some confluence of forces foreign policy relates strategically to them. It *does*—at times—but unfortunately these relatively trivial intercultural gambits are most germane to the sort of persuasion one directs to friends or allies. Bully for British plays that open in New York, or American dramas that bring standing ovations in London! Cheers also to spaghetti Westerns, Japanese versions of *Fiddler on the Roof,* USIA libraries in London, Paris and Rome and peripatetic Congressmen buying souvenirs in Lisbon! These are more or less harmless bursts of cross-cultural communication that clearly activate emotions. But any or all such emotions may be immediately quieted by *one* strategically employed block-busting bomb of the antique World War II variety, let alone a single atomic field weapon.

The measure of such understanding and amity may be gleaned best by the story of *events.* In the on-going love to hate affair we have, over the years, experienced with the USSR, the business of international understanding continues to be buffeted about by the caprices of history. Let us look at the record from America's perspective, and ask ourselves merely whether or not the degree of *understanding* (and often the proper *misunderstanding* to provide sanctions for arbitrary policies) actually produced *results* in terms either of the behavior of Americans or their decision-makers in Washington, D.C. over the long years they span.

The American Communist Party and the *Daily Worker* rarely sang the praises of the USSR louder than during the nineteen-thirties, an era that ended with the Nazi-Soviet pact. During these years the fine motion picture films—some of them propaganda pieces—of Sergei Eisenstein were loudly applauded by the American *cognoscenti* as magnificent works of art—which they were and are. During World War II, the Russians were held to be our blood brothers, and, incredible as it may seem today, urban parades were given for Soviet snipers and mass rallies were held in enormous auditoriums to support the USSR's Army. The US Army itself produced a film for soldiers in its *Why We Fight* series on *The Battle of Russia* that might well have been scripted inside the Kremlin. The Brothers Warner in Hollywood made a popular, general audience movie, *Mission to Moscow*, extolling the virtues of the sons and daughters of the October Revolution.[13] All very touching and probably quite meaningless, even in its own time, for complex and abstruse psychological reasons that need little explanation to anyone with common sense. And we are merely skimming the surface of a propaganda barrage.

Hollywood changed its tune after Churchill's 1946 "Iron Curtain" speech (foreign villians in movies were now Russians) and international espionage story writers worked-up anti-Soviet plots and sub-plots—reaching nearly psychotic proportions of hyperbole in some of Ian Fleming's British-American James Bond novels and films. But gentle hands were still reaching towards Red Square. Soviet films like *The Cranes Are Flying* deeply impressed critics and audiences. The indefatigable Sol Hurok brought to the United States an unending stream of concert musicians, dancers and other artists, most of whom were adulated and adored in New York salons. In the middle to late 'fifties, the Soviet Union took over the New York

Coliseum for an impressive exhibit treating slickly almost every aspect of modern life in the USSR. (One of the authors had an opportunity to read the Guest Book in which the visitor might write his reactions to the show, placed on the floor of the exhibit. The remarks were illuminating, especially during a period when Anglo-Saxon cuss words and obscene urban graffiti were less ubiquitous than today. What must the Russians have thought of us, despite the probability that much of the wild obscene language in the Guest Book was probably impossible to translate?)

The Cold War period was, in retrospect, quite redolent of attempts at USSR-USA cross-national understanding, the effects of which *in no perceptible way*, as far as we can determine, mitigated the psychological or political differences that waxed and waned between the two nations. There is little object in listing further tales of American "triumphs" of international amity, like the entire company of *Porgy and Bess* that literally took Moscow by storm, according to Truman Capote, who, (for reasons that have not yet been discovered) accompanied the Negro company that traveled to the USSR during this nervous period of verbal hostility. The folk opera's effects upon Soviet opinion-makers—and even Soviet public opinion at large—in matters that count (like war and peace) appears to have been nil.

International understanding is, therefore, usually a more futile—and sometimes a more risky—endeavor than sociologists, do-gooders and idealists (both the American kind who *encourage* it and the Soviet kind who *discourage* it) would have us believe. Even on the ideological front, it is difficult to assess the significance of America's recent passion for Soviet novelists like the late Boris Pasternak and Alexander Solzhenitsyn, as well as action-poets-in-the-flesh like Yevgeny Yevtushenko. Granting that such writers are dissenters from establishment politics in the USSR, they are, nevertheless, much-touted as bridge-builders between the common Soviet citizens and the American people. That their popularity in the USA counts highly in decreasing the mutual hostility between the two nations is doubtful. On the other hand, recent, well-publicized acts of violence and protests by American Jews in the USA centering on the treatment of their co-religionists in the USSR may well "call world attention" to traditions of anti-Semitism in East Europe. But, by and large, the Politburo appears unmoved by these protests *alone*. Military strategy (arms for Israel, for instance) and diplomatic maneuvering—as well as the communication by means of cash and credit exchange for goods and services—are more likely to move the Soviet oligarchs into re-thinking their attitudes towards Jews than heroic (but misused) guerrilla-style psychological warfare and open-air dramatics.

Regarding many of these matters, there has existed (and still exists) an enormous degree of mutual understanding between the citizens and the body politic of the USA and the USSR and vice-versa. Optimists who pretend to discern the seeds of *entente* between the two nations in these particular flower boxes, however, may wait for them to bloom in vain. Certainly, the Russians may metamorphose into our blood brothers once again—possibly tomorrow morning—but as the result of clear, overt self-interest and the desire for survival on the part of both nations: in the outbreak of a war, for instance, pitting both nations as allies against the "yellow peril." As insane as such a conflict would be, it just might turn the trick. But the cant of "international understanding" would have nothing to do with the matter.

Nations—like people—create strategic alliances, and then *subsequently* fall in love with convenient mythic stereotypes of other nations, just as they frequently also learn to *despise* mythic stereotypes of nations they know and understand all too well, smack in the face of reality, history and even common sense. The Poles *know* the Russians, and understand them, in all probability, better than any other people on the globe, at least the Greater Russians and Ukrainians who have been upsetting their eastern borders for centuries. And nowhere in the world today will one find greater hostility towards *all* of the USSR and her citizens than in Poland, freely and (surprisingly) openly expressed by unlikely people at the least suggestion.

But there is nothing odd in this. Discuss the Costa Ricans with the Nicaraguans, or vice-versa. Then reconsider the sociological ideal of international amity. Or talk to the Irish about the British over a pint of bitter, and be sure you have an escape route planned before you do. For conflict, one might almost generalize, appears to be an *inevitable* result of free and open communication between people who are quite similar but who differ on *basic issues* having to do either with money (in any of its forms), territory (which is often a form of money), or religion (which is often also a matter of territory). Pakistan and India, Biafra and Nigeria, the Viet Cong and Vietnam, North Korea and South Korea, and, of course, Northern Ireland and the Republic of Ireland represent but selective instances of this gloomy generalization. Such realism forces one to turn his back upon the kinds of thinking that substitutes kindly motivations for the multitude of political, social, economic, religious and military realities that permeate so much cross-cultural babel on our disordered globe.

The United Nations, unfortunately, was built upon just such shoddy and shaky aspirations, confused with international diplomacy and gut—level reality. It was therefore doomed to its present impotence and past failures. Had the UN been constructed upon a firmer structure of international law, including, as any legal structure must, *just but unequivocal penalties* for fairly adjudged transgressions, and plenty of military muscle (or "police power," if the term is preferable)—including *absolute international control* of *all* mutually surrendered nuclear weaponry—it just might have worked. Well, so much the worse for old man earth, and better luck next time—if there is a next time.

Meanwhile, we in the USA shall doubtless pursue the panaceas of love, understanding, mutual humanity and continue to call forth all the benign deities who have, since the first writing of history, been summoned to create peace in the world—but have given us less than half a century of it in three millennia, and then only when men were too tired, enervated, malnourished or sick to fight.

Another voice on tape is that of the Shavian Devil: "The plague, the famine, the earthquake were too spasmodic in their action; the tiger and the crocodile were too easily satiated and not cruel enough: something more constantly, more ruthlessly, more ingeniously, more destructive was needed; and that something was Man, the inventor of the rack, the stake, the gallows, the electric chair; of sword and gun and poison gas: above all of justice, duty, patriotism, and all the other isms by which even those who are clever enough to be humanely disposed are persuaded to become the most destructive of all the destroyers." [14]

Pennywhistle Blues

At this point, we might argue that the history of international persuasion has been for so long so ineffective, and the risks of its pursuit, in any form, so great, that the salubrious use of propaganda on a global scale is—like education for the achievement of universal civility—an impossible, quixotic dream; and that we had all best get on with the ancient, but occasionally effective, business of diplomacy, military gamesmanship and economic purse-snatching, forgetting forever the much-touted issue of the *"war for the minds of men."* This argument is discouragingly cogent, and has recently been heard, not only in the seclusion of small enclaves of political-scientists and diplomats, but from the floor of the United States Senate. It is a good case, and a good reason for concluding this book at this point with the quote above, or for the reader to close it and pick up something less confusing, like a murder mystery.

In fact, however, we have no choice, because in the months, years and decades to come we *shall* be fighting over (and for) men's minds overseas, whether or not we appropriate money and create or destroy governmental agencies for the purpose, and in spite of any policies we pretend or intend to pursue which exclude, accidently or by design, what is loosely called "psychological warfare."

One does not need to chart to illustrate the multifarious psychological components of *all* international contacts, past and present, and their inevitable role in the creation both of alliances and antagonisms between cultures.

"Psych-war," under many names, has been a constant exponent of the *status quo* since the creation of the national state, and even before then. Machiavelli created nothing new in his great essay in honor of the wise prince. He was merely writing a selective history of events as he saw them and as he understood they had been since antiquity. Neither have modern social psychologists and sociologists created, by means of scientific intelligence, a novel discipline because of their interest in what people in one part of the world *think* about people in another part. Most important, neither have our modern instruments of mass communication created new weapons of *intrinsically* different natures than these shiploads of gossips, actors, politicians, merchants and others who zipped around the Aegean Sea with distressing speed (considering modern suburban public transportation) in the Hellenic days. We are irrefutably trapped by circumstances. And the psychological component of international discourse in peace and war *is* there, because it has always *been* there.

Global Villages—whatever they are supposed to be—may characterize certain aspects of living today better than they once did. More important, however, is the force of public intervention in diplomatic processes that is greater than ever before everywhere in the world, even (and sometimes especially) in so-called "underdeveloped nations," relatively untouched by communications technology.

One of the many causes of this increasing intervention of the public, the masses, the people—or whatever you want to call the "common man"—into previously exclusive international forums is, naturally, the proliferation of communications devices to apprise them of far-away events and the voices and faces of observers in remote places who are able to reach their eyes or ears quickly.

But this particular technology is just *one* cause among many, and, when all is said and done, serves more to accelerate the *pace* of public reaction to distant events (and non-events told as events) than it influences either their impact or quality. This observation is heresy, of course, among professional international persuaders, who would have us believe their unsubstantiated fancy (because of their gadgets) that they are fighting "new" wars with "new" weapons in "new" ways, and therefore they must be most important fellows on-the-spot, and new-style VIP's. While vanity is always understandable, this particular vanity is compounded nine-tenths of bunkum, and, as the dust of recent daily experience is settling, the fact is growing more and more self-evident.

What *has* changed in the modern world is a circumstance more subtle—but possibly more potentially lethal—than anything technology may ever be used to dream-up. *First,* in the background of any realistic view of the world is the statistical truth that more multiples of so-called "common men" live everywhere (and live longer) than ever before in history. Their ratio, therefore, to the elite classes that govern them is insistently increasing. Considering the alarming popularity of breeding, these multiples will probably continue well into the next century. Mankind's great problem will probably not be feeding and housing them (problems technology *is* entirely competent to handle) but *what to do* with them (a problem apparently well beyond the scope of technology.)

Second, participant democratic *notions* in many forms, and under many names, are today ubiquitous around the globe. Note that we said "*notions,*" not "*democracy*" itself. People are easily fooled by "men on white horses" and attractive tyrants into *thinking* that their opinions and attitudes are significant to the turn of events. But whether we are talking about democratic notions as facts or as fancies matters little. What the masses *think*, and the very fact that they *do think at all* about international affairs, is at the heart of this profound change. Not so long ago (and in eras and places where instruments for spreading communications to mass proportions were not easily available), most men on this planet lived largely cut-off from most of the political, economic and military discourse of their time and place—not because of a lack of means to enter it, but due to their indifference to it. Notions of popular democracy, public assent and grassroot, self-determined government (*not* necessarily newspapers and radios, that most people around the world neither owned nor read thoroughly nor asked more of than diversion) were spread by word-of-mouth, *the most potent instrument of mass communication ever invented*. This changed the picture.

International policy, international alliances, international antagonisms and international activities of all kinds, therefore, presently require degrees and intensities of popular support never before asked of them, both in nations where relatively free speech is permitted and in titular dictatorships, oligarchies and other oppressive societies. (No living man knows, for instance, how this vital factor of popular support and non-support influenced America's conduct of the Vietnam war—whether it shortened or attenuated it, or whether it operated for good or evil from any perspective. Nor will history tell us with certainty.)

The result of these main factors—combined with others of lesser significance, like the availability of international broadcasting conduits and the like—have forced *every* national government in the world today into creating an active propaganda arm. The United States is no exception. In every nation, also, this segment of government is moving closer and closer to its policy and decision-making bodies in terms of influence and even directive power—again including the USA. Nearly everywhere—except in strong-man regimes where a stance of bluff is an indispensible social control—this move (of propagandists toward decision-making bodies) is at the same time being resisted by old establishments of traditional politics. They fear all forms of delegated power that they do not entirely understand and/or control.

A short time ago, and for the reasons above, only in states like Nazi Germany did a ruler like Hitler permit his Minister of Propaganda, not only to maintain access to the innermost secrets of government, but also call upon him for advice in determining what directions to take in such seemingly irrelevant problems as military and economic decisions that might affect the masses directly. Today, such advice is avidly sought—although not always acted upon—by almost every governing body everywhere, including the most idealistic and sage. The hazards of disregarding the psychological aspects of *all* public policy, and especially that involving other nations, is now simply too great.

President Nixon's personal visits to Vienna, Moscow, Kiev, Tehran, Warsaw and Peking in 1972 are examples. Whatever they may or may not have accomplished in other domains, their world-wide psychological value (with the exception of the Tehran visit) in terms of human attitudes and opinions was probably more significant and epochal than their military, economic or political ramifications will turn out to be *in the long run.* After all, in an age of satellite communication, and given America's relatively well-schooled pool of foreign service professionals and free-lancers, why *should* an American president have to *go* anywhere, except for a change of climate and/or personal reasons of whim? International jawboning, as a matter of fact, on summit levels, is usually about as formalized as the Catholic High Mass, with its agendas, interpreters, exchanges of amenities, state dinners and other nonsense that is nothing but colorful stagecraft and psychological window dressing.

Carefully worded and translated written messages are instruments of choice today for dealing precisely with important and urgent issues at the highest level of State, just as they have been for centuries. They lack, however, the psychological dimension that all publics everywhere have learned to demand: a feeling (however spurious in fact) of *engagement* in public policy. And this feeling is only achieved by reducing abstract power to personal contacts with which publics around the world may identify and empathize. A. A. Berle cogently indicates this point in his last retrospective book on life at the summit of international politics.[15]

So, to repeat, we have no choice—or any more choice than any other nation, big or small, has—regarding our participation in the *War of Ideas*. Rhetoric to the contrary is wasted breath. Practical politicians and diplomats naturally know this, because they are continually forced to deal with life as it is, not as they would have it be. Of course, also, they sing the blues and hanker after a bygone and more easy and comfortable time of gentlemanly international intercourse, treaty-making and civility that never really existed. They forget (or never knew) that social psychology and its long history includes in its syllabus a plethora of complexities, not easily taught in career-training schools for the foreign service. And the penalties for misjudgments in the international arena are both grave and all-too-often wide open to public scrutiny. International service is a difficult and demanding life's work, the details of which we now turn to with humility and trepidation.

NOTES TO CHAPTER 4

[1] Report by Comrade L. I. Brezhnev, General Secretary of the CPSU Central Committee, to the Twenty-fourth Congress of the Communist Party of the Soviet Union, March 31, 1971. Quoted in Gayle Durham Hollander, *Soviet Political Indoctrination* (New York etc.: Praeger Publishers, 1972), p. 196.

² We know that Lord Haw-Haw (William Joyce) was hung by the British, not as a propagandist but as a traitor, a moot matter. But whatever became of Tokyo Rose? Tried as a traitor after the war (she was a US citizen), Rose was subsequently imprisoned for half-a-dozen years and fined $10,000. Upon release, she married an American, and today is working as a store clerk on Chicago's North Side. In late 1972, a federal court denied her request for a hearing in order to prevent Uncle Sam from attaching her wages in payment of half of the fine still owing. The request was denied. See *The New York Times,* November 16, 1972, p. 36.

³ Just about every approach to every aspect of this now-waning disciplinary conceit may be found in the articles that make up the excellent anthology, edited by Heinz-Dietrich Fischer and John Calhoun Merril, *International Communication* (New York: Hastings House, 1970). One major problem in turning this aspect of communication studies into a discrete area of inquiry is that its various "experts" (present company included) describe the elephant from incompatible viewpoints—in fact, even define the word "elephant" in profoundly different and inconsistent ways. Dissonance among the viewpoints of the experts is therefore (and amusingly) greater than the misunderstandings and ethnocentric mischiefs between those countries and cultures that these same experts are supposedly clarifying. Back issues of *The Public Opinion Quarterly* (organ of the American Association for Public Opinion Research, published by the Advisory Committee on Communication, Columbia University) are the best sources for interminable evidence, over the years, of this *katzenjammer.*

⁴ One of the most rational, but parochial, documents on the subject was written by a senior editor of *Printer's Ink* whose ethnocentric interpretations of international communications do not counterbalance his good prose or considerable experience on the domestic front. It is a valid memento of this school of thought, small as it was. See Walter Joyce, *The Propaganda Gap* (New York: Harper and Row, 1963.)

⁵ The present writers, during this period, were employed in tandem to indoctrinate the writers of an American overseas broadcasting agency into radio broadcasting techniques, in order to add some color to what the agency believed was a roster of dull and uninspired programs. With considerable doubt and clear warnings, we set about arranging for them a series of seminars, drawing largely upon the skills of domestic professional radio and television broadcasters, who teach these arcane arts at various universities, with success—are assumed. The progress and outcome of this venture were too complex (and trivial) to report here. Suffice it to say that the total effect of this enterprise upon the agency's operation was zilch. The service's basic orientation to broadcasting remained what it was: a device for political persuasion, told for the greatest part by spoken lectures in abstruse ideological terms. And this was (and is) probably the only and best possible course for such a broadcasting service,

operating under its peculiar circumstances and utilizing its highly politically sensitized staff of writers and researchers, to take. The experience was interesting, but neither productive nor enlightening.

[6] Recent books emerging from academia seem to be drifting away from the constrictive and "how-to" approach in persuasion and propaganda in favor of more broadly based considerations of psychological and sociological experiment and theory. See the concise and well-organized treatment of the dynamics of persuasion in Otto Lerbinger's *Designs for Persuasive Communication* (Englewood Cliffs, N.J.: Prentice-Hall, Inc., 1972), as well as co-author George N. Gordon's more wide-ranging (and discursive) but less orthodox (and successfully achieved) volume, *Persuasion: The Theory and Practice of Manipulative Communication*. If you are buying books on the subject of mass persuasion, buy both. You will not need others—as of the present moment, at least.

[7] From a speech by Bertram Cowlan, *Thinking Small: Some Comments on the Role of Mass Media for Economic and Social Development*, delivered at the International Broadcasting Institute in Amsterdam (1971); soon to be published in *Educational Broadcasting International* (1973).

[8] See *The Idea Invaders*, p. 17–67 and Gordon's *Persuasion*, cited above.

[9] There are many books on Goebbels and his dirty work, but this particular point, his general sophistication regarding the past and present of his profession, is most clearly treated in Ernst K. Bramstead's *Goebbels and National Socialist Propaganda 1925–1945* (Michigan: State University Press, 1965.) Most other biographies, including recent ones, lack Bramstead's necessary detachment from the moralistic sermonizing, usually so attractive to writers who choose subjects like Goebbels for biographical study.

[10] See John C. Clews, *Communist Progaganda Techniques* (New York: Frederick A. Praeger, 1964), and read between the lines of the deceptively charming essay by Yuri I. Bobrakov, "From Red Square to Pennsylvania Avenue" in John Lee (ed.), *Diplomatic Persuaders* (New York: John Wiley and Son, 1968), pp. 117–127.

[11] Soundings may be heard in Warren H. Phillips' dispatch from Peking, "China's Press Corps—Discipline Plus" in *The Wall Street Journal*, November 7, 1972, p. 14. The journalists (and other information personnel) whom Phillips met in China show all the signs of rigorous training in didactic, intentional and/or manipulative communication. But a single encounter cannot provide us with information of the nature of this training or its specific content.

[12] The Moscow Politburo blows hot and cold on the matter of cultural exchange with the West. They are clearly as nervous about the inherent corruptions in "international understands" as we in the USA are sold on its benefactions. The *New York Times* headline on January 6,

1973, "Soviet Rebuffs Western Appeals to Ease the Exchange of Ideas," tells, in the ensuing dispatch from Moscow, the well-worn news that the USSR and the USA are both cracked in the same groove on this issue, but at different angles. See also the *Times* Editorial on this issue, January 12, 1973 entitled *Moscow Fears Thaw*, p. 32.

[13] Propaganda in films, domestic and foreign, shown to Americans admits of many enigmas, as do all reputed effects of movies on audiences. Film has been used in the USA mostly to *confirm* attitudes of audiences (general and specialized) that they already display, and thus may be said to "work" as persuasion—just as long as they are not required to *change* attitudes or cast doubt upon them. Two recent books on persuasive cinema are Richard Dyer MacCann's almost encyclopedic *The People's Films* (New York: Hastings House, 1973), and the less scholarly but more colorful volume (well larded with fine movie photographs) by David Manning White and Richard Averson, *The Celluloid Weapon* (Boston: The Beacon Press, 1972.) Both books are naturally better at hindsight concerning what the movies they treat *reflected* in American social and political life than how they really *influenced* the people who viewed them, their main didactic objective in most cases. The former book is largely concerned with documentaries, while the latter centers mostly on "entertainment" films, a purely formal difference of little consequence to the analyst of persuasion or to the working propagandist who uses film to achieve his ends. That each type of film attracts and moves different audiences differently is, of course, of critical importance to the propagandist, depending upon his objectives and resources.

[14] From Shaw's *Man and Superman;* the "Don Juan in Hell" dream sequence, Act III.

[15] See A. A. Berle, *Power* (New York: Harcourt Brace and World Publishers, 1969.)

PART TWO

Those Who Do Not Understand the Present Are Condemned to Optimism

5

Nice Guys Finish Last

'Though Waterloo was won upon the playing fields of Eton,
The next war will be photographed and lost by Cecil Beaton.

NOËL COWARD
(*Bright Young People*)

The United States reached, in the early nineteen-seventies, a turning point in its world-wide propaganda, information and so-called "cultural exchange" policies, an eventuality beyond dispute—if any aspect of national life may, indeed, be viewed as history while it is happening. This is possible when reason and opinion both join for a moment in a unanimous verdict. At the instant Caesar was stabbed, we may justifiably assume, for instance, that the conspirators knew that they were making history.

To *reach* a turning point is one thing. Actually to *turn*, however, is a different matter, because one has *three* options at the juncture: *not to turn* at all and be jockeyed about by fate;

to retreat to a former position in the hope that history will repeat itself; or, finally, *to pursue* a novel and untried course.

The options today are in the works. They will not be taken hastily. And one may expect feints, passes and diversions to accompany their disposition. But occur they *must*, for a number of reasons. We list them below as follows:

First, our relative disengagement from the political-military conflicts in Southeast Asia—most notably in Vietnam—will have, for years, repercussions in our international relations, not the least of which will be the psychological fallout in the minds of masses around the globe of (all rationalizations and catch-phrases aside) what is generally regarded as America's *first* military (and logistic) defeat in this century.

Second, the status and function of America's military establishment has largely, as a result, fallen into disarray. Although frantic efforts have been made to conceal the fact, all of our military services are currently victims of internal confusion and external derision, exacerbated by their classical jealousies and overlapping functions. We own, it is true, a stockpile of doomsday weapons, large and small, but even the average foot-soldier or specialist bomber pilot understands that he will probably never use one in his lifetime. As Britain lost her mastery of the seas half a century ago, so has the United States lost much of her potential *effective* military power (both real and psychological) in the last twenty-five years, largely by following, in the wrong places at the wrong times, obsolete stratagems of now-outmoded warfare. It is possible that this situation is, given the present bureaucracy that protects the American armed services from more than titular civilian control, impossible for *any* arm of the government (or all of them together) to remediate.

Third, as our country has emerged from the turbulent confusions of the nineteen-sixties, America's "image" as a major power has been altered by the severe public home-grown traumas of that turbulent decade—most of them important because of their dramatic impact upon visible aspects of American life.

In the end, they were largely moral changes that also touched every aspect, visible and covert, of our culture—one way or another. We refer to the cumulative impact of the apparent end of certain well-worn illusions: that a national economy would expand forever; that mass education may balance out mass social inequalities and might solve societal problems; that the implementation of statutory freedom often generates social evils worse than bondages of constraint; and that racial minorities (especially Negroes) aspire to be anything more statuesque than walking, diluted materialistic imitations of the WASP majority. Legal abortions, pornography, drug and alcohol addiction and female priapus-worship (Women's Lib, for short) are not recent currents in American thought and behavior. But the new social sanctions they have achieved in one mere decade of confusion and torture are but a few of the results of the death of old illusions. Add also the many demoralizing aspects, layer by layer, or the political corruption and apparent misuse of executive power by over-zealous political types in the Watergate incident during the 1972 presidential campaign. The effect of these multiple disenchantments will be felt in American culture for many more decades.

Fourth, as the liberal ideals of the first half of the century were either assimilated into custom or slapped, in failure, back at the consciences of thoughtful idealists, concerns about technology and its relationship to the environment replaced them as popular causes, programs, social and political games. Woodstock, the hippies and Consciousness IV (or was it III?) were neurotic symptoms of national breast-beating. Labeled loosely "ecology," "pollution control," "doing one's own thing" and so forth, they centered on humanity's apparent indifference to the side effects of his conquest of nature, the same indifference that had, in a former age, been regarded as *the* prime virtue that built the world's richest industrial nation.[1]

Fifth, calculating their losses in the generation since World War II, America's sentient public set about, in the public light of television, movies and the press, a well exploited re-appraisal of past errors. The conclusion was inevitable: whatever we had been doing was *wrong*. International alliances had, in masscom simpilisms, yielded Vietnam. A new isolationism was therefore in order, or, at least, not out of the question. Severe questions concerning exactly which peoples were America's allies and which were her enemies were also asked. Consequently, our programs of international rapport and alliance were also opened to scrutiny. Soundings from both the public and Congress asked that we abandon what had been, in effect, a twenty-five-year, costly, cross-cultural goodwill mission conducted by radio, cultural exchange, film and television wherever our spokesmen might gather a foreign audience. Engaged as our chief executive apparently was in making new friends out of old enemies, and subject, as the public and their representatives were, to considerable invidious derision by our former friends abroad, our past propaganda efforts seemed to have ended in failure. To extend them untouched into the future appeared to be sheer stupidity.

Sixth, the world's smaller nations (most of them dependent upon the United States in many ways) could not help but notice—by the examples of America's former military enemies, Japan and West Germany—that Mother Earth could survive (and survive well) without the export of America's technological genius, her fabled "know how," and even her (somewhat tarnished) talent for regulating international economic matters. The latter truth was dramatized the moment the USA permitted the price of gold to float free on the world's markets, thereby releasing the index finger of her iron hand over foreign currencies and inflating, in a single moment, the value of the near-mythical vaults under Fort Knox by nearly one-hundred per cent! Drama, of course, but drama symptomatic of larger truths, and, most interestingly, an expedient economic ploy that worked—for a time.

Seventh, an American citizen had stepped out of a space machine and walked on the surface of the moon, an act that, in all its ramifications (and even considering its enormous complexity), engendered more pointless international hysteria than any symbolic occasion since Lindbergh landed solo at Le Bourget Field in France.

In sum, so-called "silent majorities" and wistful conservatives notwithstanding, post-Vietnam America has become quite a different culture (as the sociologist and anthropologist evaluate cultures) from the society that emerged from World War II, with her ideals in liberal democracy, the mysticism of her capitalism and technology and her faith in the inherent civility of her people confirmed by the magic of recent military victory.

The passage of time alone does not account for the severity of these changes in our society. A formidable speculative literature has been devoted to brave attempts at other explanations, so we shall not attempt to replicate or add to its multitude of wide-ranging guessworks.[2]

Like Popeye the Sailor, we am what we am. But, unlike the one-eyed imp, we am not what we were.

The Road Back

Arguments for neo-isolationism sound better to American ears at this moment of history than they have since Washington published his Farewell Address. There are many reasons for this eventuality, and to dismiss them (as some would) is not to discredit them.

American intervention in overseas cultural, social, political, economic and military affairs has been, since the last World War, in large measure a doctrine espoused by liberals and other men and women of good will. True, some of our most successful meddling with foreign matters—the totalitarian administration of Japan by General MacArthur after the Pacific war, for instance—was actually carried out by arch-conservative businessmen, politicians and soldiers; but its general pith and philosophy was liberal. During the nineteen-thirties, isolationist notions were heard most usually from Anglophobic midwestern politicians and doctrinaire adherents of the far right. So unpopular was their position by the end of World War II, that they were hardly able to mount token opposition to our first participation in the new United Nations Organization during the late nineteen-forties.

Should we need a personified, single reminder of this liberal interventionist thrust, the authors would choose Eleanor Roosevelt, not as a woman or the wife and widow of a dynamic President, but as a public symbol of everything benign about global idealism. A public figure of extraordinary and eloquent faith, she was fazed neither by changing times, distance nor history. During and after the war—and finally at the United Nations itself—she was driven to extraordinary energy and eloquence by deep concerns for and faith in what she considered America's *obligations* to bring some measure of its prosperity—both material and political—to every citizen in every corner of the earth. Echoes of her late voice rang in John F. Kennedy's 1961 Inaugural Address, as he promised our nation that America's business was correcting injustice wherever it might be found on the globe. (Kennedy's talk was the last time, to date, that a powerful American official has spoken in quite these terms without first wincing noticeably.)

To explain what amounts to a complete doctrinal turnabout in one decade on the part of the same liberals for whom Mrs. Roosevelt spoke so eloquently simply by citing their attitudes towards the Vietnam war (as is often done) is to simplify the true dynamics of public opinion to absurdity. The comparatively rapid shift from idealistic intervention to new-isolation on the part of the liberal community has involved complex matters, almost as complicated as the corresponding seesaw movement on the part of many conservatives to their present (and unhappy) stance as internationalists.

The liberal tradition of cultural intervention in overseas affairs was a broadly based manifestation involving the coordination of highly specialized concerns, and considerable political self-interest. In retrospect, it displayed the enormous vulnerability that often occurs both in genetic and intellectual inbreeding: common weaknesses are mated, and what was once *inherent* (or, as biologists say, a genotype) eventually appears as an obvious *external trait* (or a phenotype).

For many years, the idealism and altruistic thrust of this tradition had had to grapple with one *major* reality: that American intervention in any matter anywhere in the world had, by its nature, to involve deep and lasting *economic* ramifications. This side-product, even if initiated by government or public agencies, almost invariably resulted in formidable benefits, of one sort or another, to the *private* sector of our capitalist economy, much the same way that the British, Dutch and Belgian colonialism had operated in the century before World War I.

Foreign wars, for instance, were (and are) always good business, and, therefore financial good news to certain, well-established private American interests. So was (and is) the *cessation* of warfare with its rebuilding of foreign economies and opening of potential, exclusive new markets. No matter how small or apparently benign our degree of intervention, *some* of America's business community would invariably profit from it in the forms of oil from South American countries, sugar and bananas from island republics, customers for heavy machinery, cheap non-union labor for American consumer goods etc. (How soon, one wonders, will offshore oil rigs be mounted by American petroleum companies in the mineral-rich shoals of South Vietnam, for instance? Plans, at the moment, are on drawing boards.)

American intervention abroad might, therefore, almost invariably and inevitably be called "imperialistic," at any rate as the American liberal ear had been tuned to hear the word. Problems involving political imperialism were, not so long ago, easily explained idealistically and neatly tabled: wherever we went we (supposedly) also spread democratic idealism. But economic imperialism was another matter, one that the liberal might somehow live with, just as long as it was conveniently overshadowed by a quantum of "higher morality": matters like justifying Hitler's base treatment of Jews; North Korea's devil-ish destruction of Syngman Rhee's democratic (?) government; Arab barbarities against "civilized" Europeans in North Africa; and/or African Mau-mau and/or Indian vengeance against "innocent" colonists who had implanted civilization among the heathens; and other such sentimental constructions of the history of intervention.

But the *fact* that America could not manage (with one or two exceptions) a purely *altruistic* policy of world engagement and intervention in *both* theory and practice was—and is—one well-whispered theme in the litany of the far political left that has remained consistent since the era of the Wobblies. If liberal interventionists could not ignore these voices, they could, at least, count them as negligible when held against the sum of virtues that international responsibility had historically entailed for the United States' worldly destiny.

Now, almost nothing is as bitter as the cynicism of the altruist whose idealism has turned to salt in his mouth. With the war in Vietnam, *one* of the *many* contributing factors noted above, the consciousness of liberal interventionists was turned, bit by bit (as disillusionment at home followed disillusionment abroad), towards the unpleasant (to them) results of our policies of global engagement. The period that extended from before World War II, into the postwar "isolationist-versus-globaloney" era, and up to the present, was evolving, for liberals, realistic new insights. The news that once-glamorized American heroics beyond her shores were what they had always been—not policies of liberal, social and political amelioration, but careful stratagems of military and economic self-protection—shattered insidiously the morass of myths in which many Americans had lived.

The new-style open diplomatic forum of the United Nations merely served to dramatize much unsavory diplomatic by-play that had heretofore been hidden behind special diplomatic immunities, private treaties and man-to-man handshakes. What the liberal interventionist therefore had discovered, in the wake of Latin-American revolutions, Soviet barbarities in

Iron Curtain nations, and in the upheaval, nation by nation, on the African continent, was simply that old Earl Browder, other American Communist spokesmen, the Park Avenue "pinkos" and the defunct *Daily Worker* had, all along, been dead right. The United States *was* one of the most overt, self-interested (or selfish) imperialistic nations in the world (forgetting the USSR, conveniently for the moment), and that our humanitarian façade had been, almost from the first, a mere cover for the nuts and bolts, first, of military protection (and sometimes aggression) and (worse) for raw economic capitalist expansion.

All of this was hardly news, however, to conservatives who had ingested these realities in a multitude of ways (not worth dwelling upon here). But they *were* earth-shattering revelations to men of good will who finally discovered, when all was said and done, that they were exactly what their old revolutionary enemies, whose continuing antagonisms towards them they could never comprehend, had said they were all along: namely, *dupes*. (That they also may have been "dopes" is mere linguistic serendipity.)

These reactions did not square strictly with logic. But psychologists tell us that deeply felt reactions are often untidy matters, rarely logical. Interventionists therefore created a new isolationism that was, with little ideological maneuvering, brought into line with older styles of liberal idealism—that is, it was, and remains vague enough to hold any amount of "do-goodism" required. Most of the "doing" is, however, at this writing, rhetorical promising to solve our problems *here at home* by removing something from something: removing mercury from tuna fish, heroin from bloodstreams, corruption from politics, hepatitis from clams, cancer from mice, rickets from Appalachians, violence from the streets, deceptions from consumerism, and copious other diversions, as required to keep liberal public attention on its idealistic home base.

The *real* economic (and military) imperialists today, of course (who had generally sympathized with the conservative domestic politics of yesterday's isolationists), were handed a banner they did not particularly desire to carry either. But carry it they discovered they must, sometimes (and unconvincingly) mouthing old liberal slogans of times past. As neo-interventionists, they have taken extraordinary pains to remind us in mass magazines of their overseas banks and bankers and their financier-philanthropists spreading bliss (and low-interest loans) to underdeveloped nations, their gratuitous triumphs of ecology while digging for copper and oil, their water-purification programs that bring Coca-and-Pepsi-Cola to the underpriviliged, and of their many supposedly solid *ententes* that their petroleum deals with Arabian despots (and even with Russians) throw off as side-products in the expansion of their wheels-and-deals to new and unlikely remote, foreign places. Their footwork was not—and is not—fancy enough either to be interesting or consequent, nor has it been cleverly managed or well enough sold to the public to be taken seriously. The public interpretations of their new songs fell to familiar advertising agencies and public relations creeps, who liberally applied their hoary, unimaginative formulas to what might have been a colorful era of new corporate legends. (Industries like advertising, and publicity services that are run by mousebrains, rarely engender creative deceptions. In the long run, however, we are a safer nation for this natural weakness —as long as the news does not spread too widely and while our feather merchants believe their own self-made myths.)

In this setting, modern neo-isolationism may be examined free from the kind of facile etiology that is presently espoused by liberal television pundits and professors of the political science who, yesterday, recoiled in their comfortable classrooms in shock at the "atrocities" of Vietnam, "America's longest war," the "only war we have ever lost" and so forth. How conveniently these pundits and professors had forgotten their erstwhile joy (if they were old enough) at the destruction by bombing of near-entire cities in Japan and Germany. Neither did they seem to hear themselves cheer on the slaughter of Arabs and Israeli's involved in the "non-atrocious" (we assume) on-going and apparently endless and (to some) senseless combat that undulates bloodily in the Near East. "Atrocities," it seems, relate to *where* you find them.

This rhetoric—all of it—is nonsense because, as we have noted, neo-isolation is simply *not* a reaction to the Vietnam war alone, or to our present engagement in nearby and remote countries, although *all* salient, historical factors in recent history have contributed their mite to it, including Vietnam. Its deepest roots, however, are planted in the near-total failure of those very quondam liberal illusions, once loved by so many: that civility between nations is amenable to nostrums compounded *exclusively* of good intent—like the United Nations, international low tariff commerce, the Peace Corps, cross-cultural visits of students and professors, exchanges of circuses, ballet companies and symphony orchestras—and all the other *nice* things that the American liberal may not enjoy much himself, but nevertheless has been told is "good for him" and, accordingly, must also be good for all men as well.

The best argumentative responses to recent liberal, economic, military and political neo-isolation have come, not from the Madison Avenue spokesman for conservatives, but from the liberal community itself—which is to be expected. Liberal voices have always been (and are today) among the most articulate in the nation, representing the lion's share of the faces we see, words we hear and voices broadcast on our major conduits of communication, the most articulate of our college and university "opinion-makers," and our most artful writers and skilled editorialists. But keeping liberals in lockstep is difficult. Conservatives tend usually to march to a single drummer. But, as one moves left in the American political spectrum, one meets more and more individuals who fancy themselves either independent intellectuals and/or free spirits. Thus they enjoy both the stimulation and enervation of dissention, particularly in their own ranks.

Presently a professor of history at Tel Aviv University (a veritable ivy-covered paradise, one imagines, for an American "intellectual" out to do-good), Walter Laqueur has summed up the anti-isolationist position better than most of his opposite numbers among conservatives, at least those who write for magazines like *The National Review*. A few quotes are in order (not from *The National Review*):

"Neo-isolationism as a mood is thus understable enough," writes Laqueur, "and one might go so far as to say it is in the American grain. . . . The present American policy of interventionism, the argument runs, is a reflection of some of the worst impulses in American society. It is pursued by a foreign policy establishment that is itself in thrall to the interests of big business, the prosperity of the American capitalist system depending on overseas expansion and imperial domination." (The "line" in a nutshell.)

Having slain these dragons (particularly arguments presented in Robert W. Tucker's book, *A New Isolationism*), Laqueur continues, "There is little reason to suppose that neo-isolationism will make for a more peaceful world," he writes:

> . . . and there is even less reason to suppose that turning away from foreign affairs will make it any easier for the United States to tackle its domestic problems: the urban crisis, the unsolved social and racial questions, the alienation of wide sections of American society. A confident, dynamic country can play an active part in world affairs and at the same time cope with its internal problems. A people adrift, lacking purpose and conviction, cannot do either; defeatism is an affliction which cannot be compartmentalized . . .[3]

Retreat from American commitments abroad, Laqueur notes, transcends whatever risks we may take, even the much-despised evil of economic imperialism that might yield still greater evils abroad. In words not unlike those frequently heard from the conservative side of the hall these days, he argues in cogent, but familiarly altruistic, terms, redolent of polemicism dating back to the nineteen-thirties and middle-to-late nineteen forties. Neo-isolationism, if formally implemented in foreign policy he says:

> . . . unquestionably creates a new situation. The balance of power is indeed changing—but not toward multipolarity. While America is in retreat, the Soviet Union still has a globalist policy. As the U.S. opts for disengagement, the Soviet Union increases its commitments. To this extent, regardless of America's economic performance and strategic might, the Soviet Union is now in a superior position. Nor is the hypothesis warranted that new centers of power are about to emerge. A world power (let alone a "super power") must be capable of asserting its interests and purposes beyond its borders. Yet with all their economic resources and military potential, Western Europe and Japan are not only lacking in that capacity, but in the area of defense they are even more dependent on outside help than Australia or Brazil. It is uncertain that they will succeed in weathering the coming storms once the American umbrella is removed from over their heads.
>
> There is, in short, no multipolar system emerging, unless one takes the term as a euphemism for the spread of confusion, or possibly chaos. The American retreat is causing new power vacuums in the world. How they will be filled, and who will fill them, is the great question of the decades to come.[4]

And so Laqueur is at home at last, comfortable in the altruistic dream that military power and economic greed may lead for the United States of America to a higher destiny than base interest. Oddly enough, he may be right—quite obviously for the wrong reasons.

The nation, to paraphrase Whitehead, that does not move *primarily* out of self-interest is doomed. And neither battalions of saints nor rosters of benign motives nor voluntaristic cerebrations can alter the matter one jot. As poorly as history teaches, here is one of its major lessons that is probably valid. The fundamental question upon which the instrumentation of *any* reactionary policy, therefore, pivots today is whether or not, given all factors, our nation can *afford* to pursue it, motives aside—except those of, first, survival and, second, health. Economic or political or military neo-isolation show no exceptions to our requirements and impetus for survival. And should we follow yesterday's admittedly justifiable attractions, we risk mortal combat both with the gods of history and the guns of our competitors in *all* spheres of international life, which is to say, in international competition for both the loyalties and sweat of the masses of men and women everywhere.

Hacking Ahead

No solid guideposts for America's long-range future in the international on-going *War of Ideas* have yet been erected, except, possibly for some Xeroxed think-tank contingency "studies," futurological gambits in pamphlet form, and published musings from professional brain zoos like the Rand Corporation and well-meaning (we imagine) shock artists like Herman Kahn, Alvin Toffler and Dr. McLuhan. Futurologists, astrologers, seers and psychics and all manner of haurispices naturally have their own plans for us, some of which—like Hitler's horoscopic military strategy—may serve us as well, or better than the absence of policy or tactics rooted in stupidity. Crystal balls sometimes work, in a hit-or-miss way, although they are *never* made of crystal. Just old glass.

Our present position is critical, but not hopeless, mainly because, as the old epigram says, "There is nowhere to go but up." This is fortunate, because America's genius for losing games on the psychological warfare front has become legion. As we have noted, two-thirds of the world *still* believes, to this day, for instance, that the United States forces in Korea twenty years ago actually used bacteriological weapons, simply because we have never been able to convince anybody but ourselves that we did *not*. The same sort of misconception applies to our role in the Hungarian uprisings a handful of years later, although an impartial study made by a more-or-less neutral nation, *proved* irrefutably that we did *not* instigate these abortive hostilities, either by word or deed, overtly on radio or covertly by agitation. World opinion—and even current opinion *in* Hungary—*has had* to blame someone or something for the debacle, and Uncle Sam was the convenient (and all-too-gentlemanly) patsy. Two examples among, literally, hundreds in our case-book.

We have at present, in other words, a *chance* to redeem our credibility among the nations of the world and, at last, to use various international instruments of communication effectively, granting that we manage to articulate for ourselves, at least, and other nations, at best, a foreign policy that makes consistent sense. As the astute British writer and political correspondent, Aberon Waugh, has noted,[5] the *small* part of America's international posture that floats above the water must, at any rate, *seem* to make sense, a requirement that has manifestly not been met by Washington during the past century or so.

We must first ingest the axiom that most of our so-called "allies" and all "neutral nations" would rather be "Red than Dead," and so, if our cards were all down face up, would we. Other nations do not, by and large, tend to believe our protestations of policies responsive only to "higher morality" or to the abstract defense of freedom in places where men live as slaves. Nor are they impressed by our ghost-written perorations about our obligations to nations dominated by communist oligarchs, or the many other moral imperatives which *have*, in sorry fact, served us too often as a substitute for foreign policy for many years. Waugh suggests that if enlightened America-watchers overseas believed the explanations that we give for our erratic international behavior, they would also have to accept the fact that American foreign policy craftsmen in general, and the chief executive particularly, must be quite insane. This they will not do, and therefore they accept the logical alternative: that we are chronic liars.

Now, none of these people are, of course, insane in Waugh's terms, nor are they liars. They are merely narrow-minded and short-term realists, forever concentrating exclusively upon economic, military and political emergencies as they pop up here and there. Engaged almost entirely in reacting busily to daily power shifts around the world, they rarely think to defend their chess moves in true terms—that is, as raw self-interest.

For instance, most routine revolutions and upheavals in small Latin American nations are of little purely *military* importance to the US, but they are frequently life-and-death matters in American corporate board rooms. A revolt in Czechoslovakia may mean little economically to Wall Street, but it is certain to upset some aspect of the delicate balance of *military* power in Europe. So might every move, or whisper of a move, that East or West Germany makes towards possible reunification. Taiwan is, at the moment, such a well-fused political and economic firecracker that she may, if circumstances insist, upset many American business interests, America's military position in Asia and the political games being played by the entire non-communist East. Our tactical and ideological (but all too "temporizing") positions vis-a-vis *all* of these overseas locales stem from realistic considerations of national self-interest. They extend into action the sensible hope that the West, for the foreseeable future at least, will continue on its way neither "Red nor Dead."

Set against this hard-core realism necessary for day-to-day foreign intercourse, the late Lyndon Johnson's gooey moral suasion for instance, was one of the main aspects of the late Vietnam war that the American people—particularly the young—found least palatable for the longest time, for the best of reasons. It was, fortunately for the stability of the nation, counter-balanced by equally (and sentimentalized) breast beating and emotionalism among so-called "protesters" and other stampers and yellers who had been cajoled into the position that the best way to end a war is to offer psychological solace to one's enemies. While it may have extended the war (or our part in it), the "protesting" let off steam and helped to maintain some sort of stability at home.

Most of these indignant exhibitionists were *just* twerps. As in all wars, major and minor, there exist, however, genuine military enemies residing within every combatant's perimeters. They may be counted upon invariably to join whatever "peace now" forces arise spontaneously, especially when the going gets rough, as they did heroically in Germany, for instance, during the final year of the Nazi Reich. Extremely rough estimates put the number of "hard core" international communists presently breathing American air at somewhere between ten to twenty thousand. If this number is accurate, they hardly pose a clear or present threat to the welfare of our state, *except* during periods such as the great outburst of rage at our Vietnam debacle during the middle to late nineteen-sixties. At such moments, our society might even employ the services of well-meant lunatics cast in the mold of the late Senator Joe McCarthy. But such people are never around when the United States —or any nation—needs them. They are, first, fearful of bucking public opinion. Second, they know well that their chances of becoming "men on horseback" at such times are nil. They wait until their ministrations are *not* needed, and then they prey upon the latent paranoia in every society at times when life seems unaccountably secure.

All in all, America's moral stance during the Vietnam years was, in many ways, a far more terrible atrocity than Mai Lai. In the long run, it probably caused more bloodshed in Southeast Asia than a battalion of Calleys could ever accomplish at their stupidest. What America was protecting in the East, or so those who led us into the war *thought* we were protecting, boiled down to a series of political alliances with various small, weak and inevitably corrupt (neither more nor less than other weak communist and/or capitalist regimes usually are) nations, our economic relations with them (particularly as suppliers of natural resources, potential and real), our military position (or posture) as defenders of Japan, the Philippines and vital allies and, last, our questionable image, at the time, as a protective world power.

The rhetoric of a morality turned to cynicism (due to the painfully articulated reasons at the beginning of this chapter) turned the well-meaning Johnson, for all his supposed political craftiness, from a dignified President into a man who sounded like a Texas preacher or pious liar. It "reduced his credibility," in the words of his supporters, not only to American ears but to those overseas inclined to think the best of us even when the issues do not warrant it. Our scorn here is not partisan. Richard Nixon not only inherited the war, he inherited the *reasons* for the war—good or bad—and our official rationalizations that had, by 1968, worn pretty thin. (That the *real* causes of the Vietnam hostilities may not have been sufficient for us to *join* a political-religious-ideological insurrection that the colonial French had abandoned in confusion a decade before is irrelevant both to these rationalizations and our poker-faced adherence to them to the end.)

True enough, Nixon wore our accepted, national moral stance better than Johnson. But any new face in the White House would have. It is also true that Nixon was finally highly instrumental in disengaging America from the tangle, but only after realistic *ententes* with the USSR and Red China had been painfully created, and the two or three warring factions in Vietnam were laboriously placated (or read the riot act) by means of what may well be the most complicated "peace" agreements of modern times. In the meantime, Nixon willingly hung Johnson's albatross on his own neck and weakly continued to appeal to "higher morality." He accomplished a "peace with honor" that probably might have been negotiated years before, had the American posture not demanded the shiny gloss of saved faces and pseudo-ethical justification.[6]

Dead soldiers, it seems, are less immoral (in psychological terms) than the compromise of slick principles that—in this day and age—are patent frauds! When such principles fit the requirements of time, place and the cultural imperatives of history, on the other hand, only the cynical and the clear-headed see through them, calculate their risks, and then, nevertheless, proceed ahead with what they know is a *necessary* charade. History, of course, provides one an exceptionally clear head, and it permits considerable retrospectively directed cynicism, as Barbara Tuchman has so engagingly shown in her careful reconstructions of the recent past. Moral imperatives were indeed also the issue when Rome destroyed Carthage, but it is difficult to get excited about them today. Anecdotes and conjectures about the peculiar relationship between Hannibal and Scipio Africanus are, after the passing of two millenia, more amusing than the harsh moral issues raised by the rapid genocide of half-a-million Carthaginian civilians in 146 B.C.

Vietnam is, unfortunately, more a case study of misread psychology on a global scale than a strategic debacle, or so history is likely to tell us when present passions cool—or when we blunder tomorrow into another, similar *mish-mash* that permits us a perspective of Vietnam we now have, say, of the Korean war. Lacking a viable, consistent foreign policy (and carrying all the open secrets the world knows about American capitalism, international political power and military force), we were compelled to resort to the same sort of policy guidelines that served us well in World War II, but which neither time nor circumstance could justify in Vietnam, circa 1963–5. To world opinion, we looked either like liars or fools. We may have been both, but only sympathetic observers of Waugh's stripe chose to believe the latter. To the rest of the world, we announced, in effect, that we were liars. And we were. We were *also* fools.

Our position, therefore, in the world of international psychological warfare could not, at the moment, be better. For the first time in modern history we know exactly where we stand: at the bottom of the ladder of world opinion. And our enemies (yes, Virginia, we have enemies—even among our friends) intend to keep us there for the best of reasons. Like all true believers and spontaneous saints who have received a true mission from God, *they* want to conquer the world *their* way, hopefully with ideas, but with arms, if necessary. In effect, today they count us out of the battle, although we want exactly what they want—and our preference for ideas over arms is neither greater nor less than theirs. Nothing could be clearer.

Time Out For a Bedtime Story

Once upon a time, an incredible event occurred. Of course, it could not *really* have occurred, as the reader will see. But bedtime stories are enjoyable, precisely because they deal with improbabilities that *should* have happened but for the intervention of man's prosaic, disenchanted hand.

Once upon a time, as we said, a group of learned Americans, all of them steeped in the prestigious arts of healing the sick and the lame, and all people of great reputation and deep wisdom, left their homes to travel abroad and see how other great physicians practiced their arts in distant corners of the world. To be precise, they flew in giant airplanes to remote China, long sealed off from their own country by diplomatic contretemps.

When we say that these physicians were wise, we mean that they were wise as *physicians,* clever at medical technology and procedures accepted as therapeuticly healing professionals in their own land. They were *not* particularly wise in the ways of science itself, any more than most other healing physicians in America, because science and the skills of medicine are not the same sorts of enterprises—although it was not uncommon for semi-educated people like lawyers, newspaper editors, college professors, reporters, politicians, and even doctors themselves, frequently to confuse the two. Neither—and, we suppose, this is more important to the fanciful thrust of our incredible tale—did they know much about magic—black magic and white magic.

This ignorance was not an oversight nor was it intentional on their parts, but simply the result of fashion and professional imperatives. A medical patient in America, for example, would not be heartened to hear that a high-ranking specialist to whom he (or Blue Shield) was paying a fortune for removing a tumor was a magician. Few doctors—especially prominent, expert doctors—cultivate seriously the study or skill of magic.[7] Nor, at this moment in history, are they expected to try their hands at it by their peers or patients.

Now, the Chinese doctors our American physicians visited in the former's homeland were also wise, not (possibly) as wise as their American counterparts in the twentieth century arts of medicine or modern medical technology, but wise in human matters, because these Chinese physicians were also Chinese, a situation that they could no more avoid than the fact that the American doctors were Americans.

China had, at the time of this story, recently made enormous advances indeed into the modern world of technology under a Communist government—small advances, possibly, when judged against the affluent standards of the New World, but great indeed for a populous culture that had achieved a peak of technological civilization many centuries ago, and was then subject subsequently to many invasions, destruction and finally stasis.

The wise Chinese physicians, in addition to having mastered an ancient school of therapy that anticipated modern psychosomatic medicine by a thousand years, were also, both as doctors and men, extremely sensitive—as many Orientals are —particularly *politically* sensitive, both to influences from *within* their society by politically ambitious and powerful officials to *demonstrate* to foreigners the success of Communism, and from *without*, to the degree of admiration or "face" they might muster when judged by colleagues from across the sea in the USA, where modern medical procedures and instrumentation might make many of their ancient—and some of their modern—practices seem crude by comparison.

As Chinese, these doctors were also mindful of their own traditions, including that of magic, both black and white. This heritage contains some of the cleverest feats of legerdemain in the repertoire of all modern conjurers, both Eastern and

Western. They had been raised, as most Chinese are, to respect the art of the professional magician, both as delightful theatrics and as an overt display of superiority in the effortless accomplishment of the impossible by means of clever deception. In no manner, therefore, does a Chinese audience (which often includes physicians) consider a prestidigitator to be a "fake," when he, for instance, apparently decapitates his young assistant and subsequently restores his severed head. The act is "real" *if* the audience is fooled. And moral judgments about the "deception" (more a Western than an Eastern idea) involved in cutting off heads and restoring them before an audience are quite beside the point. Let us add also that physicians in China are as likely to be fooled by a good magician as American physicians—and enjoy the game as much, but in somewhat different ways, in a different humor and in a different ethical framework.

As we said, the American physicians who had traveled to China could not have been expected to know these things about Chinese doctors, because they were interested almost exclusively in Chinese medicine as they *understood it.* Nor might they have comprehended the feelings of deep fear that our Chinese physicians experienced when they heard that their counterparts from America were coming to visit them and pry into their less than perfect (by modern standards) methods of healing, hospitals, operating rooms and health facilities. The matter of "face" was paramount to them, more important, of course, than the matter of medical professionalism. Chinese doctors do not belong to the American Medical Association, you see.

A Chinese problem was therefore solved in a Chinese way. Searching among their ancient lore for some aspect of Chinese medicine that remains to this day a mystery to Western medicine that they might display to their visitors, the answer to their problem was obvious: *acupuncture,* a weird ritual of dramatic penetrations of the human epidermis with needles that sometimes worked and sometimes did not (rather like Vitamins and Cold Remedies in the West), depending upon what was expected of it therapeutically. Of two things the Chinese physicians were certain: The snooping American doctors were certain to know *nothing* about acupuncture and/or the Goldbergian theories of sympathetic nervous reaction upon which it was founded ages ago by medicine men who knew nothing about the anatomy of the human nervous systems. Second, the American doctors were certain also to be magical illiterates!

The American doctors, therefore, after having toured Chinese medical installations and talked (via "politically sensitive" interpreters) to the Chinese doctors, were treated to a rare sight for Western eyes—or so they thought. (The sight is not rare. Its rough counterpart occurs daily at American carnivals, and nightly in supper clubs where magicians appear as "hypnotists" and "mentalists.") The Chinese surgeons had consented to demonstrate to the Americans how they had contrived a monumental blending of the ancient medical wisdom Eastern-style with the modern techniques of healing by combining the ancient therapy of acupuncture with modern surgical techniques!

Children, you can just imagine the breathless reports of the event by the American physicians—who had, incidentally, been sent on their mission by high and prescient Oriental "experts" in the United States with the poorest preparation imaginable for the kind of experience they were likely to encounter. The stories they told when arriving home are far too lengthy to repeat in this purely fictional fable.

In effect (and shorn of the enthusiasm of the telling), what the Americans *saw* was this: a conscious Chinese patient was brought into a surgical operating room. The Chinese doctors stepped aside while an acupuncturist stepped forward and proceeded to use the poor patient as a human pin-cushion, placing long needles into his flesh here and there—*but not into his abdomen*—muttering various incantations and accomplishing the placement with precision and copious theatrical élan. At the end of the puncturing procedure, the acupuncturist announced that the patient was now "ready." The latter, however uncomfortable, was still fully conscious. The Chinese surgeons then stepped forward, and, *without employing an anesthetic of any kind,* incised with their scalpels the smiling patient's abdomen and snipped out his vermiform appendix in conventional modern surgical fashion.

At this point, to relieve the tension of the enterprise, one assumes (and probably to close the gaping mouths of the American doctors), tea was served. Propped up a bit, the patient himself, fairly dripping haemostats and the usual impedimenta surgeons stuff into a body cavity from which they have recently excised an organ, joined the party, sipping tea and apparently joking with the benumbed American doctors.

The tea-break concluded, the Chinese physicians finished the job in short order, sutured the blood vessels, closed the wound and quickly sent their patient back to his ward. When asked, as they immediately were, by their American colleagues *how* this unbelievable anesthetic procedure actually worked, they gave typical orientally inscrutable answers translated by an inscrutable interpreter. It worked, and that, in effect, was that.

When the fictitious American physicians returned home, every *other* aspect of their journey to China took second, third and tenth place to their breathless reports about the strange event in the Chinese operating room! They discoursed rapturously about the wonders of acupuncture and the vast body of deep, ancient wisdom, of which the West was ignorant, now being employed in Red China, to perform miracles. The shoddy nature of many Red Chinese public health facilities, ratios of doctors to sick people, matters of training and skill, and all of the genuine professional concerns in which the American medicos had at first been interested, were now incidental.

Their eyewitness reports of their journey to Red China filled American newspapers and general magazines—not reports of the status of medicine in China, but reports of *acupuncture.* Biology professors at great universities in the United

States scratched their heads and warned their classes to be "open-minded" where the conventional anatomy of the central nervous system was concerned. Disturbed medical solons checked reputations for truthfulness of our traveling physicians, whose glowing reports they read in both the popular press and professional journals. They were spotless: all observers were top men in their fields, of faultless reputation for the integrity of their observations. From out of the woodwork, apparently, wizened Orientals—or just people, male and female, who looked either jaundiced or squinty—crept immediately to work, opening acupuncture parlors across the United States in abandoned stores and massage parlors for purposes that defy description, some of them supposedly therapeutic. The event became a legend. And acupuncture entered the annals of American medicine as a secret weapon of the Red Chinese!

It was.

Whether this obviously absurd story is true or not does not, of course, matter much.

It matters as little as the ways (many of them) that a magician may *appear* to saw a woman in half or decapitate an assistant or levitate a chorus girl or make a bird and a cage disappear into thin air.

It *would* matter, if we exposed on this page secrets currently used by professional magicians to make a living. But few magicians use the particular device employed in this bedtime tale in their performances today. (*Some* do, but you will probably not know when or how even if you see it done, *especially* if you are a physician.)

It matters as little as the *truth* matters: that the Chinese patient who had his appendix removed after being anesthetized by acupuncture *must have* been loaded in the abdominal cavity with injections of novocaine, xylocaine, procaine, their Chinese equivalents, or some other powerful local anesthetic *before he was wheeled into that operating room* for his subsequent so-called "acupuncture treatment" and surgery. (Either this, or the outside chance he was a very *special* patient whose abdominal sensory nerves had sustained previous injury and was therefore immune to the pain of abdominal surgical insult.)

For all their spectacular theatrical effects, students of legerdemain are aware that the methods of Chinese magic are often elemental and prosaic, the very reason they fool people so well. Think of the familiar, simple, but eternally effective, Chinese Linkings Rings, one of the great illusions in the lexicon of conjuring. One can be "fooled" by it even if he knows "how it is done"—if it is performed artfully enough.

So our story is, in essence, mainly a tale about Chinese magic—the mastery of the inconceivable but possible and the conquest of illusion over both logic and sense. In the twentieth century, it is difficult to conceive a group of learned American physicians transformed in a few minutes by Oriental magic into carriers of a propaganda fantasy, the objectives of which were and are obvious: to divert attention from any invidious comparisons they might make between East and West in medical (and other) matters. The Chinese intended to keep "face," employing the legerdemain of acupuncture in order to score artfully a few points in the game of international one-upsmanship, and to spread wide from reliable sources currents of belief that the Orient had mastered centuries ago neurological procedures for which Western science today has merely begun to search.

In the *War of Ideas*, of course, a notable victory was scored with little effort and much art.

Now, we all know that this incredible story could not possibly be true. This is the reason we have told it as fiction. We no longer live in an age, of course, when educated men fall victim to superstition and magic. Education, particularly the kind dispensed to neophyte healers of the sick at our great universities, could not conceivably produce, among their graduates, prominent physicians of keen mind and great prestige who could so easily and simply be turned into propaganda pawns at the hands of a decadent Communist state like Red

China. We are safe from this terror, children, because American science and technology has fortified our well-cultivated intellects with immunity to the cleverness of minds that do not think in our scientific ways and are not protected by our well-earned vanity and giant national intellect.

So sleep securely, children. Our bedtime story is over. And no nightmares, please. Nothing like this incident could ever *really* happen—that is, until next time.[8]

A Sort-of Moral for Canute Rex

Call it "information exchange," "cultural exchange," "international communications"—or exercise the American art of euphemism to the hilt of inventiveness—it all boils down to "mass persuasion," or the much-hated rubric "propaganda." Ideas are weapons: domestically, interpersonally, nationally and internationally. It is quite fair to call them other, more cosy things too: "bridges," "handclasps," and so forth. But they are also instruments of war, increasingly significant as novel devices for dialogue (particularly technological instruments) multiply and evade control by their own inventors and once-masters.

In the *War of Ideas* between nations, particularly nations competing in political matters, one new discovery has become apparent: nice guys finish last.

Most Americans do not believe this truism (born, we believe, on the playing fields of Brooklyn, now defunct), but the boys who cut the mustard in the rough-and-tumble of professional athletics can tell the professors, communications experts-cum-idealists, general semanticists and information specialists in Washington (and other world capitals) a thing or two about virtue. Americans, you see, believe in acupuncture, E.S.P., hypnosis, brainwashing and all sorts of romantic conceits that are bunk. But they are nice guys.

In the United States, we have, in the *War of Ideas*, been, for years, following a rainbow. And today we are surprised that it led nowhere. We believed—and still probably believe

—that, in the somewhat ambiguous matter of international persuasion, clean hands signify, by means of moral alchemy, eventual victory in a game played on a dirty battlefield. "*Truth,*" wrote Norman Cousins as he addressed our propaganda establishment in a naïve age some years ago, "is our *weapon.*" Recent history demonstrates that it is a weapon all right—but a damn blunt one.

There *is,* of course, the case of the British—an imperfectly told case, full of half-truth and quarter-lies—that has been held up as an ideal to Americans involved in international communications ever since 1932, to be exact. In that year, the British Broadcasting Company's External Services went on the international radio air waves, carrying the chimes of Big Ben to an empire, since vanished, upon which "the sun never set." [9]

Begging the question of just *what* the External Services' generally accepted success means concretely (other than its very longevity), its greatest accomplishment has been, so goes legend, the reputation that its broadcasts have achieved by supposedly adhering entirely to "objective news" or, as Pilate said, "the truth." The BBC's short-wave service is, accordingly, touted as the most generally credible international broadcasting system in the world—that is, most people are said to believe what its broadcasters tell them—a claim based upon a handful of dusty random surveys and an image that is rarely challenged and hardly ever tested. That most of its overseas listeners are also probably highly disposed to believe *whatever* the British broadcast, true or not, is a matter rarely discussed in intercultural circles and *never* investigated.

In the words of the External Services' present most ardent admirer, Charles Curran, Director-General of the BBC, "It is significant that, as little as ten years after the infant radio was thrust into the arena of communication, the BBC should have seen its responsibilities in this field to be international, recognizing that truth and man's appetite for it knows no boundaries, least of all geographical ones." [10]

Another writer, Chris Somersett, with less of a gift for

mixed cannibalistic metaphors adds (noting that Services are broadcast in forty languages for 720 hours a week):

> The External Services broadcast in the *national interest.* The main objectives are to give unbiased news, *to reflect British opinion and to project British life, institutions and culture.* The third objective is *not interpreted narrowly.* The image projected is that of modern Britan and covers a wide spectrum.
>
> It is not the object of the BBC to interfere in the internal affairs of any country, however opposed it may be ideologically to Britain's way of life. But listeners are not left in doubt about the *various reactions of the British public to matters of world importance* . . .
>
> The Corporation—and its many journalists—operate on a simple principle: *total accuracy* and *complete impartiality.* In 250 news programmes every day, External Services *are recognised* as *the world's most reliable source of broadcast information* . . .
>
> As a result of the care taken, the BBC's reputation for *absolute objectivity and honesty* rides higher than that of any other news service in any other country . . .

As a result of all this "objectivity," notes Somersett, strange things happen:

> The BBC has found that in many parts of the world its audience increases dramatically in times of crisis. For instance, during a recent conflict in Asia, a Government Minister told a BBC correspondent: "Everyone listens to the BBC. Even those who can't read and write have marked notches on their radios showing where they can hear it."
>
> BBC External Services (also) have *an export liaison unit,* which channels material for broadcasting in 40 languages in support of Britain's export trade. The head of the unit, Mr. L. H. Gottlieb, says: "We want to hear at Bush House (where the broadcasts originate) from British exporters about British inventions, new products, export orders, technical developments and other industrial achievements."
>
> A measure of the success of these broadcasts is that many of the more than a quarter-of-a-million letters that arrive from

overseas at Bush House every year are from people who want to know *more about what British industry is trying to sell.* The queries are passed on to the firms concerned.[11]

Virtue, it seems, is ever its own reward. "Objectivity" and "truth" pay. And how nice that superiority knows for a *fact* how superior it is!

Upon the myth—or fact (it makes no difference)—of British propaganda supremacy, America, for thirty years, has pitched its international persuasive posture in *all* phases of its activity. Not only do we believe that truth and objectivity will make us so attractive, like the British, to world opinion that lions will turn into lambs, we also send lambs into the lion's cage.

This British cynosure of inter-cultural rectitude—like many myths of British excellence—admits of severe questions, rarely asked. For example, exactly how does the BBC define "objectivity"? (The best minds in the field of American journalism admit the task is beyond their abilities.) For how long, and how much on-going scrutiny has been given to the actual *content* (and its implications) of these foreign broadcasts? What relationship exists—if any—between attitudes in the West Indies, Malta, Australia, Dublin, and other *anti-Empire* outposts of the British civility to the "truth" contained in these broadcasts? What portion of Britain's overall, world-wide information services are actually implemented by the BBC, how much by the covert M.I. 6 (England's equivalent of the CIA), and other government departments, like the British Information Agency, the Film Board, etc.? Might Britain and her status as a world power have been served *better* during the past forty years by an External Services less aloof, less smug and self-righteous in its obeisance to the ephemeral gods of "truth" than the present one? (The past forty years have seen some pretty catastrophic diminutions of Britain's posture as an important world power, comparable to those recently suffered by the

United States, at least.) To what degree is the BBC's home-brewed puffery of the External Services simply the rhetoric of well-entrenched civil servants protecting their nest—the kind of poker-faced nonsense that "Auntie" poured as heavily upon the English (and the world) back in the days when she had a monopoly on *all* broadcasting in the United Kingdom? Last, what has the exalted External Services *actually accomplished* that would not have occurred had she gone off the air a year after V-E day? (Granted, British broadcasting via the External Services *did* serve an important function during World War II in disseminating hard news to the European continent, where the exigencies of combat had made a shambles of all conventional conduits of reliable information.)

Wisely or stupidly, wrong or right, it was upon this British model of international idea exchange that the United States, entering the field of international communications after World War II, in what we now call "peace time," patterned its own general thrusts at global, inter-cultural persuasion some fifteen years after the epochal founding of the English External Services. (External broadcasting services in Russia, Italy and other countries pre-dated the BBC's effort, but they directed themselves largely to individual foreign crises as they arose, and did not continue sustaining service for long after their propaganda purpose was served.) Paying less attention to what Britain, through all her cultural arms, actually *did* than what she *said* she did, America was left a legacy of propaganda policy that possessed two main features, both of which were blindly understood to serve our advantages by presenting to the world an image of a USA that never existed in fact, a picture of all Americans as *nice guys.*

First—and probably most important—by whatever means we chose to spread ideas abroad, and/or carry on ideational warfare in peacetime (a nasty un-American sounding tautology on its face), the directive psychological aim and means of our efforts were designed to function as *servants* of foreign policy, not, under any circumstances, as masters. We created in effect, a textbook public relations effort writ large. But, unlike our *real* public relations efforts at home, we did not attempt to be "creative"—that is, psychological directives and tactical objectives were handed by our architects of foreign policy to our information personnel as *fait accompli,* from which they were forbidden to deviate an iota. Considering the arguments developed in Part One of this book, it is difficult to see how such a policy could inevitably lead our American information wizards anywhere but along the path of failure and ignominy.

Second, also following the British, it was assumed that if such a propaganda policy were properly handled, and if an accurate and careful portrait were drawn of what the United States stands for, the results would be to turn world-wide opinion in the direction of blind adoration for Columbia, Gem of the Ocean, simply because her political, social, economic and cultural attractions, truthfully mediated abroad, would prove absolutely irresistible. (Vanity of Vanities!) This assumption is naturally so filled with obvious holes of historical, psychological and logistic natures that it is difficult to dignify it with serious consideration. But romantic, absurd assumptions like these *do* apparently make sense to cocksure, insulated, monomanical bureaucrats wherever you find them: at "White's" in London, the Mayflower Bar in Washington, or over luxuriously set tables at "21" in New York—wherever the great and near-great gather to study the world by taking their own pulses.

Like the British, therefore, we were doomed to weak propaganda policies whose main pith centered on moral righteousness, not only in word but in deed—a stepchild of an equally feeble foreign policy, the vapidities of which it might merely reflect, darkly at best. Unlike the British, however, certain American international specialists (especially in the CIA) chafed under the pressure, or lack of it, as we shall see in the ensuing chapters. But, in general tenor and direction, our ideational mission boiled down to telling the world, (and selling the doubtful proposition) that America was a God-fearing nation of nice guys, square shooters, civilized politicians, benign businessmen, reverential and creative cultural leaders, far-sighted educationists and other simplistic stereotypes belied by *any single* issue of *Time, Playboy, The New York Times,* or by almost any Hollywood film (not made by the Disney organization) that has found its ways beyond our borders during the past quarter of a century. If, once in a while, we suffered troubles in the world of international politics and economics, the truth was, of course, usually reported—along with the *über-truth* that, whatever the results of this or that aspect of our foreign policy might be, our *motives* were impeccable. If the cliché candles we were lighting (instead of cursing the darkness) started international bonfires, at least *we meant well.* And this we wanted the world to know.

We are not inclined to argue here about the virtues of truth. Most rhetoric about truth is simply cant. What is true from one perspective may be false from another, or so psychologists tell us. They are probably right. Whatever bedrock we originally built our propaganda policy upon—and upon which it still rests—the overall results, it seems, ended up drawn upon a continuum—with the word "useless" on the bright end and "catastrophic" on the gloomy side.

We *could* have done better. But the past is never available for revision. The major question we now face centers upon what we are up to at the present and what our options for the future are.

NOTES TO CHAPTER 5

[1] We are not certain what the appearance, in late 1972, of the first anti-anti-pollution (or "anti-ecology," in the modern misuse of the word)

film, *Deliverance,* means or portends. Script-writer James Dickey's treat-ment of his own novel is subtle. But the movie's harsh portrayal of the "nature lover" protagonists, and clearly implied message states that, when realistic men and powerful machines modify nature to their own ends, they *may* know better than vapid sentimentalists what they are doing. For its originality alone, this otherwise lively film drama deserves recom-mendation.

² See Gordon's *Persuasion,* pp. 365–502, for a review of many of these ideas. A more detailed summary of the critical events and ideas de-veloped in the United States during the 'sixties that merit the attention of cultural historians is William L. O'Neill's *Coming Apart* (Chicago: Quad-rangle Books, 1971), except that much of the volume's type appears to have been set by a retarded computer rather than an intelligent composi-tor.

³ "From Globalism to Isolationism" in *Commentary,* September, 1972, pp. 63, 66. © by the American Jewish Committee. With permission.

⁴ "The World of the 70's," *ibid.,* August, 1972, p. 28.

⁵ See "Credibility and a Political Career" in *The New York Times,* November 3, 1972, p. 39.

⁶ The prejudices, biases, facts and fancies of the preceding pages are clearly and accurately summarized in the "Society" issue of *The Saturday Review,* December, 1972, entirely devoted to a retrospective perspective of the Vietnam war. It includes articles, representing many points of view, on "The Consequences of the War" by David Halberstam, Edwin O. Reischauer, Theo Sommer, Lord George-Brown, William H. Honan, Leslie Fiedler, Robert Lekachman, Nathan Glazer, Gloria Emerson, Sey-mour M. Hersh, Robert Jay Lifton, Francine du Plessix Gray, and (of course) Herman Kahn.

⁷ There are exceptions to every rule, and therefore the authors must apologize here to Dr. Henry Grossman, a fine gynecologist practicing in Bridgeport, Connecticut. He is also an ardent and knowing authority on legerdemain and a world-famous collector of magical memorabilia. He would be, if necessary, entirely competent to devastate the Chinese magi-cal mind, as well as to perform (if necessary) an appendectomy using con-ventional anesthetic techniques and produce a rabbit at the same time.

⁸ All fact. Every bit of the tale (including, of course, the local anes-thetic) is true in letter and spirit. And the shock waves still reverberate at the time of this writing. See "Acupuncture as Anesthetic," a cautious Letter to the Editor by Dr. Francis D. Moore of the Harvard Medical School in *The New York Times,* February 10, 1973, p. 30, noting that, in spite of the fact that acupuncture *alone* does not seem to be very effec-tive as an anesthetic, Dr. Moore has discovered that it may work com-bined with procaine. How nice! Well, so will strawberry jam if enough procaine is used! Dr. Moore also equates acupuncture (correctly) with hypnosis, another pseudo-medical, long-standing put-on, for the most part.

See the *definitive* analysis of hypnosis in Theodore X. Barber, *LSD, Yoga and Hypnosis* (Chicago: Aldine Publishing Co., 1970, pp. 135–203, 207–251, 255–277, and especially 281–318, for evidential explanations.)

The "acupuncture affair," involving the medical doctors in China, was well covered at the time in the press. But the issue of acupuncture itself for purposes *other* than anesthesia has since been blown to proportions too great (and inconsequential) for us to cite relevant material upon in this book. Our bedtime story, however, has been covered as hard and feature news in *The New York Times:* Such journalistic "heavies" as Harry Schwartz and James Reston have also leaped onto the bandwagon. See the article by Harry Schwartz in the June 6, 1971 issue of *The New York Times*, Section IV, p. 12; see the articles by James Reston describing his appendectomy and follow-up treatment, appearing in the same newspaper on July 20, 1971, p. 28; July 26, 1971, p. 1; August 22, 1971, Section IV, p. 13. In September, *The New York Times* covered the story, "U.S. Doctors Arrive in China" to investigate acupuncture. The article is datelined September 21, 1971, p. 36. Dr. Kissinger, on an early trip to China, in a piece printed October 28, 1971, p. 14, was also shown an acupuncture "procedure." A prominent American physician, Dr. Rosen, was subsequently prompted to visit China to study acupuncture for treatment of deafness. The story of his stay in China for this purpose appears on October 31, 1971, p. 20. Dr. Rosen, in the next day's press, describes the use of acupuncture as an effective anesthetic in the surgery *he witnessed* (naturally), datelined November 1, 1971, p. 14. Dr. Paul Dudley White, the controversial but eminent heart specialist, has also suggested that American medicine study acupuncture for anesthetic purposes as reported on December 4, 1971, Section IV, p. 11. When the Nixon Presidential party visited China in February, 1972, Mrs. Nixon was taken to view the use of acupuncture. She wisely spurned the suggestion that she might be interested in it for the purposes of treating headaches. (She denied suffering from headaches.) Some of those stories appear on February 16, 1972, p. 16; February 23, 1972, p. 15; and February 26, 1972, p. 10.

Since then, the press has been filled with articles, features and news reports of the uses and wonders of acupuncture for a wide range of human ailments. American practitioners, trained and untrained, have, as we have noted, gotten into the act. Book publishers, large and small, respectable and not so respectable, have commissioned writers to deliver (one way or another) manuscripts on the subject. The gullibility of the American public, suffering under the burdensome cost of health care, seems willing to turn to *any* quack nostrum as an easy way to restore health. Our community of charlatans, of which there are many, seem just as willing to turn acupuncture into a quick way to turn the buck. Meantime, in all its ramifications, legends of the mystery and the magic of the Far East has yielded a propaganda coup of broad impact in the West. The time has come, we believe, for a comprehensive book exposing the entire complex of "superstition industries" in the USA, such as astrology, hypnosis, voodooism, acupuncture, fortune telling, palm- and tea-leaf reading, exposing the industrial dimension of these frauds. Such large publishing firms as Doubleday and Harper and Row, for instance, devote vast sums of money to the publication of books encouraging the occult. If the American public were not so gullible in buying their output, perhaps such publishers would turn to honest exposés of this charlatanism. We suspect that the lure of the dollar is too strong, at the present time, even for Doubleday and other publishing "giants" to resist it and to endanger their own sales by means of an honest appraisal of their own complicity in the encouragement of quackery and charlatanism.

[9] A recent article in *Incentive*, BOAC's "house organ," January, 1973, pp. 20–21, celebrates the fortieth anniversary of the External Services in typically Anglo-smug encomiastic prose. See also the American versions in Walter B. Emery, *National and International Systems of Broadcasting* (East Lansing: Michigan State University Press, 1969, pp. 86–88); and Burton Paulu, *British Broadcasting: Radio and Television in the United Kingdom; British Broadcasting* and *British Broadcasting in Transition* (all Minneapolis: University of Minnesota Press, 1956, 1958, 1961.)

[10] *Incentive*, p. 20.

[11] *Loc. cit.*, pp. 20–21. (Italics added).

6

With Love,
From Pennsylvania Avenue

The Voice Speaks. Today America has been at war seventy-nine days. Daily at this time we shall speak to you about America and the war. The news may be good or bad. We shall tell you the truth.

ROBERT E. SHERWOOD (1942) [1]

These words alone were spoken into an "open" microphone, broadcasting through a jerry-built network of short-wave stations in the early days of World War II by a Pulitzer Prize playwright, whose best shows were bittersweet comedies written for the brilliant acting team of Mr. and Mrs. Alfred Lunt. Sherwood received his greatest accolades, however, for a panegyric biographical drama about Abraham Lincoln who, in some ways, he himself superficially resembled. Called to Washington D.C. in the frantic days after Pearl Harbor by President Roosevelt, Sherwood hastily set up the broadcasting arm of a new government agency called the Office of War Information. Its business was to be propaganda. War propaganda!

Sherwood is generally credited with coining the name "Voice of America." A brilliant, genial, articulate skeleton of a man, well over six feet tall, whose clothes looked like draping on a coat rack, one hardly expected that behind his spaniel-like countenance and, shakily trimmed mustache, there glowed the soul of a word-master. Sherwood's looks were deceiving. In fact, his initial duties as the original manager of the "Voice," as it had come to be called, were soon to become nugatory. His word skills kept him busy, working with Judge Samuel T. Rosenman, ghost-writing speeches for President Roosevelt. Hence, he gave less and less time to managing a radio station, even an international one. He was just too valuable to Roosevelt, a man with a genius for identifying talent he could use at his right arm, or near it.

Sherwood's place in the history of American drama remains today much more secure (and better known) than his role either as chief rhetorician for World War II's commander-in-chief or as the first architect of a supposedly "temporary" government agency that was to find itself still alive—and suspended somewhere from the State Department's organizational chart—with the impressive name, ten years or so later: The United States Information Agency. A far-flung operation (still known overseas, for reasons too esoteric to fathom—except that it follows the British name of the British Information *Service*—as the United States Information *Services*), the USIA, long outlived the war. It survived a history, too desultory to follow here,[2] into its present incarnation today, an unwieldly appendage to the State Department that plods through time to the present moment in three main, but relatively distinct, manifestations: a broadcasting service, an overseas public relations arm of State, and a mediator of something called "cultural exchange."

State Department Stepchild

The administrative quarters of the USIA are today spread-out through eight separate buildings in Washington

D.C. Its headquarters are on Pennsylvania Avenue, "just across the street from the White House." (*All* buildings on Pennsylvania Avenue are "just across the street from the White House," even if they are three-quarters of a mile away from it. As a matter of fact, "just across the street from the White House" on Pennsylvania Avenue sits a small park, where, on a hot day in summer, a Good Humor on a stick is about the most satisfying comestible you can purchase in the Capitol for under ten bucks.) The USIA also rents office space here and there, both in the USA and overseas, including a building on New York's Fifty-Seventh Street that is loaded with assembly-line dental surgeons and periodontists.

Over the years, the agency's Directors have constituted a mixed bag of diplomatic, executive, legal, and broadcasting-journalism types. Stars in the Agency's diadem have been Arthur Larsen, a *Time* magazine alumnus; the famous broadcaster, Edward R. Murrow, a liberal Kennedy appointee who (due to ill health rather than lack of skill or drive) served the agency mostly as window-dressing at home and abroad; George V. Allen, career diplomat, an Eisenhower-conservative; the efficient Carl T. Rowan, a journalist, and one of the first Negro high-level administrators on the Washington scene (a Johnson appointee); Leonard H. Marks, drawn from a legal career in the field of communications to the USIA by President Johnson in 1965; and Nixon's first-term appointee, the arch-conservative Frank J. Shakespeare, Jr., who, like the liberal Murrow, is a survivor of the Columbia Broadcasting System's executive suite. Shakespeare survived Nixon's first term in office talking about a "hard line" for the USIA. But he did not take well to the travails and intransigencies of a bureaucracy that seemed, by virtue both of its size and loose structure, to travel its merry path in spite of the political or doctrinal allegiances of the men (including him) who were supposed to be running it.

At the helm of the USIA, as of this writing, is James Keogh, and his presence in the USIA front office surprises nobody privy to the Washington scene. A Nixon appointee, Keogh merely moved "just across Pennsylvania Avenue" from the White House, where he had been one of the President's corps of speech-writers, called to Washington from a successful career as an author and editor. His book, *Nixon and the Press*, chronicled, with partisan zeal, the much-touted manhandling of Nixon by the press in the early years of his administration, and a film he scripted, *The Nixon Years—Change Without Chaos*, was exhibited at the shoo-in Republican Convention in Miami in 1972. A one-time executive editor of *Time Magazine*, Keogh joined the Nixon camp in 1968. And, by the New Year of 1973, he had risen to presiding over the far-flung USIA, keeping his eyes pretty closely fixed, no longer on *Time Magazine*, certainly, but on the executive cottage "just across the street."

(Where do all the ex-*Time* editors come from, who move from the little newsmag to careers in politics? An editorship on *Time*, it seems, provides excellent preparation for governmental high-level appointments; just as an editorship of *Fortune* seems prerequisite to a post as a foundation pundit and expert. Did the late Henry Luce run a school for public administrators on the side? Sociologists might be interested in a statistical analysis of this curiosity.)

Despite its neat organizational handouts,[3] (and its sometimes surprising efficiency at lower levels of organization, some of which—like travel arrangements—are often handled by the State Department), the administrative end of the USIA is but one of many faces of the agency. It is, however, the face you meet when you visit Washington to talk with USIA old-timers about American international communications. They see their handiwork as a sub-Department of State, that echoes, almost to an apostrophe, whatever the Secretary of State and/or the President decide is the foreign policy "line" of the day or year. The "line" is usually pretty vapid. We'll examine it further below.

The agency displays two other facial incarnations, however. One, the old Voice of America, is still broadcasting today to the world in some 35 languages on 250 newscasts per diem from 23 studios, employing some 2,300 people, a network costing from $40–50 million a year, utilizing 109 transmitters totaling 20 million watts of radio power, beamed to a weekly audience of 40 to 50 million people, and so forth, and so forth *ad nauseam.*

The gigantic *size* of the Voice as a broadcasting system may easily be authenticated by studying budgets and scrutinizing inventories and counting heads. The *effects* of the Voice on its listeners, other than selective and intermittant jamming of its broadcasts (particularly by the USSR) and just *who* listens to which broadcasts in what countries is anybody's guess. USIA broadcasters like to talk about these things in precise terms, and slick papers and publications for the general public (that cannot be disputed) are occasionally issued, singing the Voice's praises in conventional, American institutional Public Relations-style terms.[4] Write to the USIA for some. You will get more than you need. Kenneth R. Giddens, an old Voice hand, is presently director of the Voice of America and holds the official post of Assistant Director of the USIA.

Forgetting the formal echelon of the agency and its multifarious activities for the moment, the third major manifestation of the USIA is its wide collection of overseas operations that consist of Information Centers, Libraries, Exhibits, stationary and traveling "information officers" (Public Affairs Officers called PAOs in agency *patios*), that are so various and different one from the other—and far-flung—that the Agency Director invariably has his problems explaining, in his yearly inquisition before the Congressional Appropriations Sub-Committee (that passes on funds for the Agency), exactly what they are up to overseas. Nor do sympathetic but cynical legislators *expect* him to explain much.

Congressman John J. Rooney of New York, for instance, here cross-examines Shakespeare on his budgets for the fiscal year 1973 in open hearings in April of 1972, having just brought up the issue of apparently overpaid personnel in West Germany. (Ben Posner, who jumps into the fray reprimanded below, was Shakespeare's "facts and figures" man, a non-rotating Assistant Director of the USIA in charge of the Office of Administration—and a smart cookie):

MR. ROONEY:	This is the area where we have that fine and expensive German Club; is it?
MR. POSNER:	This area includes the country of West Germany, Mr. Chairman.
MR. ROONEY:	And that includes where all these overpaid people are located. Is that so?
MR. SHAKESPEARE:	You are referring, Mr. Chairman, to those who are overgrade?
MR. ROONEY:	That is exactly what I am referring to.
MR. POSNER:	Mr. Chairman, in Western Europe, relating the grades of the officers to the classifications of positions, there are 29, or 8 percent, who are overgrade, and 70, or 44 percent who are undergrade.
MR. ROONEY:	What is the connection? Why do you tell me this?
MR. POSNER:	The question was in connection with . . .
MR. SHAKESPEARE:	In these posts, Mr. Chairman, it is sometimes difficult, because of the availability of an officer or because of changes which occur while officers are on duty worldwide, to have in every case an officer who is of the exact rank as the allocated rank for the post. I think what Mr. Posner was trying to do was to give you an overall view in Western Europe of the percentage of those who happen at the moment to be overgrade and the percentage of those who happen at the moment to be undergrade in relation to the allocated ranks of the jobs they hold. In every case we try to select an officer for a post who is most qualified for it, and we also try to match the grades.
MR. ROONEY:	I would rather do something about the people who are undergrade. This situation has been going on for years. Why Germany, I could never figure, unless you have a lot of boating enthusiasts who like the Rhine River.

MR. SHAKESPEARE: The figures we gave you were the figures for Western Europe as a whole. We will provide for you, Mr. Chairman, the overgrade and undergrade numbers of our total American complement in Germany.

MR. ROONEY: Insert a short statement at this point indicating the number of overpaid personnel you have in Germany. Then put the next country which has overpaid people and the total number in that country. Then we shall see whether the Rhine River has anything to do with it.

MR. SHAKESPEARE: All right, sir.[5]

Badinage in Congressional Committee of this sort is often misleading. So a moment's sympathy for Congressman Rooney, please. And sympathy, also for Mr. Shakespeare, although, as a retired Director, he does not need it any more—if he ever did. Faced with an agency budget, blithely presented to him by Mr. Shakespeare, of $198,697,000, Congressman Rooney is attempting to analyze the appropriation of monies on paper, according to the USIA's Washington perspective of its own activities—all neatly itemized and categorized. Too neatly! But Rooney is also well aware that the document in front of him is—and *must be*—but a fictional abstract of the profile of a rambling operation that has been constructed by bureaucrats in such a way as to provide the impression of the sensible and methodical use of public funds. Hence, his occasional levity and cynicism at the game Shakespeare and company *must* play to defend their document.

As a matter of fact, Mr. Shakespeare knows all this too. For instance, in defending expenses for overseas trade, technological, cultural and educational exhibits, the Director's guard falls for a moment, and his biases as a gentleman and ex-broadcasting executive are clear, although slightly tortured:

MR. ROONEY: Would you venture an opinion as to whether or not these exhibits which you just mentioned are as important as having the Voice of America broadcast to the Soviet Union unjammed?

MR. SHAKESPEARE: Yes, I will venture an opinion. If I had to choose between having this exhibits program and having the Voice of America unjammed, and I had to take one or the other, and those were my alternatives, I would choose to have the Voice of America programs unjammed by a significant margin of choice.

MR. ROONEY: Of course you would.

MR. SHAKESPEARE: *That is not to say I do not believe these exhibit programs are not valuable for the country.* You asked me the question in comparative terms.[6]

What both friendly antagonists face, of course, is the defense of an enormous budget that will be spent, for the most part, by people in places *neither* Mr. Rooney nor Mr. Shakespeare will know—or possibly care—about, so as to supervise or audit even superficially. And each knows the other knows. Nor, probably, *could* either find out accurately and exactly how these funds were to be used, even if they were so inclined. And, doubtless, Mr. Shakespeare's impending resignation from the agency was already well-rumored in the Capitol. He quit about six months later. In addition, Congressman Rooney's committee had, that April, also to wade painfully through many other complex government budgets, before the Subcommittee eventually recommended passage of them to the House of Representatives. The major concern of both parties was, therefore, to deal decorously with an immensely costly and complex matter both with the greatest reasonable dispatch and parsimony. Dispatch and parsimony happen also to be, in the opinion of many, two of the major aesthetic assets of fiction as opposed to real life in other manifestations of culture, not related to government. But only an insane literateur allows himself to *confuse* fiction with real life. Neither Congressman Rooney nor Mr. Shakespeare was, as of April 1972, apparently insane.

To call the agency's third function, its operations and program on the ground-level overseas, merely "far-flung" is accurate but flip. The description does proper justice neither to the diplomatic personnel of the State Department, with whom the USIS staff works closely, or the USIA people themselves. In the field, the latter are uncomfortably detached from their native land, and often find themselved sacculated (in various degrees in different places) within American enclaves on foreign soil, where they must acquit the day-to-day job of "coping" by cultivating both contempt and happy disdain for the bureaucratic organizational charts drawn up in Washington to which they are supposedly subject. Because USIS is an arm of the Department of State, USIS office territory and operational nitty-gritty centers mostly around US Embassias, Consulates and Missions on foreign soil around the world. In day-to-day operations, therefore, USIA people use the same Telex gizmos, offices, duplicating machines, local staff secretaries as State Department diplomats and patronize the same tax-free supply stores and American Clubs. They keep their spirits (of all kinds) up at most of the same cocktail parties that State's diplomats do, eternally trading the same gossip and stale anecdotes with them in both their private and public lives.

As a result, and partially as yesterday's "old boys" in the foreign service are dying off to make way for today's new "old boys," it is often virtually impossible to sever clearly USIS personnel and services from those of "regular" American diplomats and other sundry Americans who staff and inhabit our overseas outposts. Drawing a line between a State Department "cultural attaché" and a USIS "foreign language specialist" (the "foreign language" usually being English in non-English speaking countries) is frequently mostly a matter of protocol, more important in Washington than it is, say, in Barcelona or Zagreb. As matters work out, State Department diplomats are often busily engaged at so-called "information" work, simply because they are able to sustain contacts and friends that USIS personnel do not or cannot. It is not unusual, for instance, for a fairly high-ranking diplomat, stationed in a more-or-less anti-American totalitarian nation to keep a 16mm sound movie projector in his home or apartment. There, he may project American movies (for political or purely frivolous purposes) at gatherings of local nationals who will never see these films in their own theatres, and which would be difficult or impossible to screen at formal "informational" showings in an Embassy or Consulate under the aegis of a PAO.

In much the same manner, USIS personnel often find themselves playing the role of diplomats (whether they like it or not), because of their frequent mobility in intellectual and cultural circles among foreign nationals, who do not appreciate or care much about the niceties of our State Department's organizational charts. An American visiting an overseas Embassy often has quite a task separating the "State" men and women from the "Information" men and women. He also receives little enlightenment for his pains if he does. Not only do they look alike, talk alike and play their roles as foreign service personnel with the same (often artificial) sophistication, their pay-grades and tenure regulations are similar and subject to (in the field, at any rate), surprisingly little one-upmanship or rank-pulling—mostly because, many observers agree, all feel they are in the same boat.

Foreign Consulates and Embassies, of course, are places where *many* things happen, so variegated in nature that they resist generalization. Details may best be left to novelists like John Le Carré, or Len Deighton, masters of the art of glamorizing these prosaic posts by excursions into the world of "might-have-been," as often as not. On the other hand, *something is* almost always "up" at most foreign outposts (American and others), in addition to conventional diplomacy, if only trade and economic matters and the maintenance of personal "inside" relationships that sometimes require a bit of derring-do, if not cloaks and daggers.

The United States Information Service is everywhere and at all times much involved in this colorful *ambience*. That innocent-looking reading-room and/or library attached to an

Embassy in, say, Budapest, Zagreb, Bonn, Bogota, Lima or Moscow, *may* be just what it seems—an innocent-looking reading-room and/or library. After its windows are broken and its papers pillaged a few times by local thugs, it is quite simple to entertain other kinds of thoughts about it. But such suspicions are gratuitous: rarely is anything dramatic proved and, when it is, a fuss is raised by the host country and a few diplomats are sent home without even the martyrdom of an espionage trial. They are usually replaced by others in short order.

Americans, Russians, Jordanians, Israelis are all in the same boat on Embassy Row (or Consulate Avenue), wherever they are. Mysterious strangers *do* come and go—although, logically, a mysterious stranger *anywhere*, who is up to no good, would steer a wide ambit from *all* Embassies and Consulates. The entire staff manages to maintain a tight-lipped look, in order to give impressions they are vessels of profound secrets that might hurl the world into atomic warfare in minutes if they spilled what they knew. Add to this *mise-en-scène* countless journalists and writers who daily follow "leads" from various Embassies and Consulates (and her USIS personnel often know where and when good "copy" is being made at their posts), peripatetic Central Intelligence types pretending to be tennis, water-sport, or skiing professionals, and local self-styled information merchants—and you have something of a picture of the environment in which America's propaganda activities are carried on by PAOs and their associates in the field.

(How happy our overseas information people must recently have been, when the news broke in the German magazine *Stern* that Sir John Rennie, the supposedly anonymous director of Britain's M.I.6, the Secret Intelligence Service—the man known as "C" in fact and fiction—had indeed puttered around England's diplomatic corps, in the course of his black art, as a medium-rank Information Officer, among other disguises. Ergo: "Now, take that young chap who claims to be a USIA film expert and is always off somewhere in the Ruritanian mountains supposedly photographing scenery. Do you suppose that *possibly*—just *possibly*—Keogh is a "front," and that *he* might be . . . ?")

Imagination can carry one long distances, and it does its greatest damage to those who believe their own illusions. Fantasies abound in the world of *all* foreign services. The USIS is no more (or less) a part of them than other diplomatic corps around the world. In fact, so thin a line is drawn, these days, between American diplomats and "information" people abroad, that one is inclined to wonder if (a) the line might or should be erased *entirely,* or (b) it should be darkened with a sharp pencil and torn apart. In the concluding Part of this volume, we shall return to the problem, in order to evaluate possible solutions.

Output Measures Nothing

By Congressional fiat, the USIA is prohibited from directing its guns, in any but insignificant ways, upon the American people themselves. This is the single reason that most Americans live and die in nearly total ignorance of the extent and nature of their own government's major propaganda institution. All in all, the authors agree, for two reasons, with those trepidations that underlie Congress' fear that even so benign an agency as the USIA *might* constitute a danger to the Republic had it, say, the potential power of a Voice of America *in* America, directed *at* Americans.

First, the spectre of such an enormous communications bureaucracy directed at the American public flirts dangerously with both our stated and implied freedoms in the Bill of Rights. Congress is *specifically* prohibited in the First Amendment from messing about with free speech or the press. And, in spirit if not letter, *any* agencies funded or approved by Congress are also so enjoined. So much for law.

By tradition as well, mass communications in America have been for nearly two-hundred years public and *free,* in the sense that they have been largely directed—although variably controlled—by non-governmental interests and have had to take their place in America's public competitive cultural, economic and political markets. This greatest strength is also their most notable weakness: press, films, radio and television are always at one another's throats for audiences and/or advertisers, and, as institutions, are egregiously opportunistic, divisive and sometimes unscrupulous, despite all the nice fairy tales they print and broadcast about their own behaviors. But what they *cannot* be (or are unlikely to become) is *monolithic* and *totalitarian*—that is, well-organized news, information and cultural-control services that would immediately be put to the service of a demagogue who, tomorrow, may find himself in the awesomely powerful position of President of the United States. While we can think of no *past* President of the United States either intelligent or venal enough (or both) to aspire to such control for partisan or self-serving ends, we are able to suggest a few candidates for the Presidency tomorrow who just *might* fancy themselves demagogic Messiahs. As long as agencies like the USIA are prohibited from indulging in domestic operations, *one* measure of safety in the matter is, at least, assured.

Second, both tradition and law frown upon government competition with private American business. And, like it or not, publishing, making movies, television and radio *are* all business in America, first and foremost and for better and worse. Government competition *might* be suffered and overcome by any one of these businesses—or all of them. But each would certainly have to change its present business practices, either to meet it or defeat it economically. (An exception, of course, is the U.S. Government Printing Office which presently competes with private publishers of many types in issuing countless documents on such subjects as raising frogs for food, reports on archeological digs on the Yucutan Peninsula and lengthy texts of the findings of Presidential Commissions, all sold at more or less reasonable prices. As long as the quality of these random documents, both as examples of the publishing art and non-fiction, remain at their present levels, the American publishing industry has absolutely *nothing* to fear from competition with the U.S. Government Printing Office!)

Despite these difficulties, the USIA remains a formidable and complex government agency. Those who question its results and effectiveness are not merely questioning the idle expense of a few American dollars per year on good works and good words. On the other hand, were it possible to balance the matter out, dollar for ruble, the USA probably spends *less*—far less—than the USSR does on similar propaganda operations— but exactly how *much* less, we cannot be sure. (Possibly, the Soviet Union puts the lion's share of its financial resources into *preventing* external persuasion from reaching its territory. Ben Posner estimates that, in 1973, the Voice of America will consume $2,259,000 broadcasting to the USSR alone in its five languages. The Russians will spend the equivalent of $175 to $200 million alone for *jamming* various of these same broadcasts [7] —that is, transmitting high-powered static on their short-wave frequencies from within the USSR, so that reception will be difficult or impossible for Soviet citizens who want to listen to them. Such a reaction on the part of the Soviets, may, if one wishes, be construed either as signs of success—or failure—of the Voice's programs, depending upon how you look at it.)

All in all, the total USIA budget for 1973 adds up to $205,657,000, higher than it ever has been, but, due to increased costs, nevertheless forcing a slight cutback in the agency's operations. About ten thousand Americans and foreign nationals are employed by the USIA, including roughly one thousand Americans stationed abroad. In effective power and manpower, however, the agency has shrunk in size by one-fifth to one-quarter over the past decade, and possibly a good deal more since its "official" envelopment by the Department of State in 1953.[8] (Over the years between V-J day in 1945 and 1953, the functions of the OWI were transformed, in slow but confusing stages, to "peacetime" operations by means of many shifts that are now history to its present place under the wing of the State Department. Presidential Reorganization Plan No. 8, finally drew these threads together administratively to create the present USIA.)

In matters of information, persuasion and propaganda, output often means nothing, although propaganda authorities at large often behave as if it does. Output from any sort of complicated operation is its easiest facet to measure and describe with quantitative precision. What matters, in the *War of Ideas*, is *results*. But results are usually difficult to measure, and may often be described differently (and accurately) by different auditors employing different criteria of judgment.

USIA output may be clearly *described* (for what purposes such description is worth), mainly because Congress must approve of every taxpayer's dollar spent on its operations. So let us examine it as it was planned for the year 1973, mindful of the fact that we cannot, on the basis of the data that follows, make any judgment about what any or all of this activity *accomplished*—if anything—except to note that, after two decades of experience, we are looking at a record of how USIA administrators felt, thought or intuited that their money should best be spent to achieve their ends as they understood them.[9]

USIS overseas posts (some associated mainly with Embassies or Consulates and some simply with Information Centers) number 109, distributed as follows: **East Asia and the Pacific:** 14 countries, 39 posts or offices; **Africa:** 28 countries, 38 posts; **Near East and North Africa:** 12 countries, 17 posts; **South Asia:** 6 countries, 18 posts; **Latin America:** 22 countries, 35 posts; **West Europe:** 20 countries, 36 posts; **USSR and East Europe:** 7 countries, 9 posts.

In sum, the USIS operates overseas most widely, it seems, in areas of the world where it may, or is permitted to, function most freely and hospitably—that is, among people who, naturally, are disposed most kindly towards the USA in the first place. No USIA post is maintained, of course, in Red China—yet. Few operate behind the *ancien* Soviet Iron Curtain. And yet, those world areas with the *least* posts may be, in effective *results*, the most critical ones; while those operating in Tokyo, London, Paris and Rome may be the *least* effective, depending upon one's aspirations for them. All in all, about $10 million are spent yearly maintaining our various USIS "missions" around the world, in basic costs.

The USIA Press and Publications Service consumes another $12 million. Its functions are variegated: a news and picture service in the USA, a world-wide news dissemination service, publisher of multitudes of pamphlets (mainly in English, French and Spanish, but variously translated and reprinted at field posts). More specifically, the USIA also publishes five magazines. The best known is probably *America Illustrated*, a lavish picture monthly production patterned on the defunct *Life*, printed in Russian and Polish. *America Illustrated* attempts, in a *kitschy*, non-political way, to deal with the most colorful aspects of American living that lend themselves to quasi-pictorial journalism. *Topic* is a more specialized journal, published eight times a year in French and English (for sub-Sahara Africa), emphasizing USA-African relationships—political, cultural and professional. For the Moslem world, *Al Majal* is *Topic*'s counterpart, in that it also attempts to interpret American society and culture for the Arab world. The bimonthly *Problems of Communism* is a more didactic, scholarly journal designed for intellectuals overseas, particularly, one presumes, those having "problems with communism," wherever they are. *Dialogue* is still another, but it is designed as a supposedly non-political highbrow quarterly of reprints and original material dealing with "American thought and culture" (in the USIA's words), and is printed in English, Spanish, French and German language editions.

In addition to its own staff, the USIA employs, both for its own publications and for its news-agency functions, some 110 or so free-lance writers a year. They produce news stories and articles (many of them interviews) on topics so various that they are impossible to describe, except to say that they too all concern "American life," one way or another. The freelancer writers appear to be paid poorly, in today's market, and by word-count. The USIA does not seem to value professional prose writers highly in coin of the realm.

The USIA Screen Service is involved largely with the production, contracting for production of, and acquiring rights to, motion pictures, as well as aiding the work of foreign film crews shooting footage in the United States—and also overseas when circumstances warrant. But not all USIA Screen Service films end up on screens. Some find their way to tubes. To stimulate the use of their films by overseas television stations, is one of the Service's objectives. It also arranges for foreign film showings of American movies, television shows and documentaries that might not reach the eyes of foreign viewers without American overseas intervention.

The Screen Service consumes about another $10 million yearly. This figure includes production and distribution, not only of individual television-oriented films, but series of them, like the monthly *Science Reports, Washington Correspondent, Indonesian Report for America,* the Latin American series *Ahora,* and other projects at present in the works or on the air. Television and Film Production are separately budgeted items, but the two operations are obviously reciprocal in the use of USIA equipment, personnel etc. The actual number of *films,* therefore, that the USIA produces or contracts for means *less than* nothing. Usage is here all-important, because *one* discrete movie may last from thirty seconds to two hours, and may only reach small, elite audiences. Or it may be spread to millions of people instantaneously by television transmission. It is interesting to note, however, that the USIA spends about $173,000 a year maintaining its own motion picture projectors, mostly in the Pacific, East Africa, East Asia, South America and Africa, for use in regions where open-circuit home television viewing is not widespread.

Should numbers mean *anything,* the USIA itself produces about 75 films (not including series films) a year, and employs outside contractors to produce, roughly, another 25 (a good number of which are biographical features on colorful Americans, produced individually, for an ongoing series entitled *One Man*), some at formidable costs—up to six figures. The twenty-five or so freelance filmwriters the USIA employs, incidentally (some of whom are paid as corporate entities), seem to be much more healthily re-imbursed (at from about $1,000 to $6,000 a script) than ordinary prose pencil-pushers are by the Press and Publications Service. (So much, then, for the age of McLuhan and the war between the print and visual "media." Economic matters are dictated by the same whims of fashion within the USIA as in culture at large—where hack *prose* writers drink No-Cal, while hack *screen* writers eat peeled grapes!)

The USIA's Information Center Service operates on a yearly budget in excess of $7 million. Its core is 164 Information Centers and 127 "reading rooms." They are distributed variously around the world—30 in East Africa and the Pacific; 37 in Africa; 25 in West Europe; 12 in Latin America; and 3 in East Europe and the USSR. Added to this also is a somewhat ambiguous enterprise, whereby the USIA "encourages" local publishers overseas (with financial subsidies) to reprint certain American trade and educational books translated into local languages and distributed in paperback at low prices. Called the "Low-Priced Book Program" (an apt cognomen) little, if any, indication appears in or on the jackets of these volumes that their foreign publication has been sponsored by the United States Government.[10]

Our USIA Information Centers themselves follow the British pattern: American newspapers, magazines, books, recordings and research and are provided for the asking—within reason. The thrust of most of the Centers is cultural, educational, scientific and non-political. All in all, pretty soft sells.

The pitch is a good deal harder in the so-called "Special International Exhibitions" that the USIA designs, coordinates, manages and often tours overseas at World's Fairs, International Exhibits, Trade Fairs etc. They cost the USIA about $4 million per year, and run the gamut of labor missions (arranged in cooperation with the Department of Labor), architectural exhibits, educational technology demonstrations, commercial shows, industrial technology exhibits and the usual razzle-dazzle we invariably yawn at in national pavilions at World's Fairs. Some of the exhibits are road-shows, touring major cities of the world, particularly in East Europe, and once in a while, the USSR—as well as occasional visits to major cities in Asia and elsewhere. (Few seem to find their way to Latin America.) At present, Trade Missions (delicate matters!) are handled largely by the Department of Commerce, especially where and when dollar diplomacy is involved. The USIA is therefore left mostly with mounting sometimes portable (and sometimes notable) demonstrations of American technology, education and culture, that deal mostly in selling ideas rather than making dollars.

We have already had a good deal to say about the USIA's oldest and most famous operation, the Voice of America. There is little we may add here related to the *output* of this most costly of all USIA services. Not only does the Voice broadcast in a multitude of languages etc. etc. etc., it also *feeds* various local broadcasting systems with point-to-point broadcasts, as requirements warrant, and perpares special recorded programs for placement on local stations overseas. According to Voice estimates, supposedly about fifty million people listen to the Voice every week. This is a nice statistic; but it is impossible to prove that this figure does not miss the true mark by quite a few million listeners, more or less. Nor does it tell us *why* they listen, *what* they listen to or *what* they *think* about what they *hear*. (They probably listen mostly and regularly to music and occasionally and irregularly to news, just like American radio listeners.)

To call the Voice one of the world's largest broadcasting systems is probably correct. And to note, once again, that the Voice's broadcasts are often jammed in the Soviet Union, Bulgaria and Red China (and sometimes in Cuba and Egypt), is only fair to those who count efforts to keep the Voice at bay by means of interfering with its signal as signs of success. Whatever else it does, the Voice of America is on the air for about 800 broadcasting hours per week, and its short-waves cover the entire globe. Technical Operations (capital costs aside) to keep all this going cost the American taxpayer about $20 million per year, or slightly less than half the Voice's entire budget.

To describe the operation of the radio service itself that consumes the other half, let the Voice itself speak:

> A centralized service produces VOA news programs, analyses, and feature programs. The language services edit, adapt and translate this material into foreign languages and also create original programs tailored to specific countries, broadcast programs in different languages, and prepare material for use by foreign radio stations. There are subsidiary centers in New York, Chicago, Los Angeles, Miami, Rhodes, Cairo and Beirut; and overseas regional correspondents staffs at 4 locations, which produce program material from sources available only in the geographic areas which they cover. Program operations also include the operation of VOA studios in Washington, and network traffic control.[11]

Listen to the Voice of America yourself, if you wish. It sounds best in action. Your short-wave radio set is probably able to receive one or another of its English language programs any day of the week, especially in evenings. But watch out! Don't get it mixed up with Radio Moscow. At times, it is hard to tell the difference between them—a comparison that is meant to be invidious neither to our people in Washington nor to the "American desk" of the gigantic radio broadcasting bureaucratic monolith (said also to be "the world's largest") located in beautiful downtown Moscow that, like the Voice, never sleeps.

Objectives are Not Results

As the nineteen-seventies began, murmurs (and some yowls) of dissatisfaction with the USIA and its general ap-

proach to our "information programs" were heard both from
within and outside of agency quarters. On Capitol Hill, Senator Fulbright, well inflated with a head of anti-Vietnam war
steam, called the agency a "relic" of the Cold War. And,
within the USIA itself, various bureaucrats, surveying prolifer-
ating bald spots and graying temples in their ranks, wondered
quietly and privately whether the Arkansas senator might not
be right.

In a realistic manipulation of understatement, Henry
Loomis, until recently a Deputy Director and resident philosopher for the agency, put at least part of the problem into a
rhetorical nutshell at the time. Said he,[12] looking back at the
nineteen-sixties and forward to the 'seventies, "(1) The Agency's policy objectives have become more complex. (2) Foreign
audiences and media have become more critical, affluent and
sophisticated. (3) The competition has increased in volume
and skill. And (4) Agency manpower and funds have de-
clined."

In time, these somewhat abstract (but sensible) problems
were concretized in Loomis' fertile brain, a matter for subsequent discussion in Part Three of this book. Meanwhile, however, the rank and file of the USIA has been left pretty much
without firm guidelines for change—up to the present writing.
On higher levels, few USIA people appear deeply concerned
about losing their jobs (for various reasons), but the *next to
last thing* they want to talk about, even today, in concrete
terms, is specific *objectives* for American information (or propaganda) policy during the coming decade. The *last thing* they
want to talk about is *results:* what may realistically be expected from the USIA by, say, 1983 *in terms of accomplishments rather than activity.*

Like everybody else, they are most comfortable with what
they know best, and they know their record of activity intimately, On other issues, they prefer to indulge in generalities,
some of them colorful, some of them absurd. "Senator Fulbright is good medicine for the USIA. He keeps us on our
toes," is one. "The Central Intelligence Agency has never

planted a man in the USIA" is another. Also, "Our *big job* during the next few years is to interpret the American Bicentennial year for the people of the world. The past of America! The present of America! The future of America!" Should you ask what the USIA is going to *say* or *do* about the "future of America," for instance, the not-for-ascription answer you get is, "More of the same, brother! More of the same!" In short, little of substance emerges from discussions of this sort, except to emphasize that USIA administrators are at least ready and poised today for whatever changes they may be forced to make in its programs and policies during the next decade—they hope.

The one change they fear most, and are *least* prepared to meet, is a challenge that asks them for clear policy objectives and, worse, evidence of results. In all fairness to an agency that has been literally excluded, or kept at bay, from foreign policy determination and articulation (when and if they were made) for twenty years, our information viziers feel correctly that they cannot produce what they have not been told is required, nor achieve results that have not been requested. Says Loomis, "USIA does not make foreign policy, but the agency *does* make information policy." [13] True enough. But whatever his words imply, they do not stand for much on Pennsylvania Avenue in Washington D.C. Not any longer, at any rate.

When you lack a clear plan, you extemporize. And the USIA today is a hotbed of extemporization, some of it apparently sensible, some of it mere hedging against optimism, and some of it plain absurd. Let's check out a sample of these ideas buzzing in the air "just across the street" from the White House:

1) The USIA is no longer in the business of telling the rest of the world that the American way of life is also the *best* way of life. Instead, its main job is to interpret American foreign and economic policy, so that opinion-makers overseas understand and (it is assumed) therefore sympathize with our behavior as a nation, both at home and in the rest of the world.

2) The USIA is no longer anti-communist in basic thrust, mainly because the many faces of world communism presently look so different, one from another. Following the Nixon policy of underplaying ideology, a nation's *actions* are more important (and better stimuli for policy) than its intellectual or political *stance*. Thus, we must react to Poles as Poles, not Polish *Communists;* Chinese as Chinese, not *Red* Chinese, and so on. Neither the USA nor the capitalist-socialist nations of the West function any longer as ideological bastions of holy rectitude in a struggle in the death with a world-wide communist conspiracy. Or so it behooves us (and the USIA) to believe at the moment.

3) The Cold War has, accordingly, been cancelled due to warm weather. Gone are the days of "their side" and "our side." We are all in the game of world politics together. And it behooves East and West; American, African, Russian and Oriental to maintain decorum and international manners at any cost (regardless of our morals), because all wars are possible preludes to the Final War.

4) The strident voice of the USIA—and voice of the Voice —should be replaced by, or become a vehicle of, a novel and softer dialogue between peoples (a "brand new" idea suggested in print to the public and our information oracles by the present writers in *The Idea Invaders* more than a decade ago.) To this end, "new" notions are in the air at USIA: "thematic or thesis programming" dealing with various sides of international issues—not just the USA's position; more international dialogues and face-to-face seminars involving Americans in many areas of life; "bi-national centers," (whatever they turn out to be), "library cultural services," and other agents of rapprochement should be designed to encourage this give-and-take. So might the use of international telephone communications for "talk-back shows" by satellite on Voice broadcasts—expensive but potentially effective trickery.

5) Objective news is fine, but the British control the market. What they do *not* control is mature, interpretive comment

and discussion, always Voice of America staples, but due for expansion and re-thinking. To foreign ears, interpretation is naturally construed as persuasion. So a dangerous path is opened here, unless the commentary is balanced, responsible and top drawer, genuinely representative of responsible American opinion—both assent and dissent. An editorial service of the air might be the aim here, drawing upon daily responsible press opinion across the United States.

6) In the 1940's the USIA administrators were mostly *media men*—that is, broadcasters, writers, filmmakers etc. In the nineteen-fifties they were replaced by *language and regional specialists,* who were supposed to troubleshoot audiences and give them, one way or another, information and colorful fantasies or whatever information they wanted to hear about the USA. In the 'sixties, USIA *management men* had their hands full, juggling a fading American image against the spectre of diminishing budgets, diplomatic embarrassments and minor crises abroad. For the nineteen-seventies, the burden of the agency's directors falls now upon *communicators,* people not only familiar with how to frame attractive messages in print, words and on film, but knowledgeable in employing the total dynamic of the logical and psychological powers of communications, including the idea of feedback. In short, they now have to become communication theorists. To this end, the USIA has been conducting highbrow seminars for its staff, featuring such notable communications academicians as Harold Laswell, Daniel Katz, Hideya Kumata and other gurus from the university world to provide crash courses in political science, social psychology and sociology for USIA personnel.

"Communication theory" is just a bit more abstract than Tibetan music, and slightly less eclectic than Hindu theology! Since communication theorists usually agree only that they disagree about how people communicate—and because each theorist brings mainly to his analysis of communication the arts and skills of his own peculiar *amours propre* and original discipline of training—one imagines that these USIA seminars have been jolly occasions indeed, judging by the particular participants so far called to conduct them. How they will fare in the future, and what they will accomplish, remains to be seen.

7) The USIA has, in the past two decades, been far too sensitive to its peculiar position, highly noticeable on front diplomatic lines overseas but practically *invisible* within the USA. An occasional USIA film, like the Kennedy panegyric, *Years of Lightning, Day of Drums* reached the American public (by resolution of Congress) via a theatrical release in 1964. But, by and large, the USIA has always received extremely little credit at home for what it has done *well*—and it has accomplished much superbly, given its policy limitations. On the other hand, it has drawn extraordinary criticism for its mistakes and boo-boos, whenever they have been exposed by journalists (especially overseas), ever poised to throw their verbal darts into government bureaucracies. (USIA personnel seem blind to the fact that their plight is simply a reflection of a sad condition everywhere in a complex society. Most of us live in worlds—at home and at work—where what we do *right* is taken for granted, and what we do *wrong* is celebrated beyond reason—to our way of thinking, at least.) Such sensitivities may seem absurd, but they do little to cheer morale in the bureaucratic world of big government. And so hopes are high that the USIA's new policy of international dialogue may call greater attention to the range, scope and complexity of USIA operations *within* the United States. These may also be vain hopes. And we suspect that they are.

In short, the USIA summed up its "Strategy for the Seventies" (or, to some, its avoidance for articulating strategy) in this way:

> The President's call for partnership with friendly nations, and U.S. willingness to negotiate differences with adversaries, reflect a policy based on mutual respect. It shows not only an emphasis toward understanding the sensitivities and interests of

other nations, it augurs a more discriminating—and quieter—
U.S. role in world affairs.

For the Agency, this translates, in some places, into a less
visible approach to communication with audiences abroad. For
instance, Agency officers have found that personal discussion is
most effective with opinion molders and greater understanding
can sometimes be achieved by providing an editor with background materials for his editorials than by placing an Agency-
originated article in his newspaper. . . .

And with television growing in importance in most countries, the Agency is moving to take greater advantage of this
medium by encouraging and assisting foreign television teams
to shoot their own footage in the United States and through
joint production of TV programs. An example of the latter is
"First Friday," a monthly two-way international interview show
sent via satellite. A panel of correspondents in Rio de Janeiro
questions an American guest in USIA's television studios in
Washington.

Greater use of satellite transmissions is also being made for
official U.S. Government statements as well as for coverage of
visits to the United States of visiting foreign dignitaries.

The Agency is giving increased attention, too, to the professionalism of its staff, both in Washington and overseas, which
means broadened and intensified training for both American
and foreign national personnel.[14]

An old broadcasting hand, now retired from the Voice of
America (after a seven-year tour of duty), scratched his gray
curls. He had seen radio broadcasting turn from a toy to an industry, had, at one time, written and produced old documentary and entertainment broadcasts that are now industry
legends, and was among the first of radio's creative people to
play godfather to the infant television industry early in the
nineteen-fifties. His keen perceptions caught hungry gleams in
the eye of the bright young wolves who infiltrated the commercial networks with their films and portable cameras a few
years later. Having little taste for a cow pasture, he moved to

Washington, the USIA and the Voice of America. From the big time to the small time, or so he thought then.

"Hell," he said, "I came down to the USIA expecting I don't know what. A batch of amateurs, I suppose. Peace Corps types. Boy scouts. Recreation directors. Catskill *tummlers.* Small-town radio executives. Cute ivy-leaguers who only show up for work during vacations. The only government I had ever worked for was the Army.

"Well, these people aren't amateurs—not on the broadcasting side of the fence, or the diplomatic side, or any other side. They are dedicated, hard-working professionals. Coming from commercial radio and television in New York, I suppose I didn't know what dedication really was—except to the dollar and the big 'I am.' Take it straight from me, these people *want* to do a good job. And the USIA is no federal boondoggle. The American public is getting its money's worth wherever these people are, in Washington or New York or Vienna or Moscow.

"But something's wrong down deep there. If I knew what it was, I'd tell you. And now that I've retired, I don't see it any more clearly then when I was in the middle of it."

His scratching fingers moved from scalp to neck. He looked tired, but the fatigue was simply the weight of time—of years—on a frail man.

"I guess you could say nobody *listens* to them. There they are out—all over the world—and they *know* the common people who make up what we used to call in broadcasting 'the great unwashed.' Only these 'unwashed' are really '*unwashed.*' And the USIA people live with them close-up. Get to know them closely. But there's too damn little meaningful feedback, and no input in the right places, at least not enough to be worth a damn. The State Department, the White House—even the USIA brass—go their own ways without much consideration of what *they* are thinking and feeling and expecting from the USA: those damn 'unwashed' people out there, millions of them. Hundreds of millions. Billions!

"Oh, they *think* they know what people overseas are

thinking. But do you know how they find out? They look at newspaper headlines, or digests of newspapers, read some crap from an Ambassador's secretary and listen to bullshit that the Washington diplomatic grapevine wants them to hear. Or they contemplate their navels. Then they arrive at momentous decisions about what the Czechs, Rumanians, Germans and Frenchmen *ought* to be thinking. So it doesn't mesh. Do you know what I mean? It's crap built on a foundation of crap. Compound crap.

"It seems to me—and, hell, I'm just a broken-down scriptwriter—that the USIA is just one terrific *source* of information that ought to have something to do with what America *does* and uses its influence, money—and damn it, even guns—in all those foreign countries. I don't mean spy story stuff. And I don't mean that every jerk in every Information Center in East Asia knows more than those brain-trusters over at the Pentagon and CIA. But it seems to me that, if America is going to operate efficiently in the information industry, we have to do something more concrete than simply tell everything on God's earth that Uncle Sammy loves them, and so they better do what he says. Period.

"Love is great stuff. But there must be more to this business than singing love songs, mustn't there? Something's mising down there on Pennsylvania Avenue, all right, and I'm damned if I know what it is. An awful lot of manpower—money and brainpower—is wasting sweetness on the desert air.

"You know, from what I've seen, working for the USIA sort of makes you feel you're in a vacuum. As if you knock yourself out, and then nothing happens. But for some reason you can't or won't, understand, you keep knocking yourself out anyway. I wonder if they feel that way in other government agencies too. I'll bet they don't. Most of them probably just do the best they can and go the hell home. Well, from what I've seen, the USIA never goes home, because no job is ever finished. I just wish I *knew* a little more clearly what that job

was, even now that I don't have it anymore. Maybe I would
have done it better, like the Rinso commercials we used to
produce on daytime radio in the nineteen-thirties. Now, those
were the days. 'Rinso White!'

"Say, did I ever tell you about the time that the old Lux
Radio Theatre needed a full sixty-minute script of that old
movie—what was its name?—with a twenty-four hour deadline. . . . ?"

NOTES TO CHAPTER 6

[1] See Wilson P. Dizard, *Strategy of Truth.* (Washington: Public Affairs Press, 1961, p. 33.)

[2] See Dizard's book above. Its idealism is dated, but its facts are
accurate.

[3] The best USIA document available to the American public is the
yearly pamphlet that explains (somewhat superficially) what it is up to
and where, entitled *The Agency in Brief*, the title followed by the year
being discussed.

[4] The Voice is discussed in the above document as one of the four
USIA "media" services (Broadcasting, Information, Screen, and Press and
Publications), and each is given sufficient coverage to provide the impression of equivalence between them, hardly the truth, by any critierion.
Colorful handouts on the Voice, neatly undated and anonymous, are provided visitors to its Washington studios and are updated from time to
time. They are available to the American public for the asking.

[5] *Hearings before a Subcommittee of the Committee on Appropria-
tions, House of Representatives*, Ninety-second Congress, Second Session,
Part 4. (Doc. No. 76–8760, Washington D.C.: U.S. Government Printing
Office, 1972, p. 427.)

[6] *Ibid.*, p. 319.

[7] *Ibid.*, p. 316.

[8] *Ibid.*, pp. 312–313. See also U.S. Information Agency, 37th Semiannual *Review of Operations*, December, 1971, pp. 2–3, for a summary

of how recent changes have been—and continue to—diminish that *true* size of the USIA, appropriations notwithstanding.

[9] Rather than depend upon USIA published summaries for this material, the authors have tackled the actual budget of the agency as submitted to (and approved by) Congress. We are certain that it rivals the St. Louis, Mo. telephone directory as dull reading matter. See *Hearings before a Subcommittee* etc., op. cit., pp. 320–684. Wherever possible, summaries of costs, expenses etc. have been used, and figures have been rounded out for ease of comparison.

[10] The present writers are therefore internationally famous authors, thanks to the USIA. Your local American library will almost certainly *not* contain, George N. Gordon and Irving A. Falk, (trans., Edmond Jorge), *Comunicação Pela TV* (Rio de Janerio: Forum Editors, 1969), a Brazilian Portugese translation of Gordon and Falk's, *TV Covers The Action*, which you *may* find somewhere in the USA in its original American edition, as published in 1968. Lawrence F. Costello and George N. Gordon, (trans., Marie Sinoir), *L'Enseignment Télévisé* (Paris: Nouveaux Horizons, 1970) is sold in French-speaking Africa, while the original American version, *Teach With Television* (First edition, 1961; Second edition 1965) is now out of print in the USA. But do not be misled by any of the previous million-dollar budgets quoted above. Neither the American publishers of the books above (Julian Messner and Hastings House), nor the authors, were remunerated by the USIA on a royalty basis for the translation and publication of their works. Nor were the small flat fees paid for them either generous or, to certain eyes (ours), fair, all things considered. Permission to publish them was granted, in both cases, because all parties assumed they were serving a "good cause," and, of course, the appeal of vanity. We have mixed personal feelings about this particular operation, for obvious reasons, and know little about its results.

[11] *Hearings Before a Subcommittee* etc., op. cit., p. 583.

[12] *37th Semiannual Review of Operations*, p. 3. Loomis' remarks in this document are summarized on pp. 2–5 and are drawn upon in the discussion below. See Chapter 9 for further discussion of Loomis' philosophy of USIA policy, and his ideas for the agency's future.

[13] *Loc. cit.*

[14] United States Information Agency, *34th Semiannual Report to Congress* (Washington, D.C.: January–June 1970, p. 3.)

7

Other Voices, Other Channels

> . . . (S)*uppression of information leads to entropy and total destruction. Suppression of information renders international signatures and agreements illusory: Within a muffled zone, it costs nothing to reinterpret any agreement, even simpler to forget it, as though it had never really existed. (Orwell understood this supremely.)*
>
> *A muffled zone is, as it were, populated not by inhabitants of the earth but by an extraordinary corps from Mars: The people know nothing intelligent about the rest of the earth and are prepared to go and trample it down in the holy conviction that they come as "liberators."*
>
> ALEKSANDER I. SOLZHENITSYN [1]
(Nobel Prize lecture, 1970.
Written but never delivered.)

Great words.

Brave words.

They apply with equal pith to oligarchal dictatorships: where the free exchange of knowledge is controlled by government censorship, and to republican democracies: where the similar exchanges of ideas are controlled—with equal effectiveness—by apathy, ignorance and indifferent self-contentment.

Sad words.

They lead the writers, therefore, to consider carefully:

The Advantages of Not Having Grandchildren

Neither author of this volume has grandchildren. One is

unlikely *ever* to have them, not being a father. Prospects for the other, the presumed sire of three 'teenagers, are not as fortunate. But, to the best of his knowledge, he has, to date, been spared.

If this good fortune continues, neither writer will, at some future date, find himself forced to recount to his grand-progeny the morsel of history that follows and attempt to make sense out of it. He will not have to answer those discouragingly sharp questions that young minds pose about deceptions, good motives, strange means and forgotten history. He will not have to face the still unanswered curiosities concerning two of the weirdest byproducts of what is still called (by some) the "Cold War" between the United States of America, the Soviet Union and its five satellite nations. Reference here is namely to Radio Free Europe and, to a lesser degree, Radio Liberty.

What Radio Free Europe and Radio Liberty *are* is probably less important than what they *were*. And the story of both is likely to slip into history as they are now described in the piles of homespun documents that have emerged from both organizations over the years, including two full-length books, equally distortive.[2] But memories are short, and (as Solzhenitsyn knows that Orwell knew), whatever anyone says loudly and three times turns eventually to the "truth."

Thus the "official" histories of both agencies tell us pretty much the same story. In the late nineteen-forties and early 'fifties, a group of "public-spirited citizens", alarmed by the obvious and increasing exclusivity of Soviet propaganda in East European nations dominated by the USSR, incorporated themselves into two bodies: the National Committee for a Free Europe and The American Committee for Liberation, respectively. Both organizations were well-glazed with "front" names (more and better "fronts" for *Free Europe* than for *Liberation*), and both took great pains to indicate that they were *private* organizations, unrelated to the Government of the USA *in any way*—except in terms of informal blessings from then President Truman and Secretary of State Acheson. They were, they claimed, interested only in the psychological welfare of Hungarians, Rumanians, Poles, Bulgarians and Czechoslovakians (in the case of *Free Europe*) and Russian victims of Soviet thought control (in the case of *Liberation*). In short, they presented themselves as private philanthropies—philanthropies, that is, with a decidedly revolutionary thrust, as the names of both (at the time) indicated.

Then bingo! Within the next four years or so, both organizations were suddenly proprietors and operators of two of the world's most powerful (in terms of transmission) and largest (in terms of output) multi-million dollar radio propaganda agencies, with elaborate and sophisticated offices in New York, transmitters in Munich and elsewhere and replete with an echelon of crusaders on a holy mission: to broadcast the "truth" behind the Iron Curtain in the role of national, non-communist radio voices, oriented to the particular languages and cultures of the target audiences in each area.

The size, hours of daily transmission and numbers of languages in which simultaneous broadcasting emerged from them—and continues to flow forth—are all matters of record and make formidable reading. (The language problem was particularly intense for RL, as Radio Liberation came to be known, because of the multiplicity of tongues spoken in the USSR.) To this day, if one presents oneself to the administrators of either broadcasting service, one will emerge with more diversified documentation than he would care to—or possibly be able to—read in a month. In fact, in the case of RFE in particular, one receives the impression that one is somehow being *submerged* in reports, studies, inventories, speeches and other piles of paper that serve to distract rather than clarify the main issue he seeks to comprehend: namely, "What were and what are, RFE and RL, and what are they doing today?"

As the nineteen-fifties rolled along, Radio Liberation hit one major snag—its name. According to its press releases—(that one may or may not believe for equally good reasons), the *staff* of the organization, made up, like that of RFE, of *emigrès* and former nationals of the Soviet Union, objected to the militant revolutionary connotation of the word "Liberation." The name of the broadcasting agency, accordingly, was quietly changed to "Radio Liberty." On the other hand, nobody seemed to object to the phrase "Free Europe"—at least, not in RFE's studios. And, as time passed, and with our American penchant for acronym, Radio Free Europe became, for most purposes, known by its meaningless sobriquet "RFE" anyway. The name problems were solved.

Until approximately nineteen-sixty-six (or so), both organizations insisted upon maintaining their status as *private* organizations—on paper at least. (There was nothing they could do about rumors; and rumors of all sorts flew wildly about both organizations. Most of them were wrong.) In this respect, the sachems of RL were a bit wiser than their counterparts at RFE, who boasted of their fiscal "public support," advertised their services and libertarian virtues on television, radio and car-cards on buses and trains. RFE solicited funds from the public by means of advertising campaigns, films and television spots that promised that the public's dollar was the *only* mechanism by which RFE might broadcast its truth "behind the Iron Curtain."

When faced with the question of who supported *them,* RL personnel merely managed an organizationally inscrutable expression, a slight knowing smile and indicated that "interested parties" provided the pelf. *Who* they were, *why* they were interested, and in *what* they were interested were matters one could not profitably pursue at length with RL executives or public relations personnel, mostly because of their extraordinary collective genius at changing subjects in mid-sentence.

These postures—*both* of RFE and RL—were sheer deceptions, or quasi-deceptions, depending upon how one looks at it. In fact, it is not improper to call them "lies, salted with truth." [3] Fortunately for both RFE and RL, both organizations were well-insulated, when the truth of their common aegis finally emerged, against the usual wrath of the American public at times when it discovers that it has been, for a long period, deceived.

In the *first* place, RFE, for all its advertising and publicity, did not seem to have been taken very seriously by the American public at large, although the organization (to this day) goes to exquisite (and sometimes absurd) pains to count and list, state by state and newspaper by newspaper, the exact number of newspaper articles, editorials and cartoons that appear in the American press about it. (The discouraging nose-count, for instance, from February 17th to June 30th, 1972, was 590 editorials and 129 cartoons in favor of RFE, and 32 editorials and one cartoon against it in the press in the United States. The counting and evaluating was, naturally, done by RFE itself.) [4]

Second, about one-fifth of RFE's operating budget had indeed come from private (or "public", as you wish) donations, although the exact parts of this fraction that represents *small* donations from the general public and/or *large* donations from special enthusiasts (and why are they enthusiastic?) concerned with the spread of truth in communist East Europe is still a mystery, not very clearly covered in RFE's Everest of documentation.

RL's grand deception was considerably less elaborate, and, therefore, according to how one evaluates lies, less of a blow to its integrity when the true truth (sic) finally emerged. "Interested parties" indeed had sponsored RL and its years of multi-lingual broadcasts. But the question raised by the two words in quotes poses a semantic problem best left in its untangled state. They were not "private" interested parties, by any means, unless one construes near-invisible government agencies as tantamount or equal to private organizations—a possible but poor exercise in rationalization. The interests certainly were *not* free of official American governmental aegis. And, in this respect, RL's "cover story" was as much a fabrication as RFE's, although a more ambiguous one.

Where, then, did the two budgets that rose together over

the years to a present forty-million or so dollars per annum, necessary to operate Radio Free Europe and Radio Liberty—budgets about equal to that of the Voice of America—come from?

(And this is the reason we are glad we do not have grandchildren. We are not, accordingly, forced to explain to them the reasons, rationales, circumstances and history arising from the answer to this simple question.)

The money came from the "secret" budget, appropriated by the Congress of the United States, of the Central Intelligence Agency.

Natch!

Where else?

To the present moment, both RFE and RL insist that their fifteen, or more, year relationship with the CIA was strictly, entirely and absolutely pecuniary. And the reader may believe them if he wants to, although the evidence above strongly suggests that the credibility record of neither service is not exactly spotless. We do *not* believe them—even after having been assured personally, let us add, by the operations director of each organization positively—that neither organization was or is directed or influenced, concerning policy or operations, by the now infamous intelligence agency. We prefer recourse to the old adage, "He who pays the piper calls the tune." When one pays *two* pipers sums of US currency up to forty million (or so) dollars a year, it is difficult to believe that tunes are, let us say, not *suggested,* much less demanded. But we are reporting what we have been told by sources as reliable in this matter as one may approach these days without violating the Espionage Act. We remain unconvinced.

When public disclosures concerning RFE and RL's genuine sugar-daddy hit the news stands more than a half-dozen years ago, they created, as we have noted, remarkably little stir, fuss or public outcry. The stories were, of course, buried by the far more sensational simultaneous discoveries, played to the hilt in the mass press during the early "Vietnam protest" days, that the CIA had its fingers in more *multiple* philanthropic and foundational pies than most people have fingers *and* toes, and juicier pies (from the publicity angle) than two supposedly idealistic radio services. The CIA, it seems, had sponsored and funded student organizations, research foundations, philanthropic welfare organizations and a host of colorful camouflages for their covert operations at home and overseas, the exact nature of which remain cloudy to this day. Through it all, RFE kept on its merry way, insouciantly soliciting the public for support with apparently continued and successful results. And the folks at RL just blinked their eyes, smiled their time-worn inscrutable smiles that now implied, "What else did you expect?" when their critical relationship to our (then more than now) super-secret international information *apparat* came up in conversation.

The *main* reason, of course, that a major public outcry over the deception practised by both organizations for so long a time did *not* occur has been alluded to above and is obvious. Very few—if any—Americans cared much. Although RFE, mostly, and RL, to a lesser extent, had mounted public relations arms that attempted to mediate their motives and virtues to the public, their "sells" had either been soft or inept or both, drowned out by the glut of other voices in the masscult market bidding for attention, all demanding to be heard, hawking their good works and good words on public and private channels of communication. Having sustained the ignominy of public apathy in one or another form for years, the news that these low-profile propaganda agencies were an arm of our official intelligence agency—and therefore, despite disclaimers, probably intimately connected with foreign policy positions brewed in the White House and Department of State—simply did not mean very much to the average American. The news also broke at a time, during the nineteen-sixties, when the authenticity of almost *all* information released by government agencies was generally suspect. The words "credibility gap" had become a favorite catch-phrase in our editorial echelons. In all probability, the exposure of the CIA's benevolent paternalism was received with more gusto and gloat among certain circles in Poland, Czechoslovakia, Hungary, Rumania, Bulgaria and the USSR than in the United States.

During the years that followed, RFE and RL continued along in their time-worn tracks, modifying somewhat their fictions concerning "public support" and "interested parties." They traveled their deadpan ways, asserting half-heartedly their independence from the official "line" of the State Department, broadcasting their homeland-style ideological lectures, religious services, news and commentary in much the same way they always did. The CIA continued to provide their working capital from their now "not-so-secret" budget. And everybody tried hard to pretend that nothing had happened.

But something had.

The painful moment of truth was long in coming. By 1971, the Congress, in its infinite wisdom (and responding to some public pressure—and evidently quite a bit of private pressure, impossible to trace), found itself considering a series of proposed bills designed to extricate RFE and RL from the CIA in order to fund it directly. The intent of these proposals was to establish a theoretically independent new quasi-governmental agency called the American Council on Private International Communications, Inc. that would henceforth support *both* broadcasting systems with necessary money for their services and policy guidance.

To this end (and apparently delighted to be out from under the CIA's wing), both RFE and RL mounted quite a picnic at the open hearings designed to examine the worthiness of this proposal. RFE clearly dominated the proceedings, providing the lion's share of razzle-dazzle, while RL confined itself to a few well-informed witnesses, testimonials and clear supporting data. With a peculiar bias towards the importance of RFE broadcasts to Poland (workers' uprisings in Poland had been much in the international news at the time and since 1968), testimony was given the Congress in Committee by various academicians, ex-East European diplomats, and clearly partisan *emigrés* from East Europe and the Soviet Union. They included a nuclear physicist, an economist and the president of the Polish-American Congress (!). Their evaluations of the work of both services was, needless to say, quite laudatory—in fact, enthusiastic and unequivocal. Not a word of criticism of either agency was spoken. Letters of support from familiar RFE-RL boosters—like former Ambassador to the USSR Foy Kohler, writer Paul Wohl, political scientists Leonard Schapiro (London School of Economics), Harold C. Deutsch (University of Minnesota), Valdimir Reisky de Dubnic (University of Munich), Max Hayward (St. Anthony's College, Oxford), Zbigniew Brezezinski (Columbia University), as well as other luminaries from East and West, including, *mirabile dictu,* the son of Alexander Kerensky—were either heard or entered into the record.

The show was good enough to activate Congress—on an interim basis—to create the proposed new agency as requested, ostensibly detaching RFE and RL from the CIA and its funding. It was also impressive enough to activate Senator Fulbright of Arkansas into a reaction that one would have expected from him much sooner—or from some other neo-isolationist critic of the chronic deception and secrecy into which most American international propaganda and persuasion somehow weaves itself.

Addressing his colleagues in the Senate, the general tenor of Senator Fulbright's feelings toward both RFE and RL may be gleaned in the following exerpts from a long and untidy speech, delivered in 1972, reprising an analysis of RFE and RL, that the Senator had sent to the Library of Congress (the agency officially reporting on RFE and RL to the Foreign Affairs Committee of the House of Representatives) shortly *before* the well-staged and advertised hearings described above. Noting that the hearings now completed "may have placed too much reliance on the public information handouts provided by the Radio organizations (and their own researches) themselves

—organizations which I might point out still refuse to acknowledge publicly any ties to the U.S. intelligence community," the Senator contested, in his characteristic rhetoric, RFE's and RL's neatly mounted arguments for continued funding:

> . . . (W)hat we are left with is two rather dreary commentaries on two very bureaucratic organizations whose common goal is to liberalize the governments of Eastern Europe and the Soviet Union by broadcasting "balanced news" to the peoples of these countries. The people, in turn, according to the theory, then pressure their respective governments for democratic reforms, and this, in turn, serves to create conditions for world peace.
>
> Of course, the theory runs headlong into the brutal experiences of Hungary and Czechoslovakia . . . Such a theory, I believe, is based on nothing more than an arrogant belief that people around the world will act like we want them to act if only we tell them how.
>
> Mr. President, the proper perspective on Radio Free Europe and Radio Liberty was perhaps best stated in a letter which I received recently from a retired foreign service officer, who devoted more than 20 years of his professional career to Eastern European and Communist affairs. He asked that I not reveal his name, but I would like to quote from his letter for the benefit of my colleagues:
>
> "It seems clear to me, were there no RFE or Radio Liberty now in existence, that nobody would suggest that this would be the time to establish such a station. The pattern of our relations with the countries of Eastern Europe has evolved in such a manner, that no one would pretend to argue that our interests in that part of the world would be better served by setting up such a station now.
>
> "The main argument for continuance of the station, then, is now the bureaucratic one: a large organization with an expensive staff now exists, and so must presumably continue to exist, even though the need for it (if ever there was such) has long since disappeared. But the staffs can be taken care of much more economically, with generous severance pay, than by prolonging the life of an unneeded station."
>
> I think this is a very perceptive observation and one which serves full consideration, particularly by those who, up to this

point, may have been exposed to only one side of this issue. I, of course, am persuaded that the Radios ought to be liquidated, unless perhaps our European allies are willing to pick up their fair share of the financial burden that these Radios impose—a burden which the American taxpayer would otherwise have to continue to bear alone . . . .[5]

In this particular—and lengthy—tirade the articulate Arkansan did *not* refer to RFE and/or RL as "relics of the Cold War," although this remark; made at another time and place, encapsulated trenchantly his belated outrage at twenty or so years of America's information strategy, its ambiguities, deceptions, incredible naïveté and dubious organizational distinctions. The Senator certainly made a sharp point—this time, at any rate.

And that, grandchildren who do not exist, is that. But says the logician, if philanthropic committees, "public support," and "interested parties" that do not exist wrought Radio Free Europe and Radio Liberty, might not a pack of grandchildren who do not exist also be fully as real as RFE and RL?

So—grandchildren aside, let us look more closely at these complex agencies that at last, and by an act of Congress, have finally become what they were supposed to have been at the outset—more or less, and possibly too late. In order to accomplish this, we must first turn towards the territory that is their main concern, best described as "Communist Europe."

Looking Eastward

As every American high-school student is supposed to know (but probably does not), the term "Iron Curtain" was first turned in reference to the Western borders of the Soviet bloc of nations in Europe, including East Germany, in a speech delivered shortly after World War II (1946) at Fulton, Missouri, where nothing else of much consequence seems to have happened before or since.

The words were an infelicitous Churchillian metaphor, but a "grabber," poorly descriptive of the delicate military, economic and psychological partition of Europe after the war. So was its corollary, the phrase "The Cold War," that presumably described battles of words over, and through, and/or around the very Iron Curtain that was supposed to have been lowered on the European Continent between Eastern Communist and Western Democratic (Socialist and Capitalist) nations. Had an "Iron Curtain," in any construction, existed, a "Cold War" would have, of course, been impossible. But these contradictions are the price of colorful speech. When both metaphors are referred to straight thinking, they are absurd taken alone, doubly absurd taken together. And both serve as weak shorthand descriptions of the shifting, multilateral balances of powers that were the consequence of the all-too-rapidly and thoughtlessly thrown-together agreements made at the now-infamous Yalta and Potsdam conferences of 1945. The arbitrary and poorly reckoned mule-trading carried on at these occasions in high places served well the post-war interests of neither the Western nations (the USA, mostly) nor those in the East (the USSR, particularly).

Western involvement in East Europe had become, by the end of World War II, so integrally a part of the history and traditions of the West (in Europe as well as in the USA) that no metaphorical Iron Curtain would or could sever effectively interdependences that had been evolved over hundreds of years of active and fertile cross-cultural relationships. *All* of the Eastern European, Communist Bloc nations had been variously engaged, mostly through immigration, in the growth of the United States in its "melting pot" years, and, possibly more important, in nearly all of her military and political alliances with the rest of Europe, since the American Revolution in the eighteenth century. More immediately, patriotic, anti-Axis nationals had fought shoulder-to-shoulder with the Allies during World War II. They included, for instance, Polish battalions in the Soviet Army, Polish fliers with bushy mustaches piloting RAF airplanes on bombing raids over Germany and many other, similar units. Governments deposed by Nazi invasion—

and their eloquent, powerful diplomats of many political stripes, far left to far right—had found provisional refuge in Britain and the United States. They were poised to return to their native lands when World War II peace treaties (they incorrectly assumed) would restore to their native soil a *status* that was never again to be *quo*.

The strands of historical relationships of incredible complexity (that could not even be outlined in a single volume) were neither to be severed nor short-circuited easily by an Iron Curtain mentality or (presumably) ideological Cold War.

In the United States, they yielded, however, to Churchill's simplifications. Like all great wartime leaders, the British Prime Minister had a gift for a polar, black-versus-white thinking that was to cause his eventual consignment to the political scrap-heap in the complex, subtle light to dark-gray world of subsequent peace-time Britain. On one side of the winning nations, loomed Josef Stalin, his black shadow dominating five and one-half East European nations with apparently oppressive state dictatorship; on the other side, Uncle Sam (and John Bull and friends), symbol of freedom, democracy, truth and Lockean-Jeffersonian virtues that required and resisted lucid explanations. David Low's political cartoons of the period conveyed to the public, in appropriate caricatures and harsh pools of India ink, this polarity—black and white; no grays.

Taking advantage of this simplistic spirit of the times, both Radio Free Europe and Radio Liberty were born—created by sophisticated students of foreign policy who knew (and *know*) that their mission in the mythic Cold War was not —and *could not be*—easily sloganized, as they were forced to feign as purveyors of "truth" to nations riddled by political indoctrination and censorship.

Complications immediately arose. In the case of Radio Free Europe, each of the five nations to which it broadcast was, and remains today, factionalized ideologically and politically to various degrees. The question of exactly *who* speaks for "free" Hungarians, Czechs, Rumanians, etc. from outposts miles from their borders in the great West is one that was never solved, and has not been solved to date. For Radio Liberty, these sorts of problems were no less complex. All the wisdom of America's best Kremlinologists, and intelligence reports by multitudes of defectors from here and there in the USSR, could not—and *cannot*—provide policy guidance complete enough to respond (even employing a mammoth broadcasting system) to the cultural, linguistic, ideological, religious and historical ferment that bubbles and bubbles away under the patina of Politburo unity in the mélange of states, sub-states and communities that we tend to dismiss with the (in fact) insulting name "Russia."

In only *three* main ways did the Iron-Curtain-cum-Cold War notion relate to day-to-day socio-political (or "power-play") realities of the past twenty years. And upon these hard-core circumstances both RFE and RL were founded.

First, the economies of East and West Europe are, of course, vastly different. But the differences cannot be described merely by opposing "capitalism" to "communism." The Western markets are an alliance of economic relationships complete unto themselves, with holdings, naturally, all around the non-Communist world. At their heart is the Swiss franc, the German mark and the American dollar, and the various money markets that trade in them. The blood that courses through the organ is Western trade, including what Americans called "foreign aid," but dependent for many years, until recently, upon American investments at extremely low interest rates. This latter largesse (necessary at the time) caused, in large measure, America's so-called "balance of payment" woes that have bedeviled White House budget-makers so severely in recent years. When one passes the Iron Curtain, the economic pivot of life suddenly metamorphoses into the Russian ruble, a currency apparently only as valuable as the Kremlin decrees it to be, but, for trading purposes, only as good as the economic power and potential of the Eastern Bloc nations taken together.

The Iron Curtain, by fiat, keeps these economies *reason-*

ably well separated. Of course, there are numerous leaks. But, by and large, the Communist world (that has been hardly Marxist, or even Leninist in major commercial matters) functions, economically at least, unrelated to vicissitudes of the commercial world in the private enterprise nations of the West. (The separation is dramatized even today for the Western traveler to East Europe who discovers that his dollars or francs or pounds may be subject in a ruble-based nation to any one of *multiple* exchange rates: "normal" or "tourist," and supposedly official; "courtesy" or "special," for favored travelers; "diplomatic" or "super-special," for favored visitors; and, if one has nerve, "black market" or "extraordinary," in instances where his francs or pounds fall illegally into the hands of nationals who may eventually be able to spend them somehow on the other side of the "curtain." Officially, therefore, even legitimate, non-black market rates may differ as much as 300% or so, depending upon how the East European government feels at the moment about the Westerner whose money it is changing.)

From an economic perspective, therefore two monetary blocs and their output (money) do not, resonate with one another (except in highly mystical matters, like the price of gold.) And, in the postwar world, economic alliances proved to be the most reliable lubricants of cross-cultural and international intercourse between people whose other interests in life seemed widely disparate. A curtain (not iron) *was* indeed drawn in commercial matters. But commerce in Europe did not depend upon the actual or potential wealth of *either* currency bloc. Rather, it centered mostly upon monetary speculation and manipulation in the West and government decree in the East. One may sympathize with a hypothetical Arabian Sultan, accordingly, conjecturing, at the moment, about whether to sell his petroleum to the USA or to the USSR. A hedged bet would be to sell half to each; but, as the world's economies are turning, losses on one side might well wipe out gains on the other. At any rate, the *economic* Iron Curtain is a real curtain—not impermeable nor metallic, but firm. It is made of a strong fabric, imported Polich hams and Russian vodka flowing West-ward notwithstanding.

Second, military realities seemed also to create a continual waxing and waning of antagonisms and tentative friendships along the various national boundaries of Europe within the bailiwicks either of NATO or Warsaw Pact nations. This antagonism was (and is) symbolized by the highly visible American presence (soldiers, airmen, sailors, lots of hardware and —supposedly accidentally—well-publicized "war games") in the West, and by similar Soviet sabre displays and rattlings in the East.

We say they "seemed to create" a state of confrontation, because the military muscularity displayed by both sides *may* well relate but superficially to the *real* potential military power of either bloc. Tanks, munitions and jet airplanes and—most of all—the presence of men in uniforms, mount fierce and impressive war dances. But they are all symbols of *yesterday's* military potency, the true strategic force of which *may* deal more in illusions and the exploitation of fear than genuine destructive potential. NATO air circuses and Soviet tanks possess genuine *symbolic* power, but symbolic power only. The *real* military questions of the Cold War have *always* centered on the covert, distant stockpiling of nuclear weaponry, the temperature of the psychological climate at conferences like the Strategic Arms Limitation Talks, and meticulous research, quietly conducted in the tranquil atmosphere of scientific laboratories, where biologists and chemists continue pursuits into technologies with horrific military implications—all matters that simply *cannot* be legislated into oblivion or wished away, especially unilaterally. The inexorable advance of science and technology does not, as A. N. Whitehead once observed, pay much attention to the agreements that men make about decorous behavior in their relatively peaceful moods and moments. And the military might of both the East and West may, today, be under the control of men in military garb to a *lesser* extent than in the hands of overtly peaceful souls wearing white laboratory coats.

The military aspect of the Cold War has been, therefore, since World War II, about one part active muscle to three parts (at least) well-organized showmanship—and nobody is more acutely aware of this today than military men themselves, whether they speak English, French, German or Russian. It merely does not fall to their advantage to advertise their knowledge.

Third, the Iron Curtain has, indeed, also curtailed the so-called "flow of information, knowledge and cultural exchange" between East and West, although it has never (international meta-propagandists aside), even come near eliminating it. Nor in the pre-Cold War (meaning before World War II) days, was this "flow," at any time in any way, impressive or extensive, except insofar as it concerned minor strata of the societies involved: usually the intelligentsia (that always and everywhere fancies itself "international") and the upper social and economic classes.

In the dying days of the Czars, Greater Russia was hardly drawn into the mainstream of French, British or American culture merely because English and French were spoken at the Winter Palace, or—after the Revolution—because Stanislavsky held forth to his disciples from the West in Paris salons, or because film-maker Sergei Eisenstein worked in Hollywood and Mexico. Granting Czechoslovakia's classical Bohemian and Moravian Western heritages, and the great eras of internationalism that came and departed centuries ago in countries like Poland, lines of communication between East and West Europe have, for centuries, been spotty. And whatever cultural exchange it involved was confined largely to politics, the arts and the internationalism of academia and aristocracy—not to critical life-styles, values and pressing concerns of either the middle class or the common man in the East or West.

In many ways, the Iron Curtain was, therefore, metaphorically slammed down upon conduits of inter-cultural communication that never existed in the first place. Oligarchical communists had just imposed both legal impositions and arbitrary limitations (or censorship) upon freedoms that had never been current for long in their native lands, except for short periods of unsuccessful flirtation with democracy after World War I in some instances. And, to top off the irony, organizations like RFE and RL (and the British Empire Service, the USIA and others) set themselves grimly and humorlessly to *restoring* personal liberties and cultural freedoms that East Europeans had never known. These "rights" could hardly have been perceived, therefore, by millions of astute East Europeans as inherent *civil* "rights" worth agonizing too much over, considering the pressures that so many of them have withstood so long simply to survive. Ethnocentric idealism in the West, however, could not help but encourage idealists to hanker after an era of "free exchange" and "libertarianism" for the East that, they felt, must once have flourished, even though it had not.

More than once in their histories, therefore, both RFE and RL have found themselves giving air-time and voice to former "hometown" factions much *less* libertarian, progressive and/or democratic than current ruling powers in the supposedly muted and shackled societies to which they were currently broadcasting. No shortage of such factions exist, even today. They are made up mostly of former adherents (and their heirs) of deposed nobilities, intellectual pretzel-benders (who had been driven from their homelands both *before* and *after* World War II), military higher-ups whose various quondam *coups d'etat* misfired, and even unrecognized (or identified) ex-Nazi collaborators whose latter-day exculpations involved sudden love affairs with freedom from the "tyranny and slavery" of—when all is said and done—communist governments that have (taken together and in the long run) often turned out to be *less* tyrannical and oppressive (at various times in various regions) than right-wing doomsayers predicted a generation ago—much to the distress of that same right wing. Worse, these governments have also survived in apparent health, and have even produced remarkable symptoms of intellectual and material progress in nations that had supposedly fallen into both economic and cultural degeneracy.

East Europe is not, of course, a seamless fabric (any more than West Europe is), even as it lives today under ubiquitous Politburo hegemony. From the perspectives of RFE and RL, however, does East Europe merit the special attention of the American taxpayer to the tune of $40 million a year for persuasive objectives *alone*? (Senator Fulbright says it does *not*.) And just what may (or do) the "free flow" of voices from the West, spoken in the cultural idiom of the East, mean to the people of the United States, to say nothing of those in East Europe itself?

Before we examine this picture, we must write off from our considerations East Germany, which is not, and never has been, the concern of either RFE or RL. Why? Well—for reasons as complex as Joycean prose. East Germany is the cross-cultural, psychological and geographic concern of West Germany (and vice-versa), has been for years, and will be until (and if) Germany is ever re-unified. Dismissals like this are called *Realpolitik* by academic political scientists. The term saves words and settles arguments. East Germany remains the last unexploded booby-trap of World War II despite recent agreements on partition and admission to the UN.

Czechoslovakia is, of course, still suffering the results of the abrupt end, in the spring of 1970, of its long, hankering Westward look at its end, under the Dubcek government, for political and economic reformism. This Westward gaze was interpreted (probably correctly) by the Kremlim oligarchy as an attempt by Czechoslovakia to slide unnoticed out of the Warsaw Pact and into the mainstream of economic and cultural prosperity of its NATO neighbors, a move that had been terminated in fact, but not in aspirations, by a minor, dramatic Soviet invasion in 1968. The present Husak government has now set for itself the target date of 1975 to establish a nationwide system of "political re-education" that is supposed to prevent such disquieting deviations in the future before they start. The Czechs, however, are reluctantly difficult to re-educate. And, because of proximity alone, millions of them are exposed to Western radio, television and endless capitalist corruptions of other kinds. Certainly the Czechs, and probably the Slovaks, will remain thorns in the ideological arm of the Politburo for a long time without encouragement from foreign persuaders.

Poland, Hungary and Rumania are today in much the same boat vis-a-vis the Soviet Union. The leaders of all three nations, Poland's apparently popular Gierek, Hungary's clever Kadar, and Rumania's stormy, independent Ceausescu, keep their political hands full, appeasing popular demands for ideological economic liberalization (meaning, usually, fewer or more government controls on the economy) and, at the same time, playing their role as Soviet puppets. In all these countries, Poland in particular, important eyes are looking West and, most specifically, at the USA with both questionable envy and querulous compassion.

In the light of recent signs of *detente* between Washington and Moscow, the USSR seems to be demanding from these nations increased overt displays of loyalty. It has accelerated its perpetual Agitprop machine, lest Rumanians, Poles or Hungarians get the idea that they too may soon grab the Kremlin's coattails and profit apace and equally with the USSR from increased trade, tourism and the mixed benefits of cultural intercourse with the West.

These are war-weary, world-weary nations, however. Their people are unbelievably (to Western eyes) adaptable to shifting of political winds. This malleability has been learned in a long, long battle simply to survive. In the end, they have probably lost whatever hopes they may have had, in the lifetimes of their adult present populations, of truly joining the West in economic, military or cultural enterprises, except su-

perficially. They find that accommodation to constant reminders of Soviet power is also difficult. But these East Europeans
are also *clever* and, largely, sophisticated people, capable of
swallowing and mouthing *enormous* amounts of ideology and
propaganda and, at the same time, acting immediately in ways
contrary to their verbal professions and pretenses. Americans
tend to react sentimentally to this trait, because it underscores
the many ties the US has had, over the years, with these nations. But Eastern cynicism works two ways: Polish, Hungarian and Rumanian flattery and (often) naïve admiration of the
West may, at a moment's notice, curdle into hostility, contin-
gent not upon how the West treats them or how they treat
themselves, but mainly upon the manner in which the USSR
handles its Eastern empire.

Bulgaria remains the staunchest of the USSR's ideological
allies. Rumblings of discontent frequently may be heard now
and then among Bulgarian writers and some politicians. But,
all in all, most experts consider Bulgaria a more orthodox Len-
inist-Stalinist nation than the USSR itself, and little evidence
contradicts them. Attitudes towards the West will change only
if, and when, the new East-West *detente* modifies both *official*
Soviet positions and ideology concerning her capitalist competitors. Should this occur, Bulgarians will probably react even
more slowly then her Soviet masters to any positive change in
the cross-cultural climate.

The USSR, if we are to believe the American press, is
today a nation shot-through with dissent, populated by icono-
clastic writers, poets, physicists, biologists, artists, Greek Orthodox Christians, Jews and other free spirits who spend their
days and nights noisily chafing under Soviet oppression. This
wishful thinking is, of course, nonsense. As RL recognized officially years ago, chances that an impetus for counter-revolution may be generated in the forseeable future in the USSR,
even by its most disaffected citizens, are nil. A revolution in
the USA is more likely. Dissent and argument seem as natural

to the Russian character as to the American brand. Except in wartime, journalists have as little trouble finding evidence of it in major Russian cities as in New York or Los Angeles.

Lately, malcontents of many kinds in the USSR have taken to handcopying, printing or recording on tape, proscribed literary works, articles and other materials and distributing them pretty widely in a manner not unlike the recent American "underground" (or guerilla) press and television movement in its early days. Called *samizdat* (or *magnitzdat*, in the case of tape recordings), this modification of the old mimeograph machine in the cellar has hardly reached industrial proportions—a couple of thousand *samizdat* have recently reached the West. *Samizdat* is clear evidence, not of a new groundswell of counter-revolution in the USSR, but that, despite internal Soviet censorship and indoctrination, the honorable and historical Russian tradition of intellectual subversion is not dead.

What *is* comparatively new in the USSR, is the current period of toleration of the *physical* presence of dissenters like Solzhenitsyn and scientist Andrei D. Sakharov in major cities, cultural centers and places other than upper Siberia, even though their work and ideas are often given little currency within the USSR (except by *samizdat*). Few though they are, these visible socio-political critics provide endless copy for Western journalists, who are forever on the ready to listen to Soviet nay-saying and give it inordinate amounts of publicity. But the Mendvedevs (and others) evidently do not create waves within the USSR powerful enough to upset the public tranquility or disturb the power of the Soviet governing oligarchy and its managerial bureaucrats, much less the Soviet people themselves.

So, all in all, the "Iron Curtain" was, from the start, a punk metaphor! And the "Cold War" always meant one thing in the USA and another in East Europe, as we shall see. This reappraisal of both metaphors sets the stage for our careful considerations below of both Radio Free Europe and Radio Liberty today.

Talking to the East

The future of RFE and RL depend, in large measure, upon how the Congress of the United States feels at any moment about psychological warfare directed to East Europe—its mode, its objectives, its costs in the coming years. Why, they might (and sometimes do) ask, does the USA not support a Radio Free China, Radio Free Cuba (such an organization existed once and may still be on the air), or Radio Free Uganda, Radio Free Chile—or Radio Free Tibet, for that matter?

That this crucial congressional decision—"crucial" in psychological terms—hinges on such crude questions is unfortunate, less related to the sustained future of the RL and RFE services themselves, than because the questions sidestep the issue at heart: If the Iron Curtain has indeed been a catch-phrase cover for military, economic and propaganda standoff between two ideological spheres of influence in Europe for nearly twenty years—and if The Cold War has neither been cold nor a war—what the hell *has been* going on all this time? And what excuses may one unearth for implementing agencies of yesterday's myths into a future that seems to demand the destruction of these same myths?

The gentlemen who operate (for all practical purposes) RFE and RL claim to know the answers to these questions. But they seem both conditioned and doomed to answer them by reflex in yesterday's terms, only occasionally breaking their familiar spiels long enough to indicate that they know the score, even if they are not reporting it fully and candidly to their supporters and/or detractors.

RFE's main ostensible, front-office weakness is that it is—and always has been—in love with *surveys* ("Research and Analysis" are the key words) that show how effective its persuasion is in the five East European nations to which it broad-

casts. These studies are legion.[6] They center on the following:
(1) Reactions to RFE by the press, invariably government controlled, within the target nations to their operation—reactions
that mean little, if anything, precisely because they reflect the
official policies and directives of ideological bureaucrats sacculated, for the most part, inside government agencies. (2) Responses to RFE broadcasts on East European radio and television, local and international, again inevitably reflecting merely
attitudes and policies of the governing elite that control these
communications. (3) Public opinion surveys that, from their assumptions to conclusions, should make even a neophyte student of social science research cringe in embarrassment. These
surveys and polls, almost every one, are so "contaminated" (a
sociological euphemism for the word "lousy") that one wonders
how and why they have lived and proliferated for as long as
they have, except for the fact that they are the *best* data RFE
has concerning its effectiveness within its power to produce.
The most recent clutch of them have been duly reported and
certified for reliability by Dr. Lorand B. Szalay, of the American Institute for Research, and have been given the imprima-
tur of Oliver Quale and Company, New York opinion analysis
merchants, as well as a number of "Public Opinion Institutes"
(haruspices in the "public opinion" business almost invariably
call themselves "Institutes") in Vienna, Copenhagen, Stock-
holm, London, Paris and Athens.

The pedigrees are fine window dressing, and so is the
more or less objective way RFE farms its question-asking out
to independent researchers and organizations. But the results
are sheer "crap," in the original sense of the word, because the
wine of RFE's effectiveness (if it has any) remains locked
within the minds and hearts of uncounted and uncountable
people its researchers will *never* meet, while its official inspec-
tors scrutinize with "rigidly scientific instruments" (sociological
patois for "intensive, loaded questions") the dregs of dregs:
etymologically "crap."

To the peeled eye, RFE's "own methodology for assessing

East European public opinion," in the organization's words, is a home-brewed brand of crackpot pseudo-scientism they call "CONTINUAL AND COMPARATIVE SAMPLING" (sic; RFE's capitals) of thousands of interviews of *exactly the wrong people:* East Europeans traveling in Western Europe! [7] These are *rara aves*, at best, who are moving, many of them, on short, tight leashes, for *special reasons* of one sort or another. Otherwise, they would not be permitted to travel to Western Europe, of course. Reasons for their presence in Western Europe are invariably the CRITICAL MISSING INFORMATION (sic; *our* capitals this time) in RFE's surveys.

These interviewees are then sorted out according to standard sociological categories of attitude and opinion determinants in *non-comparable* American opinion surveys (age, sex, education, *verbal* reports of political orientation etc.), all more or less irrelevant to what RFE *should want to know* about its highly specialized, extremely selective and necessarily distorted sample of respondents. These informants are next plied with all manner of leading questions, some of them, to the sociologist's eye, bordering on the absurd. *Sample:* "Why do you like Radio Free Europe?" [8]

The results of this sort of biased (and rather silly) inquisition are then carefully quantified and reported in neat statistical charts and tables that—surprise!—prove (!) clearly that RFE is a potent force in the political, religious, ideological and day-to-day lives of thirty-one million (not thirty million or thirty-three million!) East Europeans, one way or another. Love affairs with social scientific techniques, manhandled as they are by RFE, are not likely to provide the organization with much good will among politicians and others sensitive to the numerous nuances of public opinion research.

The fact that RFE's broadcasts are usually jammed in Bulgaria and Czechoslovakia, sometimes jammed in Hungary and Poland, and never jammed in Rumania (if RFE's reports on its own jamming are accurate), does indeed tell one *much* more about its impact—or potential impact—in these countries than its reams of scientific research. It examines the right things: the attitudes of national politicians towards RFE in terms of the actual damage they fear it might create among their people to their own aims and objectives at a given time. It is, however, but *one* straw in the wind.

Radio Liberty's attempts at research and public opinion sampling are no better than Radio Free Europe's. RL is simply more modest than RFE, produces less documentation, less piles of questionable statistics and assumes less of an objective, scientific posture when you bring up the matter of listeners re-actions to its broadcasts. RL must therefore be esteemed more highly in this concern than its less humble counterpart. Neither organization's evaluations of its own operations has succeeded, over the years, in convincing many uninvolved social scientists of the validity or reliability (again, social science talk for "relevance" or "accuracy") of their own estimations, *in toto*, of their *results* in international persuasion.

So much then, for the sociological over-kill that consti-tutes, by virtue of its simultaneous glut and flimsiness, both RFE and RL's worst arguments for their own futures. Let us turn instead to people, who invariably make better cases for practical policies than statistics and documentation.

According to J. Allan Hovey Jr., vice president of RFE, who functions as director of its New York Headquarters, the service's main future function will be to fill the "information gap" that faces the average citizen in East Europe today. Like RL, RFE prides itself, not only on providing information and analysis not obtainable in the five Soviet bloc nations, but also discussion of political and ideological matters that the Voice of America (as an "official" US government broadcasting agency) *cannot* deal in.

Sitting in shirt sleeves rolled up, informal, intense, in a new office still being furnished, Hoving told us: "We consider ourselves complementary to the 'Voice.'" Hovey assumes, of course, that listeners abroad are inclined to make the same kind of fine distinctions between "official" and "unofficial" sources of American information and persuasion that he does from his midtown New York office. This is unlikely.

On ideological matters, Hovey is a bit more specific, echoing a theme that American East European scholars have been chewing on ever since Messrs. Nixon and Brezshnev signed their Joint Declaration of Principles in Moscow in 1972, thereby creating an ostensible *detente* that may see the end of the Cold War mentality that has existed for so many years between the United States and the USSR.[9]

"Words like '*detente*' and '*coexistence*' can be misleading," insists Hovey sternly, "as misleading as the term 'Cold War' itself was. In East Europe, *detente* does not connote any relaxation of Soviet *ideological* pressure on her five satellite nations. It simply means that the five satellite nations expect greater trade, military alliances, and, I suppose, cultural exchange with the West—although it doesn't look that way at the moment.

"Most important, however, the ideological thrust of European communism will *not* be affected by this new aspect of coexistence with the West, especially as the USSR exercises her imperialistic instincts in Europe and elsewhere. In the West, we tend to think of the terms '*detente*' and '*coexistence*' as meaning the end of a war of ideologies, of which RFE has been, of course, a major part. We have all kinds of unrealistic visions of communist governments in the East surrendering their old notions about the inevitable triumph of international communism, one way or another. Well, they haven't up to today and, believe me, they won't. The case for RFE rests upon the fact that the *need* within Czechoslovakia, Hungary, Poland, Rumania, and even Bulgaria, for a fresh breath of counter-ideology will inevitably be just as great tomorrow in an era of *detente*—if it ever comes—as it was yesterday in the worst days of the old Cold War. Senator Fulbright doesn't seem to realize this—although, in the last analysis, he's good medicine for RFE. He keeps us alert and makes sure that our eyes are on our objectives." With a serious smile he thumped his desk with his fist and drove home his point.

Howland H. Sargeant, the polished, articulate director of Radio Liberty, makes much the same case for the Soviet-oriented agency without desk-thumping. Sargeant is a diplomat to his fingertips, a veteran foreign service advisor, and an expert on Soviet affairs whose lucid arguments for continuing RL's broadcasts flow from his discourse. His office, his person and his conversation reflect a pristine and deliberate immaculateness.

Says Sargeant, "RL has built up credibility within the USSR and, as I see it, holds today the potential power to *enhance* an era of *coexistence* rather than hinder it. The reason is simple and clear. The Russian leaders see *detente* in pragmatic terms. Here in the USA we see it as largely a psychological matter—like transactional or Essalin therapy: better communications, mutual understanding between people and so forth. All good and well, but as *ideological* differences sharpen between the USA and the USSR in the next few years, and I think they will, it will be up to RL to explain to sympathetic ears overseas that the United States remains steadfastly repelled by *any* ideology that does not permit non-conformism and civil liberties, no matter how well she gets along with such a nation diplomatically and economically.

"Also, it is reassuring to many Soviet ears to be able to listen to a broadcasting service that puts world events into meaningful perspective, independent of the Kremlin's 'official version', so that a Soviet citizen may reach a judgment of his own concerning matters that effect him. This simple charge has been, and is, given to Radio Liberty and defined by the President of the USA as commensurate with his own efforts at achieving *coexistence*."

Like Hovey, Sargeant points to the many, many times that RL has "scooped" the Soviet press itself in bringing local news to Russians before their own newspapers, radio and television stations have, citing specific examples with considerable pride. Exactly *why* Sargeant—and RL in general—takes such enormous pride in the *speed* of its news dissemination is unclear, however. "Deadlines" and "scoops" are life-and-death matters to American (and other Western) journalists who work on daily newspapers, news-magazines and for radio and television news departments. They mean considerably less to many journalists in other cultures. Most news, even (or especially) important news, may (and should) well wait an opportunity to be verified, and often requires more time-consuming analysis and cross-checking than American newsmen, in their rush to publish, actually give it. Where RL serves the Soviet Union best, Sargeant knows, is in providing news and opinion, no matter how dated or stale, that will *never* appear in today's strictly controlled Soviet press.

Also like Hovey, Sargeant minimizes to nothing the role that the CIA has played in RL's most active years. He also dismisses, a bit too glibly, the notion that RFE and RL might combine resources. "We're different operations," he says, "although we trade information and materials. Look at it this way: our coverage must extend in point-to-point (that is, from transmitter to receiver) broadcasting that covers an area of six million square miles. RFE covers an area of one-quarter of a million square miles. In the matter of technical operations alone, we are hardly comparable. And if you know anything about radio transmission, you will understand why a combination of the two, at this late stage in the game, is a false economy that might well cost more than it would save."

"Late stage in the game, Mr. Sargeant?"

"Yes, I said 'late stage', but lateness is relative." Sargeant is not only administrator, he is a pragmatist-philosopher. Those who have seen him in action know that he is not prone to self-deceit or voluntaristic thinking. Sargeant is RL's (and probably RFE's) best secret weapon, mainly because he is more than a match for any US Senator or Investigating Committee in Washington. He is an idealistic strategist of the possible and, if necessary, the inevitable.

"I don't know when," says Sargeant "and I can't speak for RFE, but, at one or another point in the progress of America's relationship with East Europe, Radio Liberty will—must—activate the long-term suicide pact it made with the future the day it was born. I take that back: *include* Radio Free Europe. Somewhere in the coming years—and, frankly, I hope sooner rather than later—*both* broadcasting services will turn off the power. And no other Voice will be *needed* from America in Communist Europe than the 'Voice of America'. "

With a knowing smile, Sargeant states "This will happen on the day that the USSR realizes the futility of censorship and the idiocy of trying to control the things about which people *think!* Then there will be no need for RL, naturally. And once our friends in Red Square recognize the inevitable, their counterparts in the entire Soviet bloc will naturally follow their lead—even in Bulgaria. Then what possible function may RL perform? Or RFE? The USIA will be busy interpreting American life and policy in its broadcasts for the East. And what might RL add? There will be no 'information gap' to fill. *Coexistence* and *detente* will be understood by the Soviets the way *we* think of it—possibly not so sentimentally—and both the United States and the Soviet Union will take their chances with destiny with all their political, military and ideological cards on the table. At that moment, the Cold War will *really* be over—without a winner."

Sargeant is entirely correct. But the *War of Ideas* will not end with the death of Radio Liberty—or Radio Free Europe. He knows this too.

Nor will the free flow of information within East Europe ameliorate, by some cross-cultural magic, the economic, military or psychological differences the man in the street in Belgrade, Prague or Moscow feels today when he looks West. Nor will it calm his fears of a re-united Germany, or a permanently divided one, or of an over-reactive America and a competitive Orient turned Red, but not *his* shade of Red. The earth of East Europe has soaked up too much blood for too many centuries to find the peace for which it now thirsts so easily, either in the mechanics of its Marxist textbooks *or* (outside the USSR) by coexisting with a capitalist world that (for all its attractions) still repels its conscience because of the brutalities of World War II. Memories that we have lost in the West but are still green in the East.

Sargeant is correct. Power *will* shift. And as the monster moves, RL and RFE *will,* in time, disappear. But other means will also, by then, be found to accomplish their same ends. The words *"detente"* and *"coexistence"* subsequently will fall into the same desuetude as "Iron Curtain" and "Cold War." They will be replaced by new terms describing power shifts and ideological confrontations we cannot now possibly anticipate, nor are our computers able to predict them for us.

At the least, the United States must be prepared for these changes—not as urgently, we think, with guns and bombs as with strategies and ideologies of our own that will withstand the bold challenges they are certain to receive at the hands of the future. At present, we apparently have none—or still rely upon old ones that ring hollow and empty. Like Sargeant and Hovey, we, the authors, would prefer the philosophical course, to build our camps on libertarian soil and extol what is in fact the *absence* of ideology: civil ideals of dissent, freedom and libertarian idealism. By all means, we join them in *preferring* faith, the faith that man left to his own devices will save his soul, his nation and his money, and repel the tyrannies, whether grounded in Rightist or Leftist dogma, that make him impotent by keeping him ignorant. We *want* to believe that men both thirst for and deserve the free currency of thoughts, ideals and faith.

Maybe they do.

Maybe not!

But the USA can do better in putting its money where it

professes its mouth is next time—if we are lucky, and if we have a next time. If given another chance, let us hope that we shall not find it expedient again to hide our convictions behind a curtain of domestic lies woven of chauvinistic do-goodism. A cheap Tin Curtain is no prettier, after all, than an Iron Curtain, even if both are figures of speech. How credible will the word of the United States be in tomorrow's forum if, like Public Relations rabbits, we hide forever the courage of our convictions in secret budgets and compose fictions about "interested parties" and phony philanthropies? In the *War of Ideas*, the voices with sticking power are those that speak openly, consistently and, within reason, honestly. All the rest, in the long run, must, in time, stutter and stumble and on the consequences of their own tissues of little white lies.

NOTES TO CHAPTER 7

[1] Various versions of this speech abound. This quotation is taken from *The New York Times*, August 25, 1972, p. 2.

[2] See Robert T. Holt, *Radio Liberty* (Minneapolis: University of Minnesota Press, 1958), and Allan A. Mitchie, *Voices Through the Iron Curtain: The Radio Free Europe Story* (New York: Dodd, Mead and Co., 1966). Gordon, Falk and Hodapp helped to promulgate the official RFE-RL "line" (albeit a bit skeptically) in *The Idea Invaders*, pp. 164–184.

[3] This entire story finally reached the floor of Congress on September 14th and 21st, 1971, where it was recorded both in full (deadpan) and with plenty of supporting evidence. See *Hearings Before the Committee on Foreign Affairs, Ninety-Second Congress, on HR 9330, 9637, 10590 and 518 To Grant Support To the Activities of Private American Organizations Engaged in the Fields of Communication with Foreign Powers.* (Washington: U.S. Government Printing Office, 1971). Printed in full, the testimony is entitled, *Radio Free Europe and Radio Liberty*, and has been published separately from other hearings as document No. 67-774.

⁴ The results of this study, which might, by stretching a term, be called a "content count," is published in Xerox by RFE apparently for its own use. No author; no date; no given publisher.

⁵ Proceedings and Debates of the 92nd Congress, Second Session, *Congressional Record:* The Senate, Vol. 118, No. 33, March 6, 1972, subtitled "Radio Free Europe and Radio Liberty" (Washington: U.S. Government Printing Office, 1972).

⁶ The following material was gleaned, in large measure, from James R. Price's obviously partisan, but nevertheless painfully detailed and well documented, study, *Radio Free Europe—A Survey and Analysis* (Washington D.C.: Congressional Research Service, The Library of Congress, 1972), issued in Xerox. Price is an analyst in National Defense for the Foreign Affairs Service of the Congressional Research Service, and a master at turning forests into hoards of trees. He also apparently believes everything anybody tells him is true, a scholarly trait to note.

⁷ *Ibid.,* p. 155.

⁸ *Ibid.,* Appendix 2, Table 3, no page.

⁹ See, for instance, the analysis and suggestions about what this era may portend in the article by Brian Crozier of the London Institute for the Study of Conflict, "The End of the Cold War?," *The National Review*, March 16, 1973, pp. 304–307, 327–328.

8

The Sound of Money

London (*Slow*) **Broil** (**1972**)

The pale sales clerk, looking more like an Oxford undergraduate than a merchant in men's-wear, surveyed the pear-shaped American traveler.

"Looks just right, sir," he said cheerfully. "Perfect fit all around."

The American peered past the full-length mirror into the morning crowd of passers-by. The weather had turned unseasonably warm. The men were not wearing top coats.

"I look, I suppose," he replied flatly, "like James Bond."

"Oh, no!" the clerk frowned. "Begging your pardon, sir, James Bond *never* wore a trench coat."

"In the novels?"

The clerk was entirely certain. "No sir! Neither the films nor the novels. No mention made of trench coats. We have made quite certain. Our firm, after all, makes *the* trench coat. We would have noticed."

The American looked again at his reflection in the mirror. "I suppose I meant Mike Hammer. Or Bogart." There was no resemblance.

"Likely sir," responded the clerk stiffly. "Wear it or box it, sir? And how do you wish to make your payment, sir?"

"Box it, I suppose. You take traveler's checks—American Express?"

The clerk smiled discreetly and helped his customer slip out of the clean, gray garment. "Right over here sir." He slid behind a Sheratonish table. "Dollars, of course. Now just a moment while I check the exchange rate." He scrutinized a card. "That will be two-hundred-sixty-five to one, as of this morning, sir."

The American blinked. "Two-sixty-five to one *what?*"

"Why, dollars to the pound, sir. The cost is sixty pounds, sir, and, as I calculate, one hundred and fifty-nine American dollars. You can't beat it, sir, in London—not for an authentic trench coat like that. Quality, sir, quality—and you can't blame the tailor for the rate of exchange."

The American purchased the coat, or rather its Regent Street label.

He did not know, of course, that four days and many jet-miles later he might have bought exactly the same coat at one of Madison Avenue's prestige men's stores in New York City for exactly $15.10 less than he paid in London, minus Regent Street label, but also inclusive of city sales tax.

The International Cash Register

Once upon a time, Britannia ruled the waves, and the American dollar ruled international commerce. Today, judging by the registry of most of the ships in the world's busiest harbors, Liberia rules the waves. The American dollar seems to rule nothing beyond the North American continent. And even there, its diminishing potency challenges the power of American corporate nabobs, the banks and the Congress and probably the President of the United States.

From our parochial, Western Hemisphere perspective, America still leads the world in international trade. Her leadership is increasingly being challenged, however—but *not* by Japan or West Germany or the Common Market or competitors she can face head on. Her antagonist is the world of commerce itself: in the form of the *multi-national corporation,* that, whether it is titularly "American" or not, knows no international allegiance in its pursuit of profits. It merely diversifies, feeds itself upon and, in turn, feeds the economies of every nation it touches around the world.

The figure of $85 billion represents the (supposed) total overseas corporate investment by American business beyond the borders of the USA. This is probably both a conservative and incorrect figure, especially if one considers (and adds to it) tourist revenues and tax preferences (which are *not* paid for by overseas holdings) that would be levied if they had been incurred in the territory of the USA. Add to this, also, our military expenditures around the world that invariably show commercial force in foreign economies. For instance, since 1965 (the year they began), we have poured $109.5 billion into Indochina alone. (The source for this figure is *The New York*

Times, Sunday, April 1, 1973). It is also, unfortunately, a *meaningless* figure because it is so enormous that the human imagination cannot conceive of what it might—and does—actually purchase for the United States in the international marketplace, or *might* have been used for at home had it not been sent Eastward.[2]

Symptoms of the power of a mere $85 billion-plus (or its equivalent in one of the world's "harder" currencies today), churning in the economies of other nations, yield numerous not-so-pleasant manifestations in the USA in statistical, monetary and day-to-day affairs. It is felt most severely by the keepers of our so-called "balance of payments" ledgers. Our massive economy is, at any moment, doing burgeoning business overseas without a subsequent reasonably proportional return *into* the economy of the United States;—in effect, much of our money is on loan overseas at about zero (or slightly higher) interest rates. The official Department of Commerce figure for the entire "balance of payments" kit-and-caboodle appeared to be edging towards $10 billion in 1970, and has fluctuated somewhat since. But the international *imbalance* represents more than the entire national budget of some other nations, many of them more affluent than Latin American Banana Republics.[3]

Closer to the American nerve than abstract statistics are the immediate panics into which venerable American investment institutions—most notably our securities exchanges—have, in recent years, been immediately thrown, either when the American dollar abroad has been devalued (to diminish, at least on paper, the burden of this balance deficit) and/or when this massive mountain of dollars abroad spontaneously(?) —at the hands of money speculators selling "short"—loses its immediate value in comparison with other, less volatile and ubiquitous currencies.

Among American investors, apparently, confidence in the US economy deflates, at these times, immediately—both at home and abroad. Stocks (and even bonds) zoom down on Wall

Street. Panic hits the banking community overseas, and assets are transferred as fast as possible to "hard and fast" investments in mystical supra-national commodities like gold jewelry and coins, diamonds, stamp collections, art works and other bric-a-brac that are supposedly immune to the "impending collapse" of the American economy—as, one imagines, economists fear it is being hatched in a back-alley by the Gnomes of Zurich.

In pocketbook and wallet terms at home, the result is an inflationary jump in the price of foreign goods on Main Street, accompanied by a near unexplainable harmonic spasm in the cost of domestic goods and services, as well as other assorted gambits designed to compensate for the chaos, such as programs of higher wages, government handouts, subsidies, boosted interest rates and so forth. Mr. Average Citizen then naturally tries to brace his *own* little economic fortress against the fate of his dollars that, he imagines, are turning to dross in his hands. In short, the spectre of inflation materializes—caused, for the most part, not by factors *within* the American economic system, but rather as the result of America's new and intimate engagement with the economy of the rest of the world.

At one time, not so long ago, American currency—supposedly reflecting buried and well-secured gold reserves at more or less controlled prices—remained the one main and last bastion of true economic isolation on the home front. Well, our buried hoard of metals at Fort Knox has recently joined the free market. It now rides up and down the seesaw of the world's international speculative community, although, in the interest of sanity, direct speculation in gold is still forbidden (at this writing the proscription's days seem numbered) in the United States and our "official" gold prices at home have been arbitrarily pegged at about $42 an ounce. (Smart American investors manage to get around these prohibitions in various ways, however.) So we must still satisfy our mystical instincts with the next "best" thing to gold: silver. But the words "Silver

Certificates" (whatever "silver" was supposed to mean on them) have, these days, even been replaced on our single dollar bills by the integrity of the Federal Reserve Bank. So our domestic dollars are openly interventionists at last. And this is no secret to either the Treasury Department or the housewife's weekly budget.

All of this may sound absurdly abstract and removed from the nitty-gritty of international trade and commerce, but financial spasms are possibly the most rapid—and devastating—forms of international *communications* operating in the world today! And the United States (with its two major economic allies, Japan and West Germany) is *the* single nation that responds most dramatically and first to any overt changes, no matter how ephemeral, in overseas commerce that may affect American business in *any* manner. In truth, almost *all* financial intercourse between the nations involved in American commerce (excluding, therefore, only those communist states that do not do much business with us) *is* the biggest and most powerful arm of business in the American economy, involving not only that enormous part of it controlled directly by the federal government, but much of it in the private sector as well. The latter is even free to swing, oscillate and vacillate, apparently and in large measure, according to forces well beyond the effective control of Washington.

The latter is true because such an enormous share of total American financial and commercial interests abroad (aside from our specific balance of payments deficits) is controlled by private multicorporations in the form of overseas investments that are more or less immune, not only from the US Internal Revenue Service, but to almost any other kind of federal regulation by the United States. And should the US government attempt to manipulate this investment indirectly by means of restraints upon home-based, American nerve centers of these multi-corporations, each and every one of them (8,000 roughly, of which—at most—a quarter may be accurately called "global" in their spread) may effectively counter the governmental threats simply by making the motions of packing up its wares—and the affluence it spreads on home ground—to seek a more hospitable nation from which to operate. This simple threat of desertion is a most effective weapon against federal fiscal controls of American-based international businesses— a sharp one that *works!*

All international multi-corporations are not, by any means, American. But the basic sovereignty of *any* such financial giant anywhere in the world is not a significant matter, because its economic involvements are crucial and primarily important only to its *own* corporate health and destiny, not to the particular place it has hung its operational hat or located its corporate headquarters. True enough, the Japanese electronics industry, for instance, has lately been cultivating new markets, far distant from its best customer, the USA, for its wares (and is, at the moment, doing so with intensity for good reasons.) But the mere *whisper* of a ten per cent tariff that *might* be placed upon Japanese (and other foreign) imports during the summer of 1971 (as part of Nixon's Phase I economic policy) was a matter of state of the highest priority in Nippon (to say nothing of Canada.) The international implications of the impending imposition caused the USA to reconsider, and then to forget, the tariff scheme and, at the same time, activated diplomats of the highest stature to scurrying between Washington and Tokyo in near-hysteria.

While *all* major multi-national corporations—Unilever, Volkswagen and various international banking firms for instance—do not live in a state of critical mutual symbiosis with the USA, American markets (primarily), capital, heavy machinery, raw materials, automobiles and other impedimenta, are important enough to these foreign corporations to impel them to subsume their national allegiances (at times) to the internationalism of their corporate enterprises—or, more accurately, to the *international, multi-corporate* business community, which, at present, is largely made up of American conglomerates.

Even on the psychological front, one discovers the paradox in which the international multi-corporation lives: American techniques and American business, for instance, are just outgrowing the United States. Titular "American" advertising agencies operate hundreds of overseas branches, employing thousands of nationals, whose yearly billings hover around the $5 billion mark, most of it "supra-national" money, in that it remains in the country of origin. All but *two* of the top advertising merchants in the United States today operate overseas, either directly or through affiliates, especially giants like the J. Walter Thompson Company—whose former executives, incidentally, have *also* found their way to the top echelons of American government. (Half-a-dozen or so were working in early 1973 as high-level White House aides to President Nixon.) Agencies like Thompson are involved overseas, not only in local huckstering, but in various types of public relations work as well for the Nixon Administration (meaning the USA) for formidable fees.

What advertising agencies export, of course, is American "know-how." And this aspect of life in the USA has been gobbled up most avidly by highly industrialized nations like Japan, Britain, West Germany and other countries where production capacity is high, affluence fairly general, but consumer demands appear to require the same kinds of kiddie-carnival techniques that have reached near mathematical perfection at the hands of our Madison Avenue tycoons.[4]

One might expect this world-wide penetration of American business techniques, American corporate style *and* American selling techniques—to say nothing of American technology and production methods—to have provided for the USA, by 1973 A.D., a steely grip upon the international cash register and effective control of international business. This is what oracles of international finance were noisily predicting seven, ten, fifteen and twenty years ago—and some of them act today as if their predictions have come true. But they were and are *wrong!*

As we have seen above, the main reason is that free enterprise business *per se* is able to afford national managerial allegiances only at times and in places when such loyalties permit maximum feasible profits for the particular corporate entity at hand. When the internationalization of an industry becomes the main reason for increased revenues and/or expansion, only *one* basic loyalty—and *one* alone—is at issue: allegiance to the balance sheet, with its profits and losses. Flag and soil are poor competitors. Invariably, the balance sheet wins.

Constellations of such victories (and the community of victors) have moved the world closer to the creation of functional supra-states than the United Nations has in its decades of equivocation and negotiation. As opposed to highly national UN game-players in the world body, economists and other representatives participating in the International Monetary Fund find themselves representing national ideologies and interests less and less and corporate welfare of their respective economies and multi-corporate interests more and more. Thus freed of any but the crudest national obligations—namely maximized profits and business and trade advantages—they can "talk turkey" in terms of profit motives, make commercial concessions, and draw up radical "deals," arrangements and concessions of types unthinkable to the conventional diplomat, hamstrung as he is by abstract policies and ideological alliances. (This is particularly true if he must operate in one of the United Nations' visible, open forums.)

Examples of this action, "diplomacy-of-the-buck," are legion: Euro-dollars are a radical departure from the ideologies and traditions of the proud nations of West Europe. But Euro-dollars have become an economic necessity. And so they shall indeed materialize. So much for tradition and ideology. Great Britain choked on bile before she finally joined the Common Market, mindful of the economic independence she had cherished and cultivated for centuries (with austere English national pride and rectitude) by generations of sons of the Empire. But join the Common Market she did, and participate she will, at the threat of economic exclusion from the supra-state economies to the East and their potential markets for British goods, and vice versa.

For a while to come, the IMF will indeed monkey around with the sliding currency scales to achieve rough forms of parity between Japanese yen, Italian lira, French francs and American dollars etc., and the fudging will work—for a time. But make no mistake, Euro-dollars will merely set the stage for World-dollars (or World-francs, -pounds or -lira), if only because world currency represents the *only* hope the IMF (or similar bodies that follow it) will have of dampening the kind of international currency speculation that forces British raincoats, for instance, to cost more (in American dollars) in London, England than in New York, New York. (But more on this subject later.)

Supra-nationalism has *not* become an idle dream, tossed on the trash heap of the UN building on New York's East River, back in the nineteen-fifties when nobody was paying attention. The international financial community does not esteem highly territorial boundaries. Big (and we mean *big*) business worships neither a flag nor a piece of printed currency, because neither is intrinsically a unit of trade and, *per se,* worth a damn to it. It pledges its allegiances to the sound of the cash register —the unmistakable noise that means business is being *done.*

All of this *should* mean that the nations of the world are, perforce, growing closer together, that age-old antagonisms are dying, and that the United States, still the most successful (or largest) mercantile nation in the West, sits in the cat-bird seat, because of her indispensible international role as master of modern technology, advertising and the arts and skills of world trade.

Well, it does not!

Business, as the old sage said, is business. And it is both complicated and ruthless. Sometimes it is also illogical.

Most of the industrial nations of the West are not highly sympathetic to the United States' balance of payments woes

—although some small non-Western nations are. (Thailand, for instance, a nation presently high on our foreign aid roster, recently *lent* the USA $100 million to even out our balance of payments with her.[5]) Nor do they appear unduly concerned that the lion's share of today's international multi-corporations are either American by birth, or are at the moment highly dependent upon America for their markets and/or manufacturing facilities and raw materials. These are all temporary arrangements that can be changed tomorrow at the behest of improved business techniques, and according to whatever inducements the global cheap labor and consumer goods markets may offer multi-corporations in the future.

By and large, America as an economic state is roundly *despised* everywhere in the globe, more disdained, probably, than Britain was at the height of that Empire's stability, which today has fallen apart. Ours is crumbling too, but, like the British, we prefer not to notice. The purr of our egos is louder to our ears than the noise of reality.

Why?

Foreign Aid in Fact and Fancy

One major factor that has influenced our position in the world's business community has been America's history of providing "foreign aid," a supremely misunderstood issue, as it has been translated from fact to newspaper copy. It remains today still another misnomer and vital factor in the difficulties we face in fiscal international relationships with other countries.[6]

Born in the matrix of World War II victory and its atmosphere of altruism, the term "foreign aid" still evokes in many, images of the bountiful Marshall Plan, bundles of wheat in the hands of starving European children and the rebuilding of farms, homes and factories amidst the rubble left by bombs and bazookas. In fact, so successful was this effort that the Congress of the United States voted, in 1953, to phase *down*-and-shortly-*out* America's foreign aid program—because its function, until this time mainly re-building war-torn economies, seemed to have been achieved. The target date for the death of America's foreign program was to be 1957, at which time extraordinary government appropriations for overseas preferred loans and gifts was to fall to zero.

In the years between 1953 and 1957, however, the focus of foreign aid was subtly changing from humanitarian to economic objectives and, bit by bit, to military matters as well. In the end, the picture was startlingly clear. America's military security—judged mostly by old-fashioned, non-nuclear warfare standards, except for our needs for missile launching sites and similar installations—now seemed to demand that, in one way or another, we finance either all or some part of both defensive and offensive forces of some *sixty-seven* other nations. Each one was understood to be *vital* to the military defense and economic advantage of the United States for various and complex reasons (many more than sixty-seven), some of them, it turned out, more political than military. (One would, for instance, be hard pressed, from *purely military* or *economic* perspectives, to defend America's long-term public investment in—or subsidy of—Israel's economy and army. *Political* reasons are manifold, although complicated.)

With the default of Congressional resolve to stick to its 1957 deadline, it was not difficult for military (mostly) advisors to talk ex-General, then President, Eisenhower to use his pressure upon Congress to, in effect, change its collective mind altogether. And, since 1957 (through one major stormy test of policy by President Kennedy in 1963), foreign aid has been an issue that generates enormous Congressional rhetoric on Capitol Hill. But it has become largely just one more of the critical international instruments subsumed by the White House into the executive arm of the government. Whenever foreign aid proposals have, in recent years, been made by the Presidents (usually with cuts and shifts here and there), after a certain amount of *pro forma* scrutiny, they are busily rushed through Congress with a good deal of noisy investigation and compromise and duly implemented at the Executive desk. The final appropriation for the year 1973, for instance, hovers around $2 billion, give or take a bit. (Note our balance of payments deficits, and remember that quite a bit of this money remains within foreign nations *as dollars* and adds up, year by year, to impressive sums.)

One might expect that this foreign aid would have, over the years, produced an enormous residue of good will for the USA around the world. This it has—to a degree: but only to that point at which the funds we send abroad are perceived as enhancing the national self-interest of those nations to which they are handed. But much of the good will we purchase *may* be—and is—neutralized by other factors. The positive psychological aspects of American foreign aid turns nugatory at exactly the moment that foreign nationals cease interpreting American largesse as altruistic, and realize that the US is purchasing political alliances, military compliances (and service, involving troop strength) and ideological deference. No price, we are discovering, is high enough to purchase national pride! This axiom explains why our foreign aid appropriations have not been able to purchase even fair weather friendship among our classical commercial and political allies, except at the grudging cost of their humiliation. And any nation—like most individuals—that must beg for its *pourboire* at the price of its self-respect and autonomy invariably ends despising its benefactor.

The general disposition of our foreign aid monies clarifies this puzzle better than aphorisms and paints a picture far different from memories that go back to the late nineteen-forties era of European and Asian recovery, a time of photographs in *Life* of bread sent to starving Italians and shiploads of rice for Orientals whose bone-ends tortured their skins.

In a recent year, three-quarters of a billion dollars went directly to the Pentagon for military assistance to Turkey (by virtue of her precarious and strategic position on the Soviet border), Jordan (our only reasonably reliable ally among the Arab states), South Korea, Cambodia and Thailand (bastions of containment—it says here—against Red China). Not a cent of the Pentagon's foreign aid funds was earmarked for South Vietnam; *direct* Defense Department appropriations were earmarked to cover her "needs"—to the tune of another $2 billion —in addition to whatever "supporting assistance" that she receives from the Agency for International Development's one-and-one-quarter billion dollars of foreign aid, money that the Pentagon never sees.

This latter lion's share of the pot (AID money) is spread around the globe according to "need." But "need" is a word that may be defined in many ways. It is most definitely *not* spent mainly to achieve "good will" among the world's masses, but rather to bolster up weak but friendly governments, provide our various military and economic allies with arms and materials to fight internal subversion (meaning mostly Communists) and to re-invigorate old alliances with more or less friendly governments in such places as Argentina (Peronist or otherwise), Algeria (worried about Tunisian imperialism), Tunisia (worried about Libyan imperialism), Ethiopia (where young Communists have lately been harassing Haile Selassie) and Ceylon (where insurgent rebels are studying guerilla tactics in the boondocks).

AID, which is largely responsible for the disposition of these funds, has used them for such worthy projects as highway construction to the ocean for land-locked African Third World nations. It should surprise nobody, however, that the bulk has, in recent years, flowed in the direction of Southeast Asia, as it will for many years to come. But Congress is just as likely as the President to construe economic aid in military-political terms at moments of panic. And, if our foreign aid money is not spent for such military and political objectives in one way, then our protean Executive branch and its Cabinet will surely find another way to distribute the pelf—more "foreign aid," but called something else. (The Military Authorization Bill of 1972 is but one example—a bill that actually died in conference, but which, nevertheless, was given *interim* funding of a *mere* $1.5 billion—until the day that it will probably rise from its ashes at some future Congress under some other name, particularly at this time, when America's participation in Vietnam's struggles no longer involves much manpower but requires mainly money and hardware.)

Now, all of this financial byplay and selective largesse *may be* brilliant military strategy. (We doubt this.) It may also bespeak a triumph of international political fiscal maneuvering in a domain of great sophistication and sensitivity about which we cannot possibly be cognizant because of Top Secret information closed to our scrutiny. (We doubt this too.)

Of this we *are* certain: it is money distributed in such a way that the "ill will" it can—and must—generate throughout the world outweighs the "good will," a consideration of *both* military and political significance. Or, as the Senate Appropriations Committee that (fruitlessly) killed the Military Authorization addition to our basic foreign aid commitment wrote with pith (and in vain):

> We cannot fail to provide adequate defense for our own country, but we can and should stop trying to underwrite military costs in 67 other countries. Buying friendship produces fickle allies and provides a corrupting influence for donor and recipient; needs are exaggerated, threats are invented and we become supporters of oppresive and brutal regimes which represent the exact opposite of every principle we hold dear.[7]

The Committee also implied that it is also *bad* business, highly detrimental both in the long and short run to America's position as an international commercial power. And that is its main relevance to the present chapter. Because most foreign aid, as it has evolved, is not commerce at all, but arbitrary influence-peddling with guns and political clout, it must defeat the very ends of commerce. It must also diminish the value of American currency and the potential power of trade to achieve international harmony between nations, West and East. The simple reason is that the USA has become a nation easier for other countries to *bleed* on spurious military and political grounds (in other words, to *blackmail*) than to do business with, *quid pro quo*.

When foreign aid—oh, so long ago—stood for the humanitarian idealism of the richest nation in the world, it meant *one* thing. As it stands today—an instrument for buying mercenary militarism and political manipulation (much of it as corrupt as it is fake) to prevent governmental upheavals (probably inevitable anyway) for dubious reasons, with arcane, unrealistic motives—it is another. This is, as we say, *bad* business, returns from which *we have already suffered* for the past decade or more—in Southeast Asia mostly, but in other places as well. (Remember the Dominican Republic?) To predict that it will serve our national self-interest as poorly in the future as in the past is not, therefore, irresponsible necromancy. It is common sense.

Foreign aid, as it is presently practiced, has also been, in effect, an albatross around the neck of America's commercial position with respect to almost every nation, save one or two loyal satellites with whom she is engaged in international commerce. Its influence under-rides all considerations made in this Chapter.

Trade, Tourism, Hard Economic Facts, and Other Fairy Tales

Partly because of the enormous impact of the USA's mercurial foreign policies, partly because modern conglomerates, production lines, advanced technology and advertising (associated, in some measure, incorrectly, all over the world with the United States and its culture), the USA is regarded globally as a materialistic megathon. The burden of wealth has carried with it opprobrium in some measure everywhere on the globe, and to the greatest in those nations most frightened or jealous of what they believe the USA stands for as a commerical nation.

In the business of business the United States has been for

over one hundred years a success. And for this sin her prede-
cessors at expert commercial enterprise, particularly the British, the Dutch, the Belgians, the Swiss, and other managers of
yesterday's now defunct mercantile empires, will never forgive
her. Most particularly, they despise her genius for effective
mass production and giantism in production, symbolized for
them by both the international multi-corporation and by Madison Avenue and the cultural fallout of both. That the multi-
corporation (and conglomerate) was a *British* invention (the
object of Bernard Shaw's wrath in prose and drama shortly
after the turn of the century), and the fact that many of the
world's major international conglomerates today are *not* American but Japanese, Swiss and English—as well as representative of other nations—does not erase this impression, current
today from Carnaby Street to Grant Road. In discussing the
national origins of heavy industry and merchants of death, foreign editorialists tend to forget the Krupps, Nobels and I. G.
Farben in favor of the DuPonts and Dows. Nor does one often
hear, in learned attacks upon America's propensity for the vul-
garities of advertising, the historical truth that advertising
(and journalism) were born in European broadsheets circulated centuries ago largely in Holland and England.

America's material wealth has been for too long and too
facilely associated with mythic images of a virgin nation, raped
and exploited by avaricious European settlers (dregs of humanity) who sat back and let profits fill their pockets, as they
bled the resources of their virgin continent, slaughtered Indians and imported yellow and black men to do their work for
them. Nothing is accomplished by citing the simultaneous imperialistic rapaciousness of European and Oriental imperialists
in counter-argument, except to provide considerable evidence
that America's commercial genius was *not* a stroke of geophysi-
cal fate, nor merely the concatination of avarice and luck.
America's commercial success largely resulted from her amazingly rapid modifications of many British industrial techniques
(and a few of her own) that threw a society into mass hypnosis

for a century, mesmerized by its own industrial genius—too distracted, unfortunately, to foresee wisely and patiently the international ramifications of its own success. America was, however, no less mindful of them than the British, Belgians or other colonial nations that were equally as busy exploiting mercilessly foreign sources of raw materials, labor and foreign markets with little more than rhetorical regard for their "responsibilities" as world powers. In all cases, from the "white man's burden" subterfuge to "co-prosperity sphere" hogwash, *no* powerful international commercial empire (including the USA) has, to date, calculated, from any perspective other than that of expediency, either the nuances and/or responsibilities of imperialistic, cross-cultural economic clout!

We require neither ecologists nor secondary-school textbooks to remind us of the tenuous thread by which our present American prosperity hangs upon her international trade alliances. Most of us are dimly aware of the fact, even if most Europeans, Africans and Asians are not. In the matter of minerals, for instance, our raw materials are amazingly scant at home: *all* of our chromium, most of our aluminum, manganese, nickel and over half of our tungsten and zinc consumed per year *must* be imported from foreign sources.[8]

Our rapid consumption of fossil fuels is an overdone topic on television documentaries. But consider, for a change, the irony that we transplanted mountains of coffee beans from Ceylon and Java to South America, so that our coffee-nerves are brewed almost entirely on foreign soil. We are totally incapable (even in collaboration with Canada) of constructing decent North American Corona-Coronas, of making crystalized ginger and candied kumquats the way the Chinese do, or growing a clove that is worth shaking onto an egg-nog. Worse ignominy, if you vivisect most of our modern, transistorized electronic equipment (color television cameras, receivers and other electronic gadgetry), the innards belie the neat American corporate names (Zenith, Philco, RCA, Sylvania etc.) on the outside casing: namely, minute circuitry and precision work involving diodes, transistors and wafers that, it seems, are most profitably and (more important) properly wired onto printed circuits best by the patient hands of (for neurological and psychological reasons yet undetermined) Japanese women, who seem somehow born to this painstaking mini-craftsmanship.

As trivial as some of these matters seem, taken in total, our dependence upon raw material and (yes) skills and technologies of our superiors overseas are all germane to what we call "the American way of life" in its materialistic aspects. We might, of course, *survive* as a nation were these lines of trade and intercourse severed absolutely—but little better than such an island nation as Britain would. In fact, because of American hyper-industrialization, the dimunition to zero of various and vital imports necessary, for example, to maintain our systems of transportation, might create *greater* havoc in so internally complex a nation as the USA than in the more self-sufficient, independent and well-pocketed England.

Survive we would. And "American ingenuity" might solve many of our problems and render us self-sufficient in time. But those of us who have tasted the mild shortages and displacements of consumer goods that accompanied World War II are aware, not only of the discomforts that arise from mild dysfunctions in a technological nation, but of the side-products of discomforts, in terms of corruption and requirements for federal controls upon all manner of private behaviors. In the end, after a decade of such self-sufficiency, America would no longer resemble herself in almost any aspect of life. The results are more frightening to contemplate than either the worlds of *1984* and/or *The Clockwork Orange*.

American commercial arrogance (a matter of style, mostly, that seems infectious), general ignorance abroad about the tenuous nature—and, let us add, the all too poor distribution—of the USA's enormous wealth and business know-how have triangulated with a spurious foreign image of the "typical American" that explains, in large measure, the near rampant and gratuitous anti-Americanism that one discovers in business circles around the globe—even among the new masters of the super-conglomerate corporations that are now burgeoning in Communist nations.

This very image is, of course, the vital fluid upon which much "Third World" rhetoric today best flourishes. But the classical envy of "have not" nations for the "haves" (the fattest of which is supposed to be the USA) is fully justifiable—*in psychological terms.*

What Third World nations are painfully and slowly learning, however, is *first,* that hyper-industrialism, mass production and standardization does not suit every clime and culture equally. They must mesh with devastatingly difficult (and slow) changes necessary in educational traditions, temperaments and tastes. *Second,* they are also discovering that these basic modifications in culture are achieved neither by firing squads nor by dictatorial fiats, guns and laws, but by the slow, grinding wheels of time that fill in, with considered judgment and experience, the painful, and seemingly invariably attenuated, transition from feudal or tribal culture to a life-style compatible with technology. This is a change, we are convinced, the surface attractions of which are indeed seductive, but which also sometimes impel a nation, however poor and remote, to exchange the worse for the worst. Kemal Ataturk knew this, because he was a wise statesman; Fidel Castro is now learning it, because he is apparently educable; and Uganda's Idi Amin Dada may never learn it, because he thinks he knows all the answers. He may therefore not survive long enough to learn!

We must grant the Third World its justified jealousy of one nation (among many) that has, at one time or another, exploited many underdeveloped peoples to its own advantages with hardly a "thank you." But anti-Americanism in less likely quarters—particularly among nations who *resemble* us in many ways—is more difficult to explain, especially when it centers on material and commercial, rather than cultural, issues.

The third *party* to triangle above—the "typical American" —is here the major guilty party, largely because the "self" he presents to the world is refracted in the world's image of American business.

Most American diplomats overseas, some journalists and writers, many professional businessmen do *not*, even to European and Asian eyes, spread this stereotype of the average American. Unfortunately, almost *all* Americans portrayed in American movies and television screens (tripe that dominates programming in so many foreign countries so much of the time that its proportion to other programming sources is, and has been for years, usually limited by *law*) encapsulate, one or another, the *least* attractive aspects of life in *every* sphere of endeavor in the United States.

Some years ago, Gilbert Seldes observed that he could not remember when or if he ever saw a character in a Hollywood movie who read a book for pleasure! Today, Seldes would be as hard-put to find a 'teenager on American television who had not been brutally corrupted by his elders in some way into cynical materialism (including the "goods" on *Mod Squad*). Nor would he discover a protagonist, male or female, in any routine film or televised series, who is not a miseducated, inarticulate, overfed semi-lecherous twerp or megalomaniac—and usually also, to foreign eyes, a disaster in the department of sexual behavior! American families in television fiction (and on slanted, selected, tasteless "documentaries" like *An American Family* (shown here on Public Television) are vapid, trivial clutches of poseurs; their children are little Rousseauan *Emiles*, spoiled rotten by money, drugs (and retreaded plot-lines). Their homes appear to be slightly enviable storehouses of esoteric gadgets their owners neither appreciate, understand, nor use properly. Exceptions exist, of course—*Sanford and Son* may be one. We can think of no others off-hand, although we wonder what is generally thought of overseas of *Sesame Street!* (And, *All in the Family*, of course, is a watered-down adaptation of a British import). But the eye of the foreign viewer of American television, tape and film is *not* peeled to seek out exceptions. The cinema of both screen and tube shows us a nation of wise-guys at best; at worst, a nation of narcotized morons. So much for this particular cesspool of exported culture, defended by its entrepreneurs as good "business for the USA."

Another question pops up here: "Why do the wrong people travel?" wrote the late Noel Coward to music. He was wrong. The *right* people travel—from the USA overseas anyway—but the wrong ones attract the attention, although they represent but a minority of the thousands of peripatetic Americans who tour the globe every year.

In the first place, we shall probably never know exactly what impact virtual hordes of children, taking advantage of airline "economies," have had upon Europeans in particular, as they swarmed upon the continent for the past half-dozen or so summers. These children, generally speaking, are not too much *worse* than European adolescents (depending upon one's idea of "worse"), but they are certainly *different* from them. They are, for the most part, perceived by foreigners (correctly) as representative of the younger generation of the affluent middle class of the United States. To the continental eye in particular, their poor manners, general uncleanliness, odd dress and hair arrangements and penchant for drugs *must* seem *strange* indeed. Stranger still are their parents.[9]

"This isn't exactly the Picadilly Hilton, sir,—but *we have* always liked it this way," said the steward of a London club in 1972 to an American arrived from an East European city still digging out of World War II rubble. (The club exchanged available accommodations with its New York counterpart, of which the American was a member at, it is fair to add, modest rates.) The London club was *not* luxurious, by any means, but a far cry from some of the pre-World War I quarters the traveler had, during the weeks previous, visited in East Europe.

The steward, however, was diffident. "I know quite well, sir" he said, "how you Americans like things a little more—well—'posh', if you know what I mean, than we often think suitable in London. But I hope you'll find things comfortable here, sir. Service we attempt, sir, not fluorescent tubes. And you'll have to use your electric razor over by the corner, I fear, sir—if you have a 220-volt converter, that is. The club doesn't provide those, by any means, sir."

The ancient club—part of a complex of structures that supposedly were built in the time of James II—was indeed not the Hilton, or even Holiday or Ramada Inns, nor a Travelodge, nor a Quality Motel. (And absolutely nothing invidious is meant by comparing it to these American hostelries, all of them suitable for Americans, particularly forced to travel as they must in the United States.) The club *was* clean and comfortable. Neither plumbing nor heating nor food (except breakfast) seemed to be taken very seriously either by its staff or members. It was as British as a "toad in the 'ole,"—as delightful a stopping-place as a traveler from the United States could ask for in terms of cheery company, relaxing quarters and obliging staff. That the latter *expected* the American to find it old, crude, uncomfortable, drafty and unsanitary is the point of recounting this minor non-adventure.

The old world has, it seems, also been able to absorb its Hiltons and Sheratons—and pizza parlors and Coca Cola culture—with remarkably little dissonance, sophisticated as it is in the art of absorption. If the Nazis, for instance, could not Germanize Paris yesterday, it is doubtful that "Le Drugstore" or "Le Supermarket" will Americanize it today. Granted that the Istanbul Hilton is something of a local curiosity, its effects on Turkish culture have apparently been minimal. And many European, Asian and African cultures have been influenced—for the better largely—by various American materialistic culture traits that are usually damned to the bone when they first appear in an old world setting: everything from hamburgers with onions to ubiquitous credit cards.

What causes conflict between cultures in materialistic matters is *not* the intrusion of architecture, gadgetry, foods or techniques that were born abroad, but, *first,* the *way* they are used and, *second,* how they *effect* and *compare* with old local or indigenous ways of doing things.

American tourists, therefore, who insulate themselves in little Americas (be they Hiltons or pseudo-Hiltons), insist on plain home cooking (which, if they mean American-style food, is neither plain nor cooked at home), and hustle from country to country and city to city around the world as noisily and aggressively as possible, *do* indeed create cross-cultural conflicts, particularly among the thoughtful. American tourists "doing" seven West European countries on a two-week (poorly) packaged, guided tour *do* often anger and annoy foreigners, proud of their cultural heritages—in much the same way that a serious American might (and should) be infuriated at the foreigner who wants to absorb *all* of the United States in a fortnight, and then employs his new expertise at home to broadcast noisily what he considers is wrong with the United States. This is boorishness, and it is both common and dangerous, no matter who the guilty party is. Because more Americans travel overseas than foreigners visit the United States, Americans are usually more often culprits than foreigners.

Tourism constitutes, of course, a lucrative form of international trade. Its commercial assets are many. The main one centers upon tourism's capacity to turn economically deprived areas of the world, with a few natural resources and questionable production potentials, into profit-making regions. Caribbean rock piles and coral reefs, once deserted even by sea urchins, are today "tropical paradise holiday islands." Soil that will not grow weeds, when covered with snow, may delight suicidal ski enthusiasts. A gambling casino and a few luxury brothels may transform an equatorial hell-hole into a haven for the rich and foolish. A dreary, decadent town, where the sewage still runs in the streets may be alchemized into "a colorful relic of old-world charm."

The basic commodity, in other words, of tourism is a highly protean ingenuity. Its cultivation depends upon the wits and skills of the international travel industry—in its way, an international multi-corporation itself, held together by agreements between cooperating agencies and complex rebate deals with airlines, hotels, transportation systems and other businesses.

All tourism is potentially lucrative. But travel entrepreneurs tend, unlike many other members of the big business community—to be short-term operators who, unfortunately, merely hit and run. This is unwise, because it eventually kills their golden geese. (They solve the problem by cultivating new geese—that is, new tourist areas and new clever "packages.") Their major chronic errors are the practice of over-sell, over-enthusiasm and deception. A Caribbean rock looks, to the average tourist, after a day or two, like a Caribbean rock. Unless the food is edible (not necessarily "plain home cooking") in "a colorful relic of old-world charm," the place is indistinguishable from a similar slum back home, and so forth. Unless airplanes run on time—and tickets are valid for the flights they are supposed to cover—the result is disastrous both for the credibility and future of the travel industry.

Nor may tourist disfavor be glossed over by colorful brochures and smiling merchantry. When word gets around that such and such a nation or island runs a chorus line of waiters, bell-boys, porters and taxi drivers who are avaricious thieves out to bilk the foreign traveler, it falls rapidly into general disfavor.

(In the United States, the single best overseas tourist agency is currently run by the Department of State and open for use, unfortunately, only to those who travel in its service. It is efficient in regard to transportations. It arranges adequate facilities within the price range government employees can afford. It oversells nothing. But if a traveler, on a government mission, has a few days to kill between assignments, modest suggestions are often made that he might—at minimal expenses—be interested in stopping here or there, according to his inclinations, to fish—for whatever he fishes for—enjoy the scenery or improve his mind. The whole operation is remarkably civilized. Crucial decisions and considerable mobility, wherever he goes, remain in the hands of the traveler—not the local tourist establishment and souvenir industry.)

American tourism abroad is most commercially attractive to tourists (and the tourist industry, of course) when our balance of payments are lowest. When they rise, tourism abroad becomes exorbitant (despite lowering trends in air fares), and the expense of surviving in countries where dollars buy pitifully little local currency creates hostility all around. Recent dollar deflations have dramatized this situation for many American travelers abroad—people like our American trenchcoat consumer on Regent Street in London, an idiot, buying the wrong thing in the wrong place at the wrong time.

As an indirect form of foreign aid, of course, tourism is most effective in the places where the least number of commercial alternatives to tourism are present to sustain or exploit the local economy. Thus the warm welcome Americans receive in some parts of Latin America, certain Caribbean islands that are *not* political crazy-houses, in much of Africa and, by and large, ex-colonial island nations in the Pacific. Tourists are also generally well-treated in all of the East European satellite nations (even Bulgaria, if you keep your mouth shut), but not (yet) in the Soviet Union, where politics so dominates every aspect of life that politeness to an American may be considered (by some die-hard party members) tantamount to subversion. If and when Red China opens up the American tourist markets, we predict that she will show a face of extreme pleasure and geniality to traveling Americans. The latter will be carefully and (inexpensively) chaperoned so that they see that part of Mao's empire which speaks best for it. The experience, we imagine, will be both comfortable and delightful, because, as we have seen, the Chinese are masters at creating (and saving) beautiful faces.

Reversing the flow of travel, however, promises even more interesting economic ramifications for the United States. For the first time in modern history, we will now benefit commercially and fiscally—to a significant degree—from a substantial flow from tourism of foreign currency *into* American coffers. More foreigners are able to afford it than ever before. Here again, the cupidity and stupidity of travel agents may well doom this enterprise—largely a flop to date, despite advertising efforts overseas and economic preferences given foreign visitors in the USA during the past decade—because of their diehard habits of over-sell, over-kill and hot air.

The United States is not a country to "see," in the conventional tourist's sense. New York is a city to *explore*. And so are Chicago, New Orleans, Kansas City and San Francisco. Boat trips on our inland waterways are miraculous experiences. So are leisurely drives through New England in summer, the Plains States in spring, and the great Northwest at practically anytime. One cannot, however, "do" them all in a month any more than one can "do" Western Europe in two weeks. Do European travel agents care?

Recent stories also, expanded by the American and foreign press and television to unrealistic, mythic proportions, concerning the violence in our cities today discourages many prospective tourists from visiting the USA. Steps must be taken to reduce the violence, of course. But, mostly, the problem will be effectively solved by taking counter-measure against the *mythology*. Cities *everywhere* are violent—for those looking for illicit "fun" and/or trouble. Acquaintances of the authors have been beaten and "rolled" on every continent in the world, and in cities renowned for their supposed tranquillity. They are the kind of people, however, who are most unattractive when "on the town" wherever they are. When in their cups, they are easy pickings for confidence-men, whores and thugs, practitioners of professions that know no national boundaries. American cities are "tough" cities, yes. Within memory, they have always been "tough," but little more dangerous, to the man or woman who minds his own business (and takes reasonable precautions with his or her possessions), than most other cities, anywhere else in the world. Their reputation, however, are parlous everywhere one goes.

Last, Americans must learn to get along with their tourists, in much the same way that the Swiss, for instance, almost invariably do, and the French (at least in the large cities) usually do *not*. This involves simple arts: politeness, modesty, discretion, sympathy and—to some degree—pride and knowledgeability.

Scandinavians also seem to understand tourists as well as any Europeans, and we might do worse than emulate them. If possible, they *try* to speak the tourist's own language—better badly than not at all. They are reasonably accomodating in most matters—but not unctuous. They do not treat the foreigner as a potential gold mine. They suggest the same economies (of all sorts) to him that they employ in their own lives. They also appear to sympathize with the tourist's chronic malaise: fright at the real and imagined threats of a strange environment. They apparently think that it is entirely natural for a tourist to be slightly frightened of *them*, obviously curious and deserving of a little extra attention and care, lest he leave Norway or Denmark—and, somewhat less generally, Sweden—with a bad taste in his mouth. They also know how to "be themselves," do not preen and crow, put up false fronts or pretend that their national social and political problems have all been solved or that they have achieved cultural paradise. They are not "on display." Tourists are guests on *their* home ground—but welcome guests.

These are not difficult attributes for Americans, in sensitive places where they meet tourists, to cultivate. In fact, most of us possess most of them already, if only the travel entrepreneurs and tourist tradesmen permit us to show our foreign visitors what we *are*, warts and all, and not what they think we *should be*.

And On to the Stratosphere

Students of the many issues raised in this chapter—including editorialists for *The Wall Street Journal* and *The Journal of Commerce*—almost invariably attempt to read into the present dislodging of world-wide trade from its old-style national moorings into the sea of internationalism (the trend that all of our observations above reflect, in one way or another) the need, in the world of modern supra-national commerce, to a court- or many courts-of "higher morality," transcendent of national boundaries and barriers.[10] In this respect, international business is not one whit different from any other institution of communication between nations: the keeping of peace, the conduct of war, the interaction of cultural life and the flow and flux of political ideas, news and culture. It is simply more *concrete*. It deals with goods and services, labor and sweat, and that omnipotent quintessence of abstract concreteness (if such there be): hard cash.

Forums and organizations for the articulation of this higher morality, its rules, regulations and penalties exist today. But, for differing reasons, *all* of them lack the encompassing catholicism that unity in world-wide trade and finance increasingly demands, as technology, transportation and communications become increasingly complex and intertwined.

The United Nations would, in theory, be the ideal instrument for the implementation of such a "membership corporation," reviewing and implementing moral and ethical agreements between nations and super-national corporations. Because the United Nations, however, must deal so openly with ideals—and is therefore so devoted to the liberal and literary debate of idealism—it also is pragmatically useless for the purposes of international commercial regulation. As a primarily open diplomatic forum, utilizing cumbersome and arbitrary vetoes, and dealing in political strategems, the earthy practicalities of economic alliances, tariffs and currency games would never withstand the rhetoric, routine maneuvering and diplomatic ploys that its forum of legations has evolved in the UN's twenty-five-year history. The UN still flexes a (frequently flabby) muscle regarding *some* matters of higher morality, but, if it works at all, it is most effective in the realm of diplomacy, treaty making, knuckle wrapping, and issues related to details of intercultural ephemera and megapolitics. Where and when it has attempted to deal with money and trade, its influence has been marginal—and will continue to be in this domain. Businessmen, for some strange reason, are loathe to surrender hegemony over their assets to diplomats, particularly those who must barter under television lights with tape recorders whirling and batteries of simultaneous translators, operating in goldfish bowls like the United Nations.

The tendency towards cooperation—or collusion; it does not matter which—has manifested itself in other, slightly more discrete recent international organizational phenomena. Their greatest weakness is, possibly, that they are not discrete enough for the tastes of their participants or the sensitivity of their objectives. Glimmers of hope are certainly evident in the (thus-far effective) actions of the International Monetary Fund, the General Agreement on Tariffs and Trade, the World Bank, the European Common Market and other recent coalitions of national commerce. (One must bear in mind their failures as well.) The two major problems that these bodies (and others like them) face are the reluctance of, and difficulty in, inducing member nations to yield commercial sovereignty to any kind of supra-national body (*less* difficult, we think, than inducing similar nations to relinquish military or diplomatic sovereignty over their internal affairs to the UN), and, possibly more important, the tendency of these committees to *react* to *dysfunctions* in international trade and monetary practises, rather than act to try to prevent them in the first place.

Whether tomorrow's *major* global international trade regulation agency is an extension of one of those that already exist or a new one is, of course, of little consequence. What *is* important is that such an agency be representative of the significant economic interests of *all* the world's nations (including those in the communist blocs, whatever their production problems, currency problems and trade problems are now, or are likely to be in the future), that it be, indeed, "supra-national"; and that it have *enough* power to regulate the flow of goods and money on a grand scale between nations in an orderly manner; and that it not encourage either the exploitation of underdeveloped nations or the speculative, gambling-casino instincts of rich, well-developed ones.

As opposed to the United Nations—where the main functional symbols of power are political alliances and (often hollow) rattlings of sabres—such an economic international agency *must have real teeth,* both for hygienic and punitive purposes. And teeth it *will* have—on the basis of *three* factors that are already operating *within* the world of international commerce today, not an artificial police power given it grudgingly by participating nations.

First, it would represent (and necessarily be representative *of* and sometimes advocate *for*) the many international multi-corporations that have already outgrown their needs for the protection or supervision of any *single* sovereign state. (The communist nations are primarily multi-corporate, in the Western sense, to the degree that their economies intertwine with those of their satellites. But, as their commercial relationships with the rest of the world grow, so will their economic engagement with it—faster, probably, than most economists at the moment predict.)

Second, the international currency mess—and the money game—must be rigidly controlled (or terminated) if communication and trade between national states is not to be destroyed by its vagaries. This has already been recognized by nearly all the world's monetary agencies themselves, public and private. Present efforts to balance dollars with yen with francs and so forth, as we have shown, are moving towards this objective by means of temporization. But the balance scale remains peril-ously unstable. And when it is upset, the world's financial com-munity runs for gold, as we have observed. It may as well turn to diamonds, Byzantine mosaics or opium, all, in the twen-tieth century, poor substitutes for hard currency that can be exchanged in kind for the trade capacity (or its potential) of a private corporation (in the form of securities) or a country (in the form of cash).

The inevitable "Eurodollar" will be, as we have already predicted, but an evolutionary step in this direction. The *World*-dollar is a better and firmer step. It must, necessarily be a currency representing the holdings of the combined assets of the international business complex of the entire world. Na-tional currencies would, of course, still be necessary for na-tional business—and even international business in transac-tions where such currency could be counted upon to maintain its stability beyond its borders. The ultimate exchange medium would be (and will have to be), however, the aforementioned "super-currency," balanced against both the immediate sol-vency of rich nations and, more important, the *potential eco-nomic value* of poor ones in terms of manpower, unexploited resources etc. Gold, silver, diamonds—and even opium—would be redeemable in World Currency at a realistic, homo-genous rate. (The international "trade dollar" or *thaler* was, come to think of it, an old, but still remarkably good, idea that got lost somewhere in the seventeenth or eighteenth century.)

Third, economic self-interest would necessarily motivate the establishment of such an economic world body primarily as a *protective* device. It would inevitably be empowered to de-stroy or counterbalance arbitrary or unnecessary restrictive tariffs leveled against industrial nations (compensating the na-tion so restricted with *other* trade or economic preferences, ac-cording to need.) This would protect the interests of multi-cor-porations within nations when and if they are suddenly taxed into oblivion or "nationalized" as the result of elections or *coups d'etat*. The body would also perform much the same function for the many thousands of other and smaller commercial units that are even more vulnerable than multi-corporations to the strong winds of undisciplined international commerce.

The inevitable—and foolish—question asked of all proposals like this one invariably is: "And exactly *who* is going to administer an agency of this sort?" The answer, of course, is "Men!" They must be men representative of the major parties already involved in matters effecting the policies and practices of world trade—selected or elected, not according to mere national allegiance, but according to the significance to on-going world trade of their particular interests and involvements. (A pox, therefore, upon professional economists unless they are *involved* economists!)

Can they—will they—be competent to arrive at effective consensuses in the delicate matters discussed above? Of course they can and will, *if their self-interests depend upon* such consensuses, and if the ultimate *desideratum* of the agency—maximizing the *profit potential* of world trade at large of all kinds for all nations—remains continually the fundamental reference point by which all policy is set and all ajudication is made.

Our stratospheric suggestion is, we think, far from unrealistic. Nor does it, like the UN, require of men that they be the good-willed supra-national moralists that they are not by nature. It construes businessmen (and institutional economists) as individuals primarily interested in the welfare of business and economy—mostly, one hopes, the particular ones in which they are personally involved. The motivating force for cooperation and agreement between them will be the knowledge that non-cooperation and agreement spells more and more of the chaos and risk that history has *already* written in their names, and that engagement means the best chance they have for insuring, for each participant, that proper measure of the world's wealth each believes he (or his constituency) deserves. All parties would be aware of course, that the scheme is a gamble, but they will, being good businessmen, find the odds attractive.

Not to mince words, the motivating force of such a "supra-agency" will *have to be human greed*, one of the most effective, powerful and time-tested instruments for opening up clear channels of commerce and communication between nations—and between men as well, even (or especially) among the powerful and rich, wherever they are found on the face of the globe.

NOTES TO CHAPTER 8

[1] October 6, 1972, p. 58.

[2] Facts and figures (rarely consistent or reliable) on international multi-corporations in this chapter have been gathered from numerous public sources. But they are all reprised, either in Herbert I. Schiller, "Madison Avenue Imperialism," in *Communication in International Politics* (Urbana: University of Illinois Press, 1972, pp. 318–338), and Harvey D. Schapiro, "Giants Beyond Flag and Country," *The New York Times Magazine*, March 18, 1973, pp. 20–22, 24, 28, 30, 32, 35, two of the best recent and comprehensive articles on the subject, as well as periodic coverage in *Time, Newsweek* and *Business Week,* too extensive to note here.

[3] U.S. Bureau of the Census, *Statistical Abstract of the United States, 1971,* 92nd edition, (Washington D.C.: U.S. Government Printing Office, 1971, p. 753.)

[4] See Schiller, *op. cit.,* pp. 319–325.

[5] Allen J. Large, "The Uneasy Future of Foreign Aid," *The Wall Street Journal*, November 29, 1972, p. 22.

[6] Material below has been adopted from *loc. cit.,* and P. T. Bauer, "The Case Against Foreign Aid," *The Wall Street Journal*, October 3, 1972, p. 22. A somewhat impressionistic editorial on the *Journal's* front page on October 9, 1972 has also been among the pieces considered by the

authors in evaluating relevant data, including assorted interviews with international financial business personnel, small-time and big-time. (One author's first experience with an international trader occurred shortly after World War II when an Arab in then colonial Algiers tried to sell him his daughter for export to America. "She will make much money for you, because she screws good anything!" said the loving father. The deal was never consummated.)

[7] Quoted in Large, *op. cit.*

[8] See the "Business and Finance" section of *The New York Times,* Sunday, November 5, 1972, particularly the article by Lester R. Brown, "Depending on others for Minerals," p. 11.

[9] The reactions of young people to foreign travel is invariably interesting—and curious. See, for instance, in the *New York Times Travel and Resorts* Section, Sunday, October 8, 1972. The feature article, "Summing Up: What Travel Abroad Meant to 5 Young Americans," explores at some length the attitude of a group of young tourists to their exploits abroad during the summer of 1972.

[10] See Schiller, *op. cit.;* Shapiro, *op. cit.;* and articles such as Edwin L. Dale, Jr., "The Search for a Durable System" in *The New York Times,* October 1, 1972, which clarifies in terse prose the mission of the International Monetary Fund and the objectives it failed to reach in the half-dozen months after the piece was written. Note also the moral idealism in reports on meeting of the General Agreement on Tariffs and Trade (GATT) in Geneva in another Dale article, "US Lists Trade Objectives and Timetable for GATT," *The New York Times,* November 11, 1972, p. 1, agreements that fell into near meaninglessness as they shifted to meet the "dollar crises" that followed the Swiss GATT meeting about three months later. Each participant nation endeavored to cover its flanks against the glut of declining US currency around the world. See the wise and witty columns of C. K. Sulzberger, in this regard, during this period. Sulzberger is at his best when he deals with problems of economic morality. Note also, for instance, reports of his incisive discussion with Japan's Premier Tanaka in Tokyo on Japan's present external trade plans and problems in *The New York Times,* March 23, 28 and 30, 1972, p. 37, 39, and 47 respectively; also, April 1 in the *Review of the Week* Section, p. 15. The article by Richard Halloran in the April 1 issue of *The New York Times* on p. 1, regarding the image of the "Ugly Japanese" is also apropos.

PART THREE

The Only Thing
We Have To Fear
Is The Future

9

American Idealism in Crisis

Hope and risk, are they too great to expect of man? I do not believe it. They constitute his shadow. They have followed him for a million years. They stood with him at the Hot Gates of Thermopylae. They shared the cross at Calvary. I think it was really there that the great wave began to gather when all else seemed lost. We are again threatened with the insidious Elizabethan malady of weariness. But a voice spoke then of hope, and of great reversals, of impending tides. May this too be such an age.

Loren Eiseley [1]

Propaganda Preparations for America's Bicentennial Year

Scrapbook Items, Assorted Clips and Wild—Track Tape Recordings:

ROBERT BRUSTEIN (*London, 1972. Construction sounds. Noise of crowds filling West End theatres*): America . . . is now in agony as a result of its past, and the afflictions of our nations are directly traceable to the errors and crimes of our history. As a result, I believe, we are becoming, perhaps without quite knowing it yet, a truly tragic nation. Our tragedy is a compound of Vietnam, of deteriorating cities, of poverty and suffering and racial strife, of drug abuse and violence, of political assassination and, further back, a heritage of the original sin of our country, the institution of slavery. A people who until very recently smiled at itself daily in the mirror, accented the positive, and demanded happy endings to its plays and movies, is now being forced, against its will, to examine its soul and live with the knowledge that the past sins are not easily re-deemable, even with the best intentions.[2]

JEANETTE SPENCER (*New Jersey Turnpike, 1973. Fog and Night. An automobile edges to a cautious 65 mph on the black, die-straight road. No scenery. Background sound is windshield wipers, accomplishing nothing*): I guess I'm the luckiest woman in the world. And I didn't just fall into luck—I was pushed. I just opened the wrong doors—all of them, and they led to the right places. That's God's way, I suppose. You think you're in the driver's seat, but *how* you make the trip, that's not your business. If I wasn't an ex-convict, I wouldn't be working now with the Fortune Society, trying to help ex-cons like me go straight and make decent lives for themselves. If I wasn't an alcoholic, I wouldn't be able to meet with other peo-ple who had drinking problems and share my experiences in shaking the addiction with them. Everything I've got—and I've got all sorts of things from life that you don't count in bank accounts—I received because of what most people would call bad luck or mistakes or just plain sickness. I think this is a *great* time in the world for somebody like me—a black woman, an ex-con and ex-drunk—because I have the opportu-nity of *doing* something about some of the "social problems" everybody else is talking about, instead of sitting on my back-side and weeping into my gin that the world didn't get around to giving *me* a fair break. People like that are pitiful. Just plain pitiful.

HERMAN KAHN (*Croton-on-Hudson, 1972. Suburban setting. Birds singing in background*): The upper middle class insists on misunderstanding all of the central issues of American life.[3]

MARY KELLY (*Moraga, California, 1973. More suburbs, California style. Automotive noises. Tortoises croak. Nobody talks about earthquakes*): We always lived in San Diego. And one day my husband came home and told me that he had a job offer here in the San Francisco Bay Area. When we *did* make the move, the children were terribly small. I was homesick and frightened, because I might have been a million miles away from where I grew up. My husband had to do a lot of traveling, and I was all alone with the children. For the first time in my life, I had a lot of decisions on my own. Now, I had started a little collection of Danish Christmas plates in San Diego, and I owned several duplicates. I got the bright idea to run an ad in the local paper and try to sell my extras. Little did I know how many people collect plates. I didn't get a chance to fix dinner that night, with the 'phone just ringing off the hook, and people wanting to buy those plates and asking about others I never even heard of. Then it occurred to me that if plates were so much in demand, this would be a good thing for me to get into. I can honestly say it was a lot of work getting started, not having much capital to work with, and we had just bought a brand new house. Of course, my husband was ready to have me committed, as he thought that I'd flipped for sure. I sweated plenty, but I was *so* determined to make a go of it. And now I have a very good business here in my home. Eventually I added other things besides plates to my stock, like figurines, music boxes, Waterford Crystal and Beleek China. I only buy what appeals to me. But my first love is the old Danish plates—funny, considering that I've never even been to Europe. I really went into the business blind, but its been a God-send for me, because I like to keep busy.

SPIRO AGNEW (*Fort Lauderdale, 1970. Microphone boom. Rattle of pages as script is turned. Pauses for audience approval. Background murmurs and spoons stirring after-dinner coffee*): We must look to how we are raising our children. They are, for the most part, the children of affluent, permissive, upper-middle class parents who learned their Dr. Spock and threw discipline out the window—when they should have done the opposite. They are the children dropped off by their parents at Sunday school to hear the "modern" gospel from a "progressive" preacher more interested in fighting pollution than fighting evil—one of those pleasant clergymen who lifts his weekly sermons out of old newsletters from a National Council of Churches that has cast morality and theology aside as "not relevant" and set as its goal on earth the recognition of Red China and the preservation of the Florida alligator. Today, by the thousands—without a cultural heritage, without a set of spiritual values, and with a moral code summed up in that idealistic injunction "Do your own thing," Junior—his pot and Portnoy secreted in his knapsack—arrives at "the Old Main" and finds there a smiling and benign faculty even less demanding than his parents.[4]

BRUCE FRANKLIN (*Anywhere, 1972. Background sounds of mass-cult magazine readers trying to think. Flipping of slick pages —fast*): Alienated intellectuals show nothing but pity or terror or contempt for most other people, particularly those spending their lives working to produce their cars, typewriters, clothes, movie cameras, houses, and bourbon. These highly cultured people are not interested in the actual lives or thoughts of the workers, whom they can imagine only looking at television, drinking beer, brutalizing their wives (all workers are men), telling racist jokes (all workers are white), and ranting about young long-hairs (all workers are over thirty and have crew cuts).[5]

TOM AMODIO (*Long Island, N.Y., 1972. Suburban noises. Pizza pies, Double-Whamburgers being wrapped, malted milks poured into waxy paper containers. French fries crackling in oil*): As raw material, I am any one of a million college fresh-men throughout the world, although my presence here results directly from a full-tuition scholarship. I am the product of a *petit-bourgoise* family and a social system that has channeled my talents into doing the single thing that I have done well for the past thirteen years: attending an educational institution. Therefore, my desire to write: although it stems from my personal feelings and hopes. Physical labor does me no harm; on the contrary, I love it. I have worked as a landscaper and as a summer employee at a large insurance company. I know, accordingly, that I cannot succeed at, or even suffer, a nine-to-five blue-or-white collar job. For further references, see my mother. The other important part of my life is people—my friends. At the moment, they are scattered across the country at college, but I am making new relationships all the time and keep in touch with old friends. I am also hopelessly quixotic, an incorrigible romantic. No matter what the impossibility rating of the dream, the believeability seems to increase as the square of the impossibility—the more impossible the dream, the more wonderful the experience of imagining it. My fantasies run the gamut from the typically sexual and the heroic type to more unusual "talkathons." These are my very own creations, wherein the characters engage in lengthy dialogues and explanations. They elaborate on everything they do. This eccentricity is consistent with my character. I have a distasteful knack for talking, especially monologues, and often too much. I literally drown my listeners in a torrent of words. My various faults are more typical and mundane; occasional grumpiness, thoughtlessness and hard-headedness. So there you have it. It has been nice talking to you.

JEFFERY ST. JOHN (*New York, 1972. Quiet. Radio studio silence. Script typed on soft paper to be edited and re-copied. No echo. Dead voice*): In the final analysis, futurists rely on fear and fantasy, the consequence of their dislike for the past and present which has produced a technological age from which they feel alienated. Their alienation is the product of their dislike of the mind, which made technology possible. In a reactionary fashion, they flee mindlessly into the fantasy of a future static society presided over by an all-powerful state which futurists, as an elite, will control much in the manner of medieval princes. The future cannot be forecast when the mind revolts from reality and natural laws. Only a love of life and respect for reality can provide men of reason and freedom and means to help shape and forecast the faint outlines of the future. The future is what men make it, so long as they never close their minds to the heroic potential of the human mind.[6]

At the bottom of things, where the foundations of destiny are built the last voice is right. One issue seems to tower over all others in regard to America's "information," "communication" or "propaganda" policies for the next decade: The future is far too important a matter to be left in the hands of futurists.

The best thinking about the future of the planet that we have discovered in recent years emerges from the fertile brain of the British scientist and naturalist, John Maddox. It may be found in his book *The Doomsday Syndrome*.[7]

Syndrome has not been a popular book (like Toffler's *Future Shock*, for instance), because it is (quite purposely) not fashionable. And the "best thinking" of would-be intellectuals and other fools who "take things seriously" follows fashion more rigidly than the boutique shop at Neiman-Marcus.

Maddox's incisive arguments are complex. They center on the ecology-hoax of the past decade (*not* upon scientific ecology, a different matter), but his fundamental message is civilized, sane and clear.

Maddox believes, *first* of all, that technology is *not* destroying mankind, and that the kind of steps men have taken in the past to contain the destructive side-effects of their inventions will inevitably continue apace in the future. *Second,* the modern "doomsday men" (as Maddox calls them) are preying upon our fears and guilts that have somehow resulted from the facts that, despite increased populations everywhere in the world, a greater percentage of the earth's population today live longer, eat better and participate in what we call "progress" (in a material sense) more fully than ever before in history. *Third*, our future-specialists, with their computer simulations and science-as-fiction models of tomorrow's world, are misguided mythologists who are dealing with incomplete data in both unscientific and irrelevant ways in order to validate absurd hypotheses that fashion alone dictates. Most of them lack a sense of history in their constructions both of the present and the future.

In contradistinction to their gloom, Maddox writes, we should be today heartened that mankind has—through three millennia of recorded history—developed a truly remarkable "technology of survival" to which the doomsayers pay little attention, more successful in recent years than ever before. Rather than squander our Research and Development upon the highly popular (but absurd) prevention of doom, Maddox urges the implementation of *this* already vital technology, now at the height of its powers.

The humble and close student of history may cautiously marvel at how his race *has* avoided extinction in its history—amidst ecological imbalances and environmental disasters that were so severe as to be almost unthinkable today—and concentrate his intelligence upon the conservation of the technological tricks and caprices of survival (many of them accidental) that our collective experience has demonstrated *work*, rather than squander money and time on contingency plans for illusory futures.

To those who would cancel all bets and claim that the present moment has *not* evolved from the past, that men in "future shock" are different from all other men who ever lived, that nuclear bombs, nucleic acids, pesticides, birth control pills and electronics have severed mankind's connections with his past experience as a species; and that modern men are somehow different from their fathers and mothers in essential human qualities, because their instruments and tools are different—to these "visionaries," one is impelled merely to re-

spond with a Buster Keaton-style deadpan face. Such individuals must think most highly of themselves to regard *their* little
moments in time (between birth and death) so precious and in
such cosmic esteem.

Coming Down to Earth

Of all the lessons men—and, by extension, nations—come
in time to learn, humility is among the most difficult. A broken
man may, as he puts the pieces of his shattered self together
again, discover humility and live with it, as Fitzgerald told us
so clearly in *The Crack Up.*

Broken nations face a more difficult job. After a decade
passes, most of them re-learn the sin of pride (and all pride,
in the mill of history, is false pride); in a generation, they are
swaggering with ego, gall and power. Sometimes. In this
respect, one conjectures that perhaps Germany and Japan
really *did* truly *lose* World War II—but so did France and the
USSR and the USA. The real winners are so obscure as to be
laughable: Norway, Denmark, Poland, Rumania, Austria and
other places where egos fit aspirations, and where men are
governed by people who, one way or another, cannot *afford* to
substitute national pride for their sense of perspective and re-
membrance of reality.

The present moment is therefore potentially the finest in
the history of the United States.

America is, at the moment, not broken. But she has been,
in the recent past, severely crushed, not only in material matters
(like the depression of the nineteen-thirties) but in the countless cultural, social, economic, educational and legal beatings
she has suffered during the last decade of disillusionment, apparently and mercifully past and over—ending with a bang,
not a whimper in the word "Watergate." We have said many
times in these pages that her image abroad is at a nadir. Her
image at home is worse.

In these worst of times, one discovers, however, the best of
times. Regeneration is possible when the last dead roots have

been pulled from the soil and the weeds cleared away. A time for greatness *may* be coming, because it is within the power of the humble alone to be great. They have nothing to lose in the grand gamble. The USA has, we hope, passed through its last "agonizing re-appraisal" and now no longer needs to torture herself in reviewing the painfully clear reasons she has reached her present era of demoralization on more fronts than we care to count. The next item on the agenda is what to do about it.

In regard to the *War of Ideas,* the first issue at hand centers upon foreign policy. In the wake of the Vietnam debacle, and in the glow of the Nixon Doctrine, we *seem,* at last, to be evolving one. But this may be just another illusion, another reflex, another temporization between yesterday and tomorrow —not policy.

Eugene Rostow and many many others have, quite correctly, laid numerous realistic foreign policy alternatives for the USA on a continuum. Whatever path we choose, we will have to find our place on this scale and, for the first time in our history, live with our choice and stay where we stop. Otherwise our policy will continue along in the absence of policy (except to "trust in God and keep your powder dry"), as chancy a way to have lived yesterday as it is today and will be tomorrow.

At one end of the continuum are the isolationists, as easily dismissed (for pragmatic reasons) in the world-as-it-is as the world federalists on the other end. Both center their visions upon *theoretical* constructs of policy, and are therefore equally as satisfying psychologically, but equally absurd practically— at the moment. They require revision in *time* (forward or backwards) to acquire reasonableness. And man has not yet learned how to move clocks forward or back.

To the left of isolation (the political "left" to be sure, but one might as well say "north" or "east") are those who would deal with foreign policy as an on-going challenge to survival. They regard peaceful relationships between nations as pseudo-wars at worst, games at best, and accordingly accept the demand to *win* as the desideratum of these contests. Much history recommends this view, if not as desirable, at least as tenable. Machiavelli was its first (and still most articulate) spokesman. But the policy for which his philosophy and rhetoric spoke is also evident in pre-Hellenic Mycenean mythology. Its main drawback lies in the simple truth known to all gamblers: No matter how many games you win, you are bound eventually to lose *one*. If the one you lose is played for high enough stakes, it will eliminate your winnings, no matter how many games you have won nor how long it took to amass your winnings. Every state, large or small, that has followed this policy has, accordingly, also been destroyed by it, as surely as the imprudent gambler ends up broke. As Ring Lardner said, "You could look it up!"

Slightly more sophisticated are the many modern strategists who follow, largely, nineteenth-century models of what they believe is *Realpolitik*. Rather than *play* the game of pseudowar, they *supervise* it by placing pressure here or there in order to maintain a "balance of power." As a result, the stakes never rise, and no participant wins or loses *enough* to devastate his opponent. Such a view, of course, construes international amity in terms of short-term spurts. Peace, it implies, is the absence of *bad* warfare. History has shown that such nonhostility may be obtained for short periods. And nothing in history denies that the periods may not follow one another without devastating intervals of destruction. Conflict, yes. Destruction, no; because the power balance will be benignly shifted (by one or another super-power in our time, one assumes) before the steps to a much-feared major war are actually taken by a power strong (or foolish) enough to take them. Contrary to the best current opinion among the newspaper and television pundits, we do not believe first, that such a crude Metternichian return to former ways is contemplated by our foreign policy architects. (The reason for galloping agreement on the subject among our international commentators seems to be, mainly, that Henry Kissinger once wrote a book on Metternich.) Nor do we believe, second, that the so-called "Nixon Doctrine" points definitively in this direction—that is, its relaxing stance in Southeast Asia and the dramatic employment of the strategy of *entente* with our erstwhile enemies seem (to us) both naive and poor preparations for the role of international umpire and gatekeeper that such a "balance" would demand of America, should it be attempted.

Moving along the continuum in the direction of idealism or liberalism, one stands on middle-ground with those who speak for the generally accepted "common wisdom" (in Galbraith's sense) of a flexible foreign policy, capable of swinging wildly in *any* direction at the behest, largely, of conventional morality as construed by "public opinion"—that is, these days, as mediated by newspapers, middle-brow magazines and television *to* the people and their opinion leaders. Morals themselves change vastly in time, but moral stances do not. (The discontents for instance, against "middle class morality" espoused by Mr. Doolittle in *Pygmalion*, in the early years of this century, displayed vastly different *content* compared to similar complaints today. Middle class moral *stances* remain, in Britain at present, as distinct from the morality of the other classes as fifty years ago, and as restrictive upon contemporary *parvenus* as they were upon poor old Doolittle, years ago.) Morality appears, thus, always to be changing; it does indeed, but only as culture changes. So foreign policy guided mainly by moral imperatives is, in content, extremely shifty and inconsistent. The moral stance upon which it is based, however, is firm.

In the case of most Americans, their "higher morality" is a belief that democracy and representative government are suitable ideals for all nations, and anything America does that propels a country in this direction is justifiable. Obviously, this is a pretty vague and ephemeral theme for policy (semantics intrude, and their complications ramify into politics, race problems, economics, military matters etc.), but it *is* anchored to a moral *stance* of some stability. It is often construed by its exponents as an ideology, which it is *not*. Ideology de-

mands far more precision and rigorous dialectic than a protean morality can withstand, no matter how firmly rooted
psychologically the moral stance is in the minds of men.
(Countering a charge, for instance, that the best arguments
America's anti-communist overseas broadcasters could provide, in order to answer Hegelian, Marxist ideology, was *anti*-
Hegelianism and *anti*-Marxism, a highly placed government
official recently turned blankly to the present authors and
asked, "What's the matter with American ideology? Don't we
have one?" His rhetorical question was not answered.) In the
instability of *all* ideological arguments based merely upon
moral postures lies their greatest weaknesses, although one
may make a case for a *type* of strength in such postures. It *has*
in the past served us well in countless instances. But their dramatic failure in the past decade to deal with the complexities
of Asian political life and warfare have underscored their vital
shortcomings.

As one moves further left along the continuum, one meets
democratic idealists of different breeds and shades whose
objectives, one way or another, spell "world federalism,"
achieved through a variety of means. They are not to be dismissed offhand—neither "world citizens," die-hard long-time
exponents of world government (like Norman Cousins) nor
transnational mystics. One must remember the seriousness of
those multiple efforts that have been made in the present century to institutionalize in formal ways some phases of this idealism, most notably the League of Nations and the United Nations. Its power is also symbolized in many less dramatic
international relationships, where national sovereignty has
been subsumed to professional interests, self-survival, religion
or do-goodism. World government is unquestionably a trend in
the air, and one that may be hastened by the universal potentials of technology, the spread of which tends always to be international in potency. Launching stations for rockets on the
moon would, for example, move the world quite rapidly in the

direction of global federation—possibly not the ideal kind cosseted by visionaries, but world government, nevertheless.

In federalist idealism, however, the exact political, economic and social nature of the institution of world government is usually of much less significance than its matrices: the abolition of nation states, world passports, the use of an international language like Esperanto and so forth. In general, federalism holds that the junction of sovereignty is, of and by itself, both benign and ameliorative, and that close and open contact between individuals sharing any *sets* of major life interests will dispel most of the dysfunctions that presently beleaguer the world. This rationale stems from the etiology that assumes that international conflicts are *caused* primarily by the very *existence* of national states that, in turn, cause misunderstandings, poor communications between people, rivalry, megalomania and other symptoms of disaster. These, in turn, cause warfare. Here is an attractive chain of reasoning, and one that is accepted *in part* (and this *partial* acceptance is also the source of the world federalists' deepest grief) by most statesmen in the world today. Most practical diplomats at work, however, desire *both* federal sovereignty *and* internationalism, interwoven among their major concerns. Infuriated, the world federalist thinks this is impossible. He is (for better or worse) quite right.

At the extremes of idealism—and the far end of our continuum—there looms a shadow world, where it is often difficult to discern differences between idealism and pathology. We are not referring to the gentle souls who, quite reasonably, would "rather be Red than Dead." But we *do* include the pathological pacifist who would, when all is said and done, rather be dead than alive. (Only the mystic—see below—can afford this luxury, either because he believes his life is worthless, that life is part of a cosmic stream of consciousness, or because he is convinced that his real rewards and true existence will only be actuated in some manner in the hereafter.)

Like all such generalizations, the hyper-idealist's shibbo-leth that "all war is immoral and unjustified" connotes a dis-connection with his species and the domination by blind faith of reason. This is a common psychotic symptom, and, in its ex-treme form, it is Utopian; in its hyper-extremism, it becomes "scientific" or "mystical" Utopianism. The rational "systems" of B. F. Skinner and Nicolai Lenin are examples of the "scientific" brand—extremely attractive to the lay public, because they are the *only* schemes that men have been competent to evolve that actually and inevitably *solve* the foreign policy puzzle—except those, of course, that are given unilaterally by the word of God. Policy derived from scientism is thus construed *only* in terms of that which directly coordinates with the achievement of a *super*-desideratum. A *single* Marxist-communist state, therefore, is never a success (or validation of communist theory), because material-dialecticism addresses itself to a field which *must* be international, lest forces from a corrupt "outside world" pollute the systemic perfection of its scientific social or-ganization. *One* Skinnerian colony (like *Walden II*) cannot hurl all of mankind beyond freedom and dignity, nor, admits the seemingly rational Dr. Skinner himself, does a single Skin-nerian state.

Similar to the world federation enthusiasts, Utopians can-not equivocate with their Utopias. Unlike the federalists, they hold that they are in possession of an *ultimate truth* about the state of man and how he should conduct his civilizations—usually quite precisely drawn—and all moral "goods" are predicated upon those events and policies that legislate the truth and prohibit falsehood. The Utopian's foreign policy, while obviously predicated upon morals (as the Utopian con-strues them), contains a *specific* agenda made up of the prereq-uisites for the ultimate legislation of *truth*.

To some Utopian idealists, ends are everything; means are nothing. Short-term losses (revolutions, assassinations, purges and other delights) will eventually be counterbalanced by long-term gains. Others are more scrupulous about balancing ends and means, but the thrusts of their policy articulation is almost always in the direction of achieving ends regardless of the means used.

The horrors of the numerous medieval crusades are clear instances of long periods when the establishment of nobility in Christian Europe accepted a Utopian idealistic foreign policy. They tried with enormous zeal (and failed) to coordinate their ends and means, in an effort to save the world they knew from the inevitable destruction and doom that they were certain would result were their ideals not vindicated politically and socially. (Economic matters seemed beside the point to the degree that countless personal fortunes were destroyed for this Utopian ideal.) One may no more accuse the Crusaders of not knowing *exactly* where they were going and what they were setting out to achieve than one may accuse the Marxist-Leninist of the same sin today. It may also rub the reader the wrong way to ask him to think of Adolf Hitler as an idealistic Utopian, but, from Hitler's iron-hot pseudo-scientific convictions in *Mein Kampf* to the drama of his suicide, he followed an almost perfect Utopian model of social idealism to its near-invariably absurd and horrible end.

Like it or not, American foreign policy must find its place on this none too encouraging continuum during the next generation. And it will, just as it belabored to uselessness the "moral-ideological" part of it during the past one.

That the USA will now enter a more conservative phase of international statesmanship seems both probable and desirable to the authors. Americans are, naturally, not ready (yet) to throw moralism entirely to the winds. But the Vietnam war indicated clearly to them the weaknesses of a foreign policy dedicated only to doing the "right thing." *First,* one often finds oneself doing business with (and allied with) the wrong people and antagonistic towards the right ones, from the moral perspective. *Second,* the sands of morality invariably and quickly shift. Then, one finds oneself defending (in excessive ways) agreements, treaties, resolutions, guarantees and alli-

ances made in a former moral climate—or under the impress
of moral imperatives that have changed. Spreading democratic
idealism (whatever it is) and republicanism (no matter how
corrupt or poorly it works) around the world is as futile and as
inevitably disastrous a course as that recommended by those
who might interpret America's manifest destiny as the imposition of a capitalist free-enterprise economy on the entire globe.

(Not beholden to moral commitments, the French, for instance, recognized the nineteen-fifties that Southeast Asia was
a social, economic and political cesspool and, in typically
French style, ceded her claims to empire and moral destiny at
the price of a minor military defeat and the dissolution of her
famed Foreign Legion. It was a good trade—for the French.
Twenty years later, the caper allowed France to play the role
of elder statesman to the USA in extricating the latter from the
remains of their Vietnam mess, into which America had, literally, blundered in the defense of moral idealism. We were saving, or so we said we believed, the Oriental world from conquest by Red China. How little we knew. Nor did we realize
how many more effective ways were open to us to achieve that
end, other than a military partnership with the mercurial politics of South Vietnam.)

Our present retreat from moralism will also necessarily
bring us farther away from idealism, but not, we repeat,
merely into nineteenth-century gambits and war games in
order to maintain a "balance" of super-powers, an absurd notion when you think about it a bit. A student of Metternich
would be the *first* to recognize how different are the fundamental rules between the European chess matches of yesterday
and today's awesome global power confrontations between nuclear empires. For technical, political, ideological, cultural,
economic and historical reasons, a three-party stalemate between nuclear giants simply *cannot* be balanced as a game
by modern Disraelis, Gladstones or (heaven forbid!) Neville
Chamberlains.

We will be—must be—responsive to a strategy of *Realpol-*

itik, but one dependent upon a *limited entente* and wider areas of interdependence between these powers, whereby national welfare and security of all the three will literally depend upon the survival and health, in *specific* and *delimited* areas of national life, one upon the other. In other words, a standoff. But one predicated upon the vital self-interests and good faith (what our complex treaties and protocols boil down to) between the super-powers in certain critical areas of culture—or areas that are *perceived by statesmen* as critical.

These will probably involve: (1) military technology, nuclear weaponry (and, therefore, stabs at serious agreements, like the present Strategic Arms Limitation Talks), the latter constituting but a fraction of the multitudinous military considerations involved; (2) world economy and the ways interdependence may *continue* to raise standards of living within and without the borders of the super-powers, on a global basis; (3) hegemony over third world and so-called "uncommitted" and "underdeveloped" nations regarding many matters, military and economic ones being the most important; (4) guarantees and enforcement procedures for political and social and cultural sovereignty *within* the areas controlled by the super-powers in spheres of endeavor where the stakes are *low*—development of transportation systems, the GNP battle, popular culture, literacy rates, demonstrations of national solidarity etc. and; (6) stimulation of the illusion of *intense* cooperation, also where the stakes are *low* (or non-existent), such as international pollution control, ecology programs, cooperative medical technological research, *panem et circuses* (as long as the latter are not too highly ideological), traveling poets, acrobats, athletes, violinists and similar side-show fare that will, in the long run, effect the fate of the world not one bit.

The super-powers, in other words, will have to learn to do business with one another, leave each other alone in areas of sensitive abrasions, and even to stroke one another gently, to the degree that public assent for on-going foreign relationships are enhanced by displays of such mutual admiration.

Upon this basis, and upon such limited aspirations as a policy of this sort permits (hopes for a peaceful world, if not a free one; contentment with a fairly well-fed world, if not a prosperous one; prospects for an explorable world, if not an open one, etc. etc. etc.), a new and viable era of modestly moral and incidentally idealistic American foreign policy is, we think, about to begin. It may, if it is successful, carry us intact to the year 2000 A.D.

George Kennan wrote, some years ago, a penetrating statement of what he believed (and apparently still believes) was the source of our moral-idealistic *raisons d'être* for past foreign policy. In the light shed by the experiences during the years since it was written (1951), it stands as a prophetic prediction of the policy blunders from which we are emerging today—and also as an agenda for the reconstruction of them today, at the latest:

> As you have no doubt surmised, I see the most serious fault of our past policy formulation to lie in something that I might call the legalistic-moralistic approach to international problems. . . .
>
> It is the belief that it should be possible to supress the chaotic and dangerous aspirations of governments in the international field by the acceptance of some system of legal rules and restraints. This belief undoubtedly represents in part an attempt to transpose the Anglo-Saxon concept of individual law into the international field and make it applicable to governments as it is applicable here at home to individuals. . . .
>
> It is the essence of this belief that, instead of taking the awkward conflicts of national interest and dealing with them on their merits with a view to finding the solutions least unsettling to the stability of international life, it would be better to find some formal criteria of a juridical nature by which the permissible behavior of states could be defined. There would then be judicial entities competent to measure the actions of governments against these criteria and to decide when their behavior was acceptable and when unacceptable. Behind all of this, of course, lies the *American* assumption that the things for which other peoples in this world are apt to contend are for the most

part neither creditable nor important and might justly be expected to take second place behind the desirability of an orderly world, untroubled by international violence. To the American mind, it is implausible that people should have positive aspirations, and ones that *they* regard as legitimate, more important to *them* than the peaceful and orderliness of international life.[8]

Aims and Means; Deeds and Words; Policy and Propaganda

One belabors the obvious (and the *Sitzfleisch* of the reader who has followed the arguments so far in this book) to observe that, as American foreign policy is reconstructed—some would say "constructed"—so too will information, persuasion or propaganda, in policy and practice, also require reconstruction.

Men on the firing line—or those who have just left it—tend to argue eloquently for the continuation of the *status quo*, on the basis, mainly, of an inherent belief (in their own arguments) that today's practical propaganda structure is flexible enough to accommodate whatever twists American foreign policy undergoes tomorrow—providing that they are not reversals of main thrusts. Thus, the Hoveys and Sargeants and the USIA establishment spokesmen—and their consultants, experts, researchers, professional testimonialists and others—argue for the maintenance of tried and tested policies and programs, with not unconvincing tried and tested rationales. But the important element implicit in their justifications for stasis is what they do *not* say: their faith that the changes they know will blow their way, along with shifts in international policies, may be assimilated with ease and facility into the organizations they now control. None are so naïve as to believe that sea-changes are not in the wind. The phlegm of their conservatism reflects merely their faith that they are competent to accommodate to new climates.

The attitude is well encapsulated, for example, in the informal observations of Henry Loomis, once head Deputy Director of USIA (in other words, he apparently ran it), who, from his present "hot-seat" as chief of the Corporation for Public Broadcasting, can afford a little armchair ratiocination without warnings that his realism is not for ascription.

"*Everything* has a public-relations arm, doesn't it?" asks the youthful, quick-trigger Loomis. "Big businesses do; big special interests do; political parties do. So, in this age of the public image and mass media, the United States had better pay attention to its public relations arm too, support it and listen to it. Exactly *how* it operates will be determined largely by the same forces that determine *all* matters of foreign policy. And these days, like it or not, this is a reflection of the thinking of the man living in the White House. Back in President Kennedy's administration, the Voice of America, for instance, became pretty important to the Chief Executive's office when it remained the *only* way of getting the truth about the Cuban Missile Crisis to the people of Cuba! Nixon is another strong President, highly sensitive to the role of public relations in his new *ententes* with the USSR and China. What may be missing in the White House is sufficient *input* from agencies like the USIA *to* the President's ear. But this may change. And even this depends upon *who* speaks for the USIA, his formal and informal relations to the Secretary of State, and how close *he* is to the President. This is the way things *are* in an age of expanding executive power, especially when men like Kennedy and Nixon—and Johnson too, I suppose—play the roles of the *real* decision makers in international policy. What's most vital is that these public relations (or, as *you* say, 'propaganda') agencies are in good shape to respond to the needs of foreign policy at any moment and in any way necessary."

Another way of looking at Loomis' analysis is to consider *all* of America's information and propaganda conduits— governmental, quasi-governmental and private—as channels involved for most of the time in a holding action, at least from the policy viewpoint. They vamp along, mediating by radio, press and film news, commentary, publications, cultural exchange and other harmless vessels of do-goodism and virtue, playing minor ideological games here and there, and merchandising as much good will as they can, within the limits of their budgets. Vis-a-vis the *real stuff* of international exchange (diplomacy, economics and military alliances), they are cosmetic in function and practice, like much (or most) public relations in the private domains of national life. As *open* channels of communication, however, they serve another purpose as well: They are always ready for use when they may be urgently required for more serious matters than cosmetics. (Back to the Cuban Missile Crisis of 1962 again, but with recent echoes in the Middle East, Poland and Southeast Asia, where American intervention—or lack of it—in explosive confrontations has required open conduits of explanation to local public opinion.)

Faced with the charge that the long-term maintenance of elaborate and expensive information structures like the USIA, RFE, RL and others, only to use them at times of crisis, appears a trifle fruitless and wasteful, men like Henry Loomis have at their fingertips an analogy that reasonably meets such criticism. Says Loomis, "We keep an Army going, don't we? But we only *use* it in times of military crisis. Well, psychological statesmanship demands exactly the same type of thinking." Granting his premises, he is correct.

The main faults inherent in all of these arguments—and in the viewpoint for which they speak—are discovered in their traditional assumptions concerning foreign policy in the age of mass communications. They construe the role of information and propaganda as mere words, cosmetics and devices for the *enhancement* of policy, rather than elements *integral* to policy. In fact, mass communications are one of the reasons that contemporary foreign policy must change modes of procedure that were suitable for yesterday's world to those consonant with the realities that the USA (or any super-power) must face in the world today.

One of the conditions of contemporary international intercourse is the communication of ideas (not necessarily of ideologies) *between men.* At issue are the *demonstrable effects* that these communications have, not only upon distant masses listening to transistor radios in the Artic tundra or "opinion makers" in world society at large, but also in the thinking and behavior of diplomats, business tycoons and high-echelon statesmen themselves. In our opinion, Nikita Khrushchev was the last formidable world figure to appreciate fully this fact of contemporary life, a manifestation of his peculiar genius that baffled his more conservative Politburo associates and, accordingly, was a main cause for his retirement from the international scene—unfortunately, we believe.

In the USA, however, others are aware of the serious and enormous directive force of communications technology. Although his professional prowess lies in the field of corporate manipulation, Frank Stanton, erstwhile Columbia Broadcasting top-cat, is both outspoken and inclined to thinking pragmatically about large, long-range issues involving communications. As an expert in the internal clockwork of broadcasting, his analysis *of but one aspect* of the total configuration of mass communications as an active factor in modern international *Realpolitik* is worth considering—and then multiplying by many hundreds of jots of concern in order to grasp the relevance of the entire issue to the articulation and implementation of a viable foreign policy in the last part of the twentieth century. Stanton, a short time ago, was concerned about the policy implications of a "far reaching new technology that has opened a new era of human progress, the miracle of satellite broadcasting." Continued Stanton:

> The satellite television broadcasts we receive today come into our homes through networks and individual stations. Through such world wide linkage, over 600 million people on six continents saw the moonwalk on television—a significant reminder of the enormous potential of satellite transmission.
>
> The capabilities of satellite communication are such that individual receivers may one day be able to supplement reception of locally originated signals with broadcasts direct from satellites 22,300 miles in the sky. Such broadcasts could make it possible for people in every corner of the earth to share in the

free flow of ideas, the free communication of knowledge and information.

And yet, ironically, the prospect of this very type of satellite-to-home television broadcast has been made the occasion for an effort to negate the principle of international freedom of communication. . .

The Foreign Minister of the Soviet Union, Andrei Gromyko, submitted for the consideration of the United Nations General Assembly the text of a proposed international convention governing satellite television broadcasts directly into homes. What this proposed convention asserts is that governments have the right to control television broadcasts from abroad via satellite to their own people by controlling international broadcasts at their source. It is an unfortunate fact that the leaders of too many nations have a deadly fear of information which could lead their people to topple the regimes in power. Understandably, these leaders are interested in stringent preventative measures. Hence the efforts of the Soviet Union have been encouraged by the acquiescence of other nations to a similar proposal from UNESCO. . .

It (the USSR) envisages not merely jamming incoming broadcasts, but also taking action directly against satellites themselves outside a receiving nation's territorial jurisdiction. The Soviet Union asks UN member states, including our country, to agree that any nation, on its own initiative, may destroy satellites to keep broadcasts from coming directly into the homes of their own people. This would make censorship a principle of international law. . .

The (U.S.) State Department's attitude is perhaps best described as "embarrassment" over the prospect of opposing the desires of developing countries, which support the (UNESCO) Draft Declaration. What the Department obviously has in mind is an attempt to avoid a head-on confrontation and give everybody a tidy diplomatic out. But I submit that the central issue here transcends that kind of diplomacy. Delaying tactics, pleas that haste is unnecessary or further study is required, are entirely out of place when the fundamental principle of free speech is at stake.[9]

Now, Stanton's immediate objective, at the time of the speech excerpted above, was to encourage American objection to the specific UNESCO declaration that would have affirmed a principle (impossible, incidentally, to enforce consistently or efficiently) permitting sovereign states to exercise self-determination in controlling the dissemination of *all* types of communication released within their borders. A master at the use of the world "censorship" to resist controls upon any type of broadcasting (no matter how irresponsible), Stanton claims that US approval of the UNESCO Declaration connotes an un-American encouragement of the denial of freedom of speech (or, more correctly, *access* to free speech) within other nations.

(Not mentioned by Stanton is the fact that the Declaration would also expose many millions of dollars worth of American electronic hardware whizzing around the earth, the "property" of publicly owned corporations like COMSAT and possibly the CBS, to instant destruction by guided missiles.)

Whether or not, as Stanton seems to assume, America's constructions of free speech *must* be imposed upon other nations, whether or not the destruction of such satellites is, in fact, "censorship" (as the term is used by men other than Stanton), and whether or not sovereign nations may legitimately protect themselves with harsh means against the impedimenta of psychological warfare, are all tacky questions of international law—unfortunately beyond both Stanton's competences and ours. They are *not* solved either by slogans or appeals to patriotism. But the emerging, exigent and pressing problems they raise for the United States are clear. Let us examine some of them:

From the psychological perspective, the Vietnam conflict was not only the longest military engagement in the history of the United States, it was also the most valuable, because, unlike the elementary lessons we have taken from other conflicts (all axiomatic *before* the outbreak of hostilities), Vietnam provided an experience that might be learned nowhere but in the crucible of experience. In the *patois* of the 'sixties, news commentators called it an "unpopular war," a cynical phrase, but symptomatic of a not-so-cynical truth if one examines the psycho-dynamics of the term "unpopular." (It is possible to conjecture that during the same decade the United States might have found itself engaged in other, more "popular" circumscribed hostilities, some not unlike Vietnam—the defense, for instance, of the State of Israel at the time of the "six-day war," had the UAR forces been better prepared for it and well supported by Soviet "military advisors.")

The Vietnam experience raises one central foreign policy issue for the future, intimately related to the psychological aspects of all American foreign policy—the problem at the heart of Stanton's concern. Briefly stated, it centers on a few obvious conditions of modernity, in no manner fundamental to the skills and objectives of either diplomats, soldiers or international tradesman, but vital to their endeavors.

Like all major issues, it represents the sum total of constituent elements, that, boiled down, are:

(1) In conditions of modern warfare, popular assent is a necessity for support of hostilities, particularly those of lengthy duration. In the long view, for instance, the difference between both the conduct and means of termination between the Korean conflict and the Vietnam conflict centered on the divisiveness and turmoil into which the latter engagement threw the civil population of America. This inevitable consequence on American soil was as much a part of the military strategy of the Viet Cong and North Vietnamese as their supply lines—quite logically and sensibly so, from their position. Under such circumstances, attenuation of the conflict could lose them little—in that the "war" had been going on for years before the American presence. And any encouragement they might add to the inevitably well-publicized divisiveness within the USA was, in their eyes, correctly perceived as a hard and fast military advantage. (Thus, their seemingly senseless tactics at the Paris Peace Conference during the Johnson years, their gleeful exploitation of sympathetic American celebrities who "protested" for "peace," and various special consideration given sympathetic newsmen and others who would feed the flames of

apparent rampant near-revolutionary disunity in a USA, as mass communications, at least, told the story, particularly in the period from 1967 to 1970.)

(2) Whatever principles apply to conflicts with guns, apply also to other sorts of conflicts—possibly more so. Public assent in its various forms (on the positive side) and public dissent (on the negative side) are both intimately involved in all forms of international commerce in its widest sense. We are not merely repeating the time-worn dictum that all public policy produces public opinion. Of course it does. And it has since antiquity. What is *new* in the modern world is the intense and immediate *power* of mass communication (particularly in disseminating widely and instantly persuasion disguised as "news") to, often immediately, *direct* public policy at all levels in international affairs. Not only may it subtly prolong and acerbate warfare, it wields the power to alter trade routes, destroy economies, murder minority groups and hurl masses into fruitless (or fruitful) revolutions.

One minor sub-point: the *nature* of the communications instruments involved (McLuhan's "media") is but *one* aspect of this power. Of equal importance are, on the one hand, the rise around the world of sentient, semi-literate masses of quondam lower-and-middle class, yea-sayers, who, today, *believe* that they have political power and are continually reminded of it by the very existence of mass communications. On the other hand, a change has occurred during the past generation, not only in the access of the masses to information concerning the flux and flow of their power, but in their genuine understandings (with the spread of education) of the implications of how their particular sovereign state—and others—uses power for the betterment or detriment of the average citizen's central concern: himself. One symptom of these trends is the growing extent of official censorship *within* modern nations, usually exercised by governments and/or strong economic interests, that has been the subject of considerable editorial comment in the United States—ironically, because the same sort of tendency towards censoring ideation (under the cover of "clearing the news of bias") has been as noticeable in America as in those nations that men like Stanton so glibly accuse of squelching the free exchange of ideas.

(3) The concept that controls may, in any long-run construction, be exercised upon mass communication technology in order to eliminate, manipulate, or channel its psychological effects is absurd, wishful thinking. One invariably hears it from the mouths of men out of their depth, who know nearly nothing about the technological and psychological facts concerning the present state of the arts of radio and television transmission, methods of coding, storing and transporting written materials (to a population where literacy is growing every day) and disseminating pictures and ideas in many forms past both national boundaries—and past any nation's statutes and laws. When we speak about the "underground press" of the world of today or tomorrow, we are not talking about mimeographs in cellars (or even *samizdats,* although they are portents of what is to come), but about giant international communication networks, legal and illegal, of considerable sophistication and magnitude, utilizing technologies already feasible today. That a man in the nineteen-sixties, for instance, was able, quite easily, to record a tape in an American radio studio that would be broadcast the following day both locally in North Vietnam and to the world by short-wave transmission, gives one an indication of the malleable nature of the relatively crude mass communications instrumentation of *yesterday.* There is no sense in dilating upon the magic available today and tomorrow: pages of books, reduced to microdots, transmitted as electronic information and entire motion pictures recorded on 4″ x 5″ file cards etc. just begin to tell the long, incredible story.

Technology alone, naturally, means nothing. What men do with it is everything. And what they *will* do with modern mass communications technology is to lay bare for all mankind to hear (or at least receive impressions of) the manifold ways in which the world's cultures are, at any time, interacting, one with the other. Neither international agreements, the protocol of diplomacy, nor "Top Secret" stamps in the hands of generals will vitiate communication technology's power, when all is said and done, to *create conditions with which foreign policies of every nation must eventually recognize a priori*. Nothing, as the French sociologist Jacques Ellul has trenchantly shown, can muster enough power to stop them except weapons of total lethal destruction.

Those statesmen and diplomats, therefore, who are still making their cases for "expanded inter-cultural programs" and the need to "sell America overseas" are currently talking in a language as dead as Sanscrit.

Mass communications at large are, in fact, a general condition of existence in the last quarter of the twentieth century. To bisect them into "internal" and "external" communications, as book publishers and university professors still do, seems archaic: quaint but harmless—if one understands that such divisions are as fruitless as dividing public health or weather prediction (or any phenomenon dealing with forces ignorant of national borders) into "internal" and "external" categories. International mass persuasion is as much a matter involving Mrs. Mary Kelly and her porcelain business in Moraga, California, as it involves a disillusioned drama critic suffering under (to him) an intolerable British production of an American play, and/or a Washington whiz-kid dealing with millions of dollars in the hopes of manipulating, to his own esoteric ends, various attitudes among ballet lovers in Belgrade, Yugoslavia. Mass communications are seamless webs that today cover the entire earth. They affect, and are affected by, everything that happens under the netting.

Their contemporary wellsprings—like this Chapter—begin and end at home base.

Welcome to the Crisis

In 1976 the United States of America will be 200 years

old. Not very long, but (next to Switzerland) the oldest federal republic in the world. The Roman empire remained a viable bureaucratic state for about 500 years. (Had it had a bit more sticking power, it would, about now, be celebrating the 2,000th anniversary of the *Republic* of Rome. As things worked out, the Republic lasted only about a dozen years after the murder of Julius Caesar.)

In the Orient, the great dynasties of Han, Tang, Sung, Yuan, Ming and Ching ranged in life-span from about 100 to 300 years, give or take a little for each.

Great Britain traces her national ancestry back for more than 900 years. But the statistic is equivocal. Her republicanism is just slightly older than in most other erstwhile monarchies on the European continent.

In the continuum of governments, two centuries is a formidable span of time. A dangerous age as well.

The record of history seems to show that governments, like men, age, wither and die. Much has been made of these analogous periods of growth: childhood, youth, maturity, old age, senility etc. Most of the analogies are, however, inadequate, simply because governments are not flesh and blood. They neither grow, survive nor degenerate in the same ways that living organisms do.

Governments, in the last analysis, are what philosophy teachers call "processes." In fact, this means that they are on-going agreements between men to utilize their resources in certain ways and according to certain limitations for their common welfare. When the agreements fail, the processes cease to function. Then, due to many *ostensible* (but not necessarily real) reasons, one government is replaced by another: that is, by a new set of agreements between some (at least) new parties.

Our American bicentennial year is notable. It occurs in the early period of an era that will be dominated by four major considerations in international life: (1) super-powerism, the logical extension of former (largely American) concepts of "unconditional surrender" and "total war"; (2) sophistications of technology, unforeseeable at the moment, that men will interpret as god-like and mythical determinants of their personal destinies; (3) millions of people abroad, emerging from primitivism, whose aspirations will be led toward the extension of that technology into their personal domains; and (4) the mediation of ideas, words, dreams and nightmares between peoples across the face of the earth who will profoundly misunderstand what they have to say to one another. Our management of the dysfunctions that this period produces will determine whether our progeny celebrate a tricentennial year.

Our bicentennial year, however, occurs also at a time of crisis, the likes of which no people who have ever lived can possibly have known, because the very means for the knowing did not exist. The crisis is not one that can be "solved." (Oh, how Americans love to isolate their problems and then "solve" them!) It is a crisis through which we *may live.* The crisis will remain untouched. But the United States will not be the same when and if she emerges on the other side of it—say, twenty or thirty years from now.

We have said that America's information policies and practices begin and end on our own soil, and we say it again. If, as a people, we display one major shortcoming in our international relationships it is our endemic ethnocentric arrogance and lack of humility as a member of the community of nations. By this, we do not mean our much exaggerated braggadocio concerning our high standard of living, wealth, "know how" or technological expertise. These are old clichés. Most of them have been put to rest by such recent events as Vietnam and our various economic woes. No, we are referring to other matters that we often construe as virtues and are, unfortunately, as American as apple pie.

Our arrogance has many symptoms—but they are merely symptoms: the breakdown of what was once a reasonably efficient educational system into a madcap collection of playschools that, given their own objectives, *do not work;* the peculiar fact that *every* so-called "social problem" to which our ameliorists put their brains—and our government puts its money—either to containing or curing simply gets worse, usually in rough proportion to the sum of money spent on it; the spread of simple vulgarity (masquerading behind the sweet phrase "civil liberty") into almost every aspect of our culture —not violence, but the delectation *in* violence in our popular culture; not sex and pornography, but our exploitation of the universal neuroticisms of voyeurism and exhibitionism in the name of sexual "liberation"; not inhuman incivilities of man to man, but the institutionalization of bad manners (manners, friend, not morals) by example of the intrusive unmannerliness of most of the celebrity caste and their sycophants who command our eyes and ears.

As we say, these are but symptoms. The reader may not consider them as heinous as the authors do. Or he may dismiss them as overly generalized dramatizations of passing mores. They are neither, but that is beside the point.

Consider, then, the really rough stuff—to many, the *serious* symptoms—still, just symptoms: millions of American black citizens (and members of other minorities) who have been forced into a reactionary retreat *away from* the mainstream of American culture and life, (to our eyes, out of sheer desperation), many of them today onto the brink of armed rebellion; an epidemic of drug addiction which (if one includes those lethally addicted to alcohol) rivals in virulence (but exceeds in pathos) the plagues of the dark ages—and about which we are, at these moments of history, powerless to do anything except talk, appropriate funds for nonexistent cures, and wait for the scourge to pass—if it does; the merciless destruction of the nucleus of all great cultures, our cities, largely at the hands of irresponsible architects and warped visionaries who profoundly *hate* cities and apparently intend, one way or another, to strangle them—and so forth, and so forth and so forth.

Symptoms of *what?*

Were we merely to say a "loss of faith," we might as well pack up our Bibles and go home. But the term is not so banal that it must be dismissed offhand.

Some years ago Leslie Fiedler spoke of "an end to idealism." But even this clear literary thinker did not credit how great was the residues of idealism most Americans still kept in their traveling bags during the years shortly after World War II, or how much further our disillusionment had yet to travel. What Fiedler meant was an end to the kind of beneficent socialistic liberalism that had sustained countless otherwise disillusioned Americans through the great depression of the nineteen-thirties.

Today, it is not only the ideals of liberalism that have failed, gone also is the implicit faith *behind* the old-time liberal's visions of social progress.

In its place is arrogance.

American arrogance, as it shows its face today, is nothing new in man's history. It is the sense that every aspect of national experience is a "challenge" that will be "solved" by superior intellect, that every curiosity worthy of printing in a newspaper is important and novel, simply because it is happening *here* and *now*. In short, it is a pathetic discontinuity with the past, with one's country, one's civilization. It is the arrogance that would sever the present instant from its roots, hurl it into a think-tank or computer and be done with it, in the stupid, blind confidence that, by a miracle of modern science, it will be analyzed, hypothesized and eventually solved.

All childish. All futile. All rootless. For confirmation, audit a class in "current social problems" at your local university—or what's left of it.

Many voices have sounded warnings over the years, but few have listened. Walter Lippmann has for decades been calling for a viable philosophy of public life in America. Where may one find it today? Millions of copies of David Riesman's *The Lonely Crowd* have been sold in paperback editions, original and revised. But its readers (and, apparently, as the years went by, even its author) have missed its point: shallow "other-oriented" men are ghosts of men, incapable either of independent thought or simple civility. Ortega y Gasset's *The Revolt of the Masses* is now in its umpty-umptyeth printing. But who, in modern public life, would publicly stand up to the Spanish philosopher's brave observations concerning the inanities of the contemporary mindless worship of specialism, science, youth, experts and barbarian, artless art?—prophetic wisdoms written in the early nineteen-twenties. Ortega—who predicted with deadly acumen the rise of fascism in Italy and the Nazi mystique!

Hundreds of other voices from the dead still beg us to consider the follies of our age. Their words are marketed by the ton in paperback. How different the destiny of our nation might be were this glut of books *read* instead of *collected!*

From today forward, America will, we think, move into the history of the future as one of the *least* idealistic nations in the world.

Let us, nevertheless, ring bells to celebrate our bicentennial year. Let us read extracts from the Bill of Rights and the Constitution in pear-shaped tones. Let us issue suitable quotas of postage stamps, medallions, coins and limited-edition fancy plates to mark the occasion. (Put them away carefully, friend. They are likely to turn out to be good investments in tomorrow's collectors' markets.)

We are a large nation and remain, to this day, a confederation of many different sorts of people. This is our best strength. In the force of numbers and disparity of life-styles, values and aspirations, we are, however, left with few common denominators in the department of ideals.

We are also but *one* potent nation among *three* superpowers—and but one among *very* many others with legitimate title-claims to all of the old virtues we used to cherish. Like all of them, we have a right to survive and, if possible, prosper in all matters affecting reciprocal relationships between cultures. If we go down, it will be most probably, we think, from implosion—the inability to handle our own affairs.

So things stand. Whatever we may reasonably expect from other nations will be neither more nor less than they will ask of us. Like it or not, in the *War of Ideas,* old debts are mostly cancelled, and so are many of our obligations. In the future, if we must fight ideologies apparently incompatible with our survival, we shall have to fight them in open combat: with words, we hope. But guns and bombs remain ready for a "popular" war, make no mistake.

As Americans, we can export neither a viable ideology nor the fragments of our shattered idealisms, as we have attempted for the past generation. What we *can* show the rest of the world is the true record, warts and all, and let ideologists and idealists elsewhere make of it what they will. For once, honesty is not only our best propaganda policy—it *is* policy. We have no choices.

Our best hope, then, rests in a return to the same pragmatism that sustained us through the caprices of our first 200 years. A foreign policy *may* be built upon an allegiance to an intelligent use of man's impulses for morality—the urge to do the "right thing"—*and* upon an appreciation of the pull of *Realpolitik,* one vector ceding necessary power to the other, as modest intelligence demands.

In the age of *entente,* therefore, America's first steps must be to establish *entente* with the remnants of its *own* heritage. Then, on to Russia and China!

If our information and propaganda arms accomplish no more than dramatizing the discovery of ourselves for the rest of the world, the agenda for the *War of Ideas* has already been clearly drawn for the next generation. But our *first* move demands an *apercu* we have never before attempted, except in the superficial language of the television set and slick magazine: a searching look at our native, American constituency, not at its image but at its guts.

Nobody on the face of the globe, in their heart of hearts, gives one hoot about America's "image"—any more than you or I care about the Russian "image" or the Chinese "image." What they care about, and are hungry to comprehend, is the internal dynamic of our civilization: what keeps us going, our pleasures and pains, our vanities and prejudices, our dreams and our disillusionments and, most important, what (if anything) we have learned as a people, both from our enormous failures and our spectacular successes.

Mass communications as a *constituent* of foreign policy face their *first* severe tests in history during the coming years. Their failure to perform the tasks expected of them will be catastrophic. Their successes will be, quite possibly, unnoticed by all but the wise and sensitive.

At any rate, the *real War of Ideas* is just beginning. Are we ready for it?

NOTES TO CHAPTER 9

[1] "The Hope of Man" in *The New York Times*, November 6, 1972, p. 4.

[2] "Britain Discovers America—and Finds?", *The New York Times*, Arts and Leisure, December 10, 1972, p. 15.

[3] Interview with Jonathan Ward in *Intellectual Digest*, September, 1972, pp. 16–19.

[4] *Time*, May 11, 1970, p. 20.

[5] *The Saturday Review*, July 15, 1972, p. 45.

[6] "Fear and Fantasy in Future Folly," *The New York Times*, December 5, 1972.

[7] John Maddox, *The Doomsday Syndrome* (New York: McGraw-Hill Book Company, 1972.) See also Melvin J. Grayson and Thomas R. Shepard Jr., *The Disaster Lobby* (Chicago: Follet Publishing Co., 1973.) for an

incisive presentation of what can be called "the retreat from reason" during the 'sixties to the ludicrous excesses of the "environmentalist religion" and the last of other movements it has inspired to the detriment of mankind."

[8] George Kennan, *American Diplomacy* (New York: The New American Library, 1952, pp. 93–94), Italics added.

[9] From a speech delivered at the *WREC Fiftieth Anniversary Ceremonies*, Memphis: October 4, 1972.

10

Suggestions and Recommendations Anyway

We know enough today to know that there is infinite room for betterment in every human concern. Nothing is needed but collective effort.

H. G. Wells

No, we shall not violate our own previous and best admonitions against attempting to "solve" problems that may not, in the usual sense of the word, be solvable.

We shall not try to collate various data and present the results of our research. We believe, unfortunately, that nine-tenths of what social scientists, these days, consider "data" are merely cold-storage *rerum* ("things"), and most of what passes for "research" in our time and place is, in A. N. Whitehead's phrase, mere "pacing a mental quarter-deck," meticulous recording of floating flotsam, unworthy of a competent junk dealer.

In the past, we have attempted to isolate and discuss some

of the major problems that the United States—and, we think, the rest of the world too—presently faces in various sorts of meetings between different nations and cultures as they are likely to take place in the future. Our emphasis has been, broadly, upon the *psychological* effects of these meetings, what results similar events have caused in the past and how best the United States may carry them out in the future. Our obvious biases result both from our special interests and manners of training. That much of this cultural intercourse will occur over great distances (and at second or third hand) by means of modern mass communications techniques is incidental to the fact that it *will* occur. We are also both eager and willing to state (and re-state) that much of important international communication that will be accomplished tomorrow will take place on a person-to-person basis. We have been concerned about *all* of it, because we cannot clearly delineate where one type ends and the other begins, and we believe they are interdependent.

As the reader has seen, we have not centered on simple problems that may be resolved into formulae or "systems" which, drawing upon a lexicon of available pre-programmed "solutions," may be resolved like crossword puzzles or questions on an objective examination. They are discursive, subtle, multi-faceted, fomenting problems, hopelessly (at times) intertwined with issues seemingly irrelevant to them. Most seriously, they are both delicate and fragile problems. To consign them to classical formats for solutions by the numbers (or by committees or task forces or the consensus of experts) so distorts their very definition and articulation that whatever recommendations or alternative strategies such treatment produces are worse than ridiculous. They are useless.

In relatively concise fashion, however, let us present below some considerations for the reader to ponder that have emerged from our discussion, offered in the face of our warnings above and in full awareness of them.

Some may seem to the reader self-evident, others absurd. But they all represent our careful and necessarily cautious judgment concerning steps that, we think, *should,* as soon as possible, be taken in the domains of policy and practice by the various American interests involved, in order to facilitate their roles via international communications in the social and economic relationships with other countries that will involve the USA in the coming years. They follow—in no particular hierarchical order of importance or pith. They are *all* important, equally so, in that we find it impossible to read the future in order to isolate the *most* critical concerns in foreign affairs affecting the United States tomorrow. We do not believe they will prove, in time, to be equally well-taken or sage. They are, however, all motivated by the same sense of present urgency —our belief that unless our information and propaganda policies are reviewed from scratch, *de novo* and *now,* the United States may soon experience on the psychological front greater future losses than she has suffered in the scorched militarized zones from which she recently retreated with, we are told, "peace with honor."

These are our suggestions and recommendations (accompanied by short justifications):

1. A call for further research and development of anything is always safe, as professional scholars know. *Priorities* of research and development programs are another matter. We believe that one of the most urgent areas for scientific and humanistic investigation facing our nation centers on methods of controlling what may be called "post-atomic" methods of warfare—that is, psychological, agricultural, meterological and other methods of manipulating the natural world to accomplish strategic ends that, in the past, have been achieved by military means. This issue has been discussed in Part One of this book. It urgently requires methodical, disciplined consideration—not visionary quasi-science futurology or airy speculation. Intrinsic to this intensive program, is much-needed study of contemporary mass communications technology—centering right *now* mostly upon the press, radio

and television—sophistications of their new devices of instrumentation and the parts they play in the formation and change
of attitudes—less at home in the US than abroad, but certainly
in America, as well as everywhere else that such intensive study
is practical. We *do* indeed know a *bit* about the psychological
potentials of mass communications, but not as much as we
think we do, by a long shot. We need to understand much
more.

2. A new policy of *entente* with former antagonists (as
well as the maintenance of former alliances) will require the
development of new world-wide psychological atmospheres of
so-called "public opinion," involving, we think, low-pitched
sentimental expectations, but promising visibly high dividends
in terms of practical results. In simpler terms, a psychological
climate must be developed among our people (and in other
countries, if possible)—encouraged by education and mass
communications—that accepts a reasonable measure of *fundamental moral and ideological differences and antagonisms in
values between people and nations as the natural state of
things.* This is a theme exactly the opposite of the official "line"
of American academic and popular "cross-cultural" anthropology for more than two generations. On the other hand, we
must recognize and advertise that mutual respect and international honor are prerequisites for *ententes* of any sort, even old
ones. We do not need to *love* our neighbors in order to *live* in
peace and prosper with them and to indulge with them in circumscribed degrees of reciprocity. An atmosphere of this sort
in international matters is relatively new to the American consciousness. It will not occur spontaneously.

3. Commensurate with a hoped-for formidable decrease in
military spending, the US should, within the next decade, reac-
tivate its Congressional objective of the early nineteen-fifties:
gradually to decrease foreign aid spending—that is as "foreign
aid" *per se.* Whenever opportunities permit, the use of foreign

aid funds for indirect military purposes should be shaved to the bone, with the corollary objective of arriving at suitable agreements with other large powers through normal diplomatic channels to decrease the need for such spending in the world's "hot spots." (Such appeals to economy—if reciprocal—will, in the proper international climate, be less difficult to achieve, we think than many believe. They must, of course, be motivated by self-interest on the part of all parties involved.) Other types of American foreign aid may well be necessary—selectively— especially in instances of disaster and for humanitarian purposes. A good portion of funds saved by the elimination of our present foreign aid program, however, should be channeled directly into low-interest loans (not gifts) to stimulate the economies of underdeveloped and/or "third world" nations. Such aid may also take the form of subsidized trade, tourism and loans for the development of local industry, until such time that these nations may handle their own economic destinies. Our objective should be to help others only to the point that they are capable of helping themselves. At that point, foreign trade, for many reasons, is far preferable to foreign aid. By 1985, at the latest, our foreign aid program should be a museum relic.

4. To ask, as prerequisite to an international communications policy, for an end to creeping demoralization in American life is a tall order—possibly impossible. Certain steps *will* lead us in this direction, but they are large ones and will strain muscles. Many of us are slowly learning that we cannot solve cultural problems with money alone or by the random application of sociological "know-how"—we mean so-called "social" problems like the worst aspects of ghetto life, our drug culture, suicide, homicide, auto-accident rates etc. Almost *all* such primitive do-goodism and pseudo-scientific attempts at amelioration should at once be thrown into low gear—at least as far as federal subsidy and direction are concerned. Community problems are best shared and contained by communities, ac-

cording to need and feasibility. (Is Daniel Moynihan the only professional sociologist in the USA who comprehends this empirical truth?) The modern state, also, is only as valuable to its citizens as its educational systems, in sum total, are worth. We shall not attempt to write a tract on education here; but the *inverse* of creeping national demoralization is *enlightenment*. For too long, we have suffered the on-going failures of our schools by calling their living, breathing and walking results (or lack of results) first, " 'teenage culture" then, "youth culture" and now "consciousness raising." In truth, these galloping monuments to the academic failures we see around us simply indicate *educational* non-results: the fact that a high-school diploma in the USA today has paper value only, and/or that a legitimate college degree may be presently obtained in the USA by demonstrating proficiency at chicken-plucking. Men and women of intense stupidities are even, these days, handed thousands of doctoral degrees a year. Our elementary and junior-high schools have functioned as Disneylands long enough! They should be places where kids learn the basic skills of straight thinking. Our high schools should be turned from catch-all time-killers into places where a selection process occurs: either *out*, because a student cannot, or will not, cut the mustard (and away with the stigma of the "dropout"; to retire gracefully at an early age from a way of life you cannot, or do not, want to pursue is no disgrace) and onwards to a terminal vocational track or to further university studies. Were we to attempt, at this point, to reconstruct our various types of universities and colleges, this book would be longer than *War and Peace*. Suffice it to say that, if every college's list of course offerings were reduced by fifty per cent, we would be on our way to solving these institutions' main current weaknesses. Again, we quote Whitehead: "Do not teach too many subjects . . . (and) what you teach, teach thoroughly." Are you listening, professor?

5. While it is permissible to talk about international communications and psychological warfare as "public relations,"

such locutions should be reserved for rhetorical purposes alone. In no manner or means, should our international persuasion policies, or the direction of their constituent programs, be placed in the hands of home-grown advertising experts, American public relations personnel, or men and women who have made their fortunes and reputations in the insular, domestic maelstrom of the American mass culture machine—radio and television in particular, and the newspaper, magazine and book publishing industries to a lesser degree. *All* of these people are primarily *business* men and women, trained and specialized as finely as thoroughbred race horses, to excel in, and deal with, their own peculiar, competitive and highly distinctive *American* areas of enterprise. Move one of them one jot from his hot-house, and he will either wilt or fall victim to the Peter Principle. At present, many such creatures are, unfortunately, involved *intimately* in numerous facets of America's international communication policies and practices. If any of them can point to records of achievement, they are probably accidental. As we hope this volume has illustrated, talents and skills that international affairs demand, particularly in the sensitive area of the mediation of ideas between cultures and countries, require special aptitudes, sensitivities and training— quite obviously nearly the exact *opposite* of those necessary to thrive in the business world of dream-merchandising, so distinctive of the American mass culture establishment. (That certain politicians may find legitimate domestic partisan uses for PR men, television types and feather merchants, we do not doubt.) The introduction also, in recent years, of public relations firms (not all of them American) to represent various insurgent groups and governments around the world, we find among the most discouraging (and possibly dangerous) curiosities of recent history. *This sort of tomfoolery must not happen at home!*

6. We have not based the following assumption on any semi-serious put-on like the *Report from Iron Mountain,* but we *do* believe that mankind *will* eventually find (or *have to*

find) viable alternatives to warfare. They will take the form of various sorts of *competition*—and we are not referring to weak-tea-like Olympic Games or international chess matches. From a psychological perspective, the best policy for *entente* between powerful nations is not necessarily one of tenuous, potentially explosive cooperation, but one of engaged competition that is not likely to explode into war. Cultural affairs programs, participation in World's Fairs, international exhibits, libraries, professional delegations of good-will merchants and so forth are harmless, and possibly benign, gambits ancillary to international policy. We grant their efficacy *in limited domains* —among educators, fashion designers and architects, for example—but these domains, are and will remain, *severely* limited. For this reason, we believe that many of our present intercultural programs should be continued, but on a considerably curtailed basis. A ball-park figure of about half the money presently spent upon them seems to us sufficient to let the Poles, Nigerians, South Americans, Cambodians and even the Red Chinese know that the USA cares (officially) about their cultural life, and that musicians and mathematicians, no matter what their nationality, all, in the old cliche, speak the same language. The money is not the main issue here; the philosophy and motives behind these intercultural missions and gambits are. Their main difficulty is that they are almost invariably considered "successes"—that is, foreigners involved in or exposed to them are almost always enthusiastic about them. But the measure of "success" usually ends exactly there. We have, it is assumed, somehow managed to exchange with a foreign nation a quantum of affection for a quantum of exported culture. And that is that. No other measure of accomplishment may be generally applied to them. The nation, accordingly, that holds us closest to its cross-cultural bosom one year may be rattling sabres at us the next because of political and military matters. The reasons have nothing whatever to do with the enormous success of, say, an international meeting of neurosurgeons that the USIA (or some other agency) had sponsored months before. Cooperation along culture levels of this kind is feeble glue. This is exactly what is wrong with it.

7. *Competition,* to refer to our assumption above, is stronger adhesive—by no means *absolutely* binding either, make no mistake. Competitive trade of any sort, as sentient Americans know, brings out *both* the best and worst in people. But the best is at least *there*. And successes and failures in this domain may be observed, measured and counted with some precision. Trade (opposed to "culture" as defined by international propagandists) is also something the man in the street —the average citizen—understands with greater ease and enthusiasm than airy bursts of communal affection that cross-cultural harpsichord enthusiasts show for each other. True, much of the emphasis in America's present participation (largely under the aegis of the Department of Commerce), in trade shows around the world *is* one way or another, competitive. By no means should appropriations for participation in these get-togethers be cut. In fact, they should be expanded. However, other types of harmless but vigorous competition exist, as well as trade. They concern such nuts-and-bolts matters as scientific and technological inventions and discoveries; and softer, cultural matters like the production of films (and honestly run international film *competitions*—not festivals), as well as developments in other, older arts (including literature and drama), methods and theories of physical and psychological therapy, advances in architecture and urban planning and so forth. A competitive *spirit* in international relationships in these areas is certainly cheaper and easier to achieve than an unctuous cooperative one. And competition is, again, what the common man understands best, especially if he is encouraged to become engaged in both his nation's wins and losses. (The so-called "space race" is a recent example.) Olympic games and other sorts of athletic contests and tournaments are satisfactory devices at times too, except for the artificial nature of their settings, manifold opportunities for cheating in the con-

struction of terms like "amateur" and "professional," and their eternal opportunities and invitations for self-serving publicity (as exploited, for instance, by Hitler in 1936 and the Black Septemberites in 1972), the ultimate objective of which is all too easy to achieve: headlines of the world's press.

8. Despite much mutual back-patting in our psychological fraternity and better Rand-style think factories, American intellectuals (and their hangers-on) have always been and are still pretty naïve in matters concerning psychological warfare. The still-simmering acupuncture scandal, Korean biological warfare myths, and Khrushchev's capers while visiting the USA in the nineteen-fifties are recent, egregious, examples of our losses on this front. We can cite plenty of others. Less important than our graduate seminars, conventions and numerous publications on "psych-war techniques" and "psych-war case histories"—most of them, to our eyes, academically interesting but infertile—is a pressing need to audit expertly the relatively sophisticated daily, ongoing uses of various subtle and effective means of mass persuasion by *other* nations in the international communications arena. To this end, either graduate university departments of psychology (or sub-bureaus of one or another government agency) should be encouraged (that is, *financed*), not merely to monitor foreign broadcasts and make fruitless quantitative "content analyses" of them (more nonproduction), but to study, in both their affective (or artistic) and in their cognitive modes, how, when and where those nations most skilled at international persuasion actually operate. We should investigate thoroughly, not only the field of anti-American propaganda, but how persuasion resonates and varies from culture to culture around the globe as it is directed, by those most skilled at it (the French and Chinese, for instance), *to* other nations, particularly to receptive ears and eyes in the "third world." Of course, the CIA, USIA, RFE and RL are all involved in various projects of this sort at present. Whatever they turn up with, most of their findings are used for limited

objectives and die on the vine. They are not called to the attention of skilled, cross-cultural social psychologists who, in the loneliness of their own mental think-tanks, may translate them into counterpersuasion when necessary, or sift them for cues for action by our information establishments and foreign policy experts. Research into the ongoing tonus of cross-cultural persuasion at depth—and conducted with *imagination*—is *sine qua non* for *all* of our information and propaganda policies and activities, both at present and in the future.

9. We think that the United States has outgrown its ancient, creaky British models of "Information Services" and "External Radio Services," upon which both our official and unofficial propaganda agencies have been patterned for more than a generation. The major drawback of the British format is its typically English inflexibility. Now that we have built, for instance, a full-blown information installation and library in the African nation of Niger—constructed at a time, long past, when we thought it was needed—how on earth do we get it *out* of Niger, now that this agency has outlived its usefulness? The answer is that we *cannot*, unless we are willing that our retreat be misinterpreted as a diplomatic insult by the citizens of Niger. So we are, in a manner of speaking, stuck there. Space does not permit (nor are we inclined) to spell out in detail exactly what alternatives to the British-type services we recommend. Common sense dictates any number of them. Of one thing we are certain: these services must be both extremely flexible and protean, accenting short-term commitments rather than solid, elaborate installations manned by numerous specialists and involving large capital expenses. We are not British, nor have we undertaken some kind of mystical moral obligation to establish American libraries and information services all around the world. Our private airlines and travel organizations may be competent to handle the latter task pretty well (and might well be provided with federal monies to do even a better job.) A rented movie theatre may accomplish things that

a library cannot—in areas of the world where literacy rates are low. And books may be distributed or loaned without creating libraries. Angles within angles present themselves to the imagination, once one disregards the inevitable necessity of following the old British models, even in the realm of international radio broadcasting. Must the VOA, for instance, pay obeisance to reporting forever "objective news"—news that our most significant listeners do not believe *is* truly objective anyway? (And, quite often, they are right.) If the BBC has an unshakable reputation for objectivity, honored by friend and foe around the world, must the United States forever trail behind Auntie? Radio Moscow does not incessantly claim to be objective: it merely insists that it tells the *truth*, quite a different matter, and understood full-well by those who, at times, enjoy listening to it, including the present authors. At any rate, we have offered just a few sample issues contained in a larger problem, one that may be solved, we think, more simply and economically than appears at first glance, if it is re-constructed from scratch.

10. Because information policy *will* be such an insistent constituent of foreign policy in the years to come, America's chief federal sachem of persuasion (whatever you want to call him) should have, to whatever degree possible and considering the prejudices of the man who is President at the time, parity with the Secretary of State in the *articulation* of foreign policy. His *input* to international strategy is as vital a matter to careful decision-making as that of the Defense Department or the Department of Commerce or State itself. Are we suggesting a Cabinet rank for the Director of the USIA? Possibly—or Cabinet rank for the particular Minister who might supersede the present Director in responsibility and function for foreign information policy matters. If and when the National Security Council ever regains its original functions and role as an *active* advisory group to the Chief Executive, our Minister of Information (or whatever) should be given an equal seat beside

diplomats, soldiers and businessmen. The notion of an expert in social psychology among the high councilors of government may sound odd to the conservative ear—even smack of science-fiction—but there is nothing new about the practice. It has simply never been the policy of "well-meaning" nations to advertise their reliance upon propaganda specialists in the construction of their world policies. Hitler made no bones about the presence of Dr. Goebbels at his elbow (*not* in his capacity as *Gauleiter* of Berlin) at his military and political strategy meetings. One of the Führer's failings was, rather, that he did *not*, frequently, give sufficient credence to Goebbels' input at these sessions but allowed himself to be swayed by more "practical" men (thank God!). Just as history demanded that, in the USA, the Cabinet ranks of Secretaries of Army and Navy be merged into the post of Secretary of Defense, it is now time that the *persuasive* arm of the Department of State be cleaved from the *diplomatic* part—at least on top, policy-making and enhancing levels. On lower levels and in the field, these differences matter little, as most American foreign service personnel know they must, and as we have indicated in this book.

11. We can already hear shrieks of agony that the following suggestion will produce (because arguments against it have already been formulated, Xeroxed, printed and rehearsed *ad nauseam*), but we believe that *all* American overseas radio and television propaganda and/or information agencies should be sheltered *under one roof and one chain of command.* Our recommendation is *not* based upon economics. It is probably cheaper to maintain the present posture of separation between the Voice of America, Radio Liberty and Radio Free Europe than to join them—but not *much* cheaper. We center our considerations upon two factors: (a) potentials for flexibility at the time that East Europe may (and probably will) become a less important target for American persuasion than other parts of the world. At such a time, many (but not all) former RL and RFE personnel and enormous transmission facilities will be

able to alter their sites and aim their resources in new directions with a minimum of disorientation, and (b) a better divi-
sion of labor may be achieved in handling different *types* of
radio (and, tomorrow, satellite television) services in different
ways, permitting experimentation with novel techniques in
broadcasting, moving towards better control, scrutiny and policy coordination than obtains within and between these agencies, taken together, at present. To those who cosset the apparent and formal "independence" of RL and RFE from the
"official" Voice of the United States, let us suggest that these
individuals are dealing in illusions, only viable (or arguable)
on American territory. In East Europe and the USSR, these illusions (and the technicalities and assumptions upon which
they are based) are not generally appreciated. Most overseas
listeners to our so-called "independent" radio services know
quite well that they are hearing a voice that is beholden to
America's foreign policy of the moment, and not to the ideals
of a bogus "home-town" local-type radio service. They are not
—nor have they ever been—as stupid as we have liked to
think they are. In any event, the present independence of RL
and RFE is also a nasty reminder of the deceptions practiced
upon the American people during the Cold War years, of the
least attractive aspects of the CIA's methods of accomplishing
its ends, and an unnecessarily rigid (in the eyes of many other
nations) preoccupation with both Soviet ideology and her hegemony over five countries. This excessive concentration connotes a neglect of other nations that might profit from short-
term, "Radio Free" style broadcasting arms. A combined
agency, budgeted at (presently) about $60 million per year,
might easily provide these services as needed—employing the
expertise of former RL and RFE staffers in political, psychological and technical matters. All American international
broadcasting is, and will continue to be, most effective, we
think, when it attempts to articulate a (literal) "Voice of America," rather than pseudo-voices of constituencies that neither
expatriate broadcasters nor master propagandists can speak for

with a genuine appreciation of their target audience's immediate interests. A true "Voice of America," on the other hand, may concentrate its guns upon the wide range of responsible (and some irresponsible) editorial, socio-political and cultural foment on our shores, highlighting the range, sense (and nonsense) of dissent from the established practice and thinking in America. Concerned with intellectual and political discourse (especially), its main objective should be to clarify both the blessings and headaches of America's attempts to achieve both free speech and libertarian democracy. This is the what *we* like best about the United States, and in our travels, these are the aspects of American life that are most—often grudgingly —admired around the world.[1]

12. An *old* idea now—one first proposed by the present writers a decade ago, to which many people listened, and about which nobody *did* anything, including us. President Nixon is no major epigramist, but what he said in 1968 about Americans talking too much and listening too little was wise advice. We have—and shall have in operation for many years to come—a fairly formidable *Voice* of America. Good and well. We need to speak in a clear voice in the babel of words that criss-cross the world's ether. What we do *not* possess is an *Ear of America*. We are, and have long been (as a culture), remarkably isolated from ideas, aspirations, values and much of the best thought that has been freely available to us from the rest of the world—except by means of a handful of foreign (mostly British) imported television shows, some highbrow films (usually French, Swedish or Italian) and a near inconsequential exchange of literature read by a miniscule part of our population. Much of this output has also been especially designed—or modified—for American "tastes," and is, accordingly, more redolent of what foreigners *think* American culture is like than indigenous to its country of origin. Americans do not care to listen to voices from the rest of the world. Hence, our immunity from much radio propaganda directed to us. But,

as lines of communications between nations increase, our
stand-pattism in this regard becomes more and more irksome
and dangerous. One of its causes is that agencies like the USIA
are, for commercial reasons (as well as a fear of government
controls upon domestic communications) enjoined from operation of *any sort* that may compete with powerful American
broadcasting, motion picture, newspaper or publishing interests. We think this protection of American industry, on the one
hand, and safeguard against the threat of officializing an *internal* American propaganda arm of *any* kind, on the other (the
United States Government Printing Office excepted), are reasonably sensible notions, by and large. In the first instance, private communications competing with federal counterparts
somehow runs against the American grain—granting that a
modification of this scheme works pretty well for British television services and in other countries. In the second place, as
executive, Presidential power increases in the United States,
one's trepidations about recommending what would, in effect,
be a communications complex at the right hand of our President (whoever he may be), with Congress scrambling for "equal
time," is not a happy thought. Congress has, however, *already*
chartered, and the President has funded, a Corporation for
Public Broadcasting that, simplifying many of its unbelievably
sticky problems, nobody, at the moment seems to know what
to do with, including the Carnegie Foundation, whose 1967
report triggered the whole present mess. Might not such an
"educational" or "public" non-profit television (and radio)
quasi-network devote a quarter to one-half of its broadcasting
time to opening up, for those Americans (a minority, of course)
who are interested in such matters, a service that provides daily
a healthy taste of what is happening on television screens, radio
studios and newspaper offices in major cities around the world,
including those as remote from us as Kiev and Cairo? Plenty *is*
happening, both politically and culturally, aside from re-runs of
old American television films, and much of it is inventive, enlightening and—God save the word—"entertaining." Problems

of translation of languages loom, but they always loom everywhere and every time cultures mix. With a will, they *can* be solved quickly and cheaply; so may problems of editing, time-delays, satellite feeds etc. In other words, we are appending to our ancient suggestion of an *Ear* that we establish an *Eye of America* as well. We do not envision these services as mere appendages to existing propaganda arms of the US government, but as a new *raison d'être* for the now-floundering *katzenjammer* that we once called "Educational" or "Public" radio and television. Facilitation of them would fall into the hands of the (potentially) financially viable Corporation for Public Broadcasting, that at the present writing, obviously has not found an identity as a parent network (and directive force) for the squirrel-cage in which America's two-hundred plus "Educational" television stations are today trying to live. As a pathway to salvation for Public Television, we think than an *Eye* and *Ear of America* beats *Sesame Street,* and its expensive imitations, hands down.

13. We think that we have already made our best case for construing international trade as a vital part of international communications and for monetary controls, even if the United States, (as one of the world's major trading powers) has to make concessions to this end by taking initiatives in enduring short-term losses. (The general nature of the monetary policies we have recently pursued by floating gold and dollar prices in the *long-term hope* of stabilizing relationships between world currencies indicates our willingness to take such risks, we think.) The antecedent to our previous and somewhat heretical notions of a World Trade body or agency equivalent to the United Nations, and the idea that it act (among other functions) as a global currency court-of-last resort, rests upon our conviction that international trade is, in many ways, the *most potent* form of international communication (and, hence, persuasion) yet developed by mankind. It is of equal (or greater) importance, we believe, with mass communications,

psychological warfare and the use of agitation or propaganda or both for political and ideological objectives. We rest our case upon the lessons of history and the role of cross-cultural trade in its most significant moments, pure and simple. The great age of world exploration in the fifteenth, sixteenth and seventeenth centuries was grounded, mainly, upon a search for trade routes, raw materials and, eventually, even markets. The rise of the great European Empires may have been energized by God's will and men's ambition, but they were implemented and paid for in the interests of commerce. To refer to Marco Polo as a Venetian export-import man, makes a facile quip, but Marco's fundamental, *economic* motivations opened up a cultural and ideational *rapprochement* with the distant Orient that shook both Byzantine and European life, in their day, to the cores. Although we disagree with those who see economics as *the* basic impetus for *all* international relationships, we are inclined to believe, in spite of frequent musings to the contrary, that most people most of the time will do almost anything for money—or for the things that money can buy, meaning almost anything. Orderly, competitive international trade, propelled by national, economic self-interests, it seems to us, is a necessary condition for (and constituent of) *any* type of foreign policy and intercultural exchange that will not, in short order, run downhill to the gulf of warfare. Modern tariff systems need not be destroyed for it, when and if protectionist devices are vital for the survival of national businesses. They need only to make *sense* in a court of highest recourse, devoted to fiscal matters, that has suitable powers to enforce its policies—enforcement, curiously, that does not require guns—merely cooperation. (Exclusion from participation in world trade may become the mightiest of weapons in tomorrow's world!) Neither does the game of currency speculation (again, within reason), industrial competition and/or international money-lending, international security trading and world banking (with its most arcane ceremonies and cabals) require abolition—just stringent controls. Ideas follow money, as every expert at mass persuasion knows. And sometimes (under certain conditions), the most potent ideological weapon a man may possess is a ham sandwich—or a freighter-load of tinned hams, or a check book to buy them.

14. Throughout this book we have taken great pains to denigrate traditional American appeals to "higher morality" when they are asked to serve as fundaments of either foreign policy or communications practice in the conduct of the United States' international affairs. We have written this way with considerable sadness. And every blunder and idiocy that we have placed at the feet of diplomats and statesmen impelled to accomplish the "right thing" (usually the wrong way) at the sole behest of his moral convictions of the moment has caused us a jot of agony in the telling. We *are*, however, firmly convinced that moral conviction is *not* a substitute for foreign policy. We shall not bore the reader by reprising our reasons. We do not, however, underestimate the necessary role morals play in *all* of men's concerns—whether they be personal, national, or international. And next to good manners we esteem morals as among mankind's (extremely) few most significant inventions—antecedant as they are to ethics, laws, political structures, all ever-mysterious psychological centrifuge that for millenia have kept villages, towns, cities and countries from flying into fragments no sooner than they were built. Morals, we believe, unquestionably take a *most* important place in foreign affairs and international discourse, in both personal and mass concerns. But, considering the parlous circumstantial political and military stand-off in which the world finds itself today, *morals alone* remain poor fundaments upon which to base public policy of *any* kind, particularly when one attempts to deal with people living in other cultures, whose moral orientations differ markedly from one's own. The past decade has illustrated in agonizing fashion how a nation—*our* nation—may travel part-way down the road that leads eventually to revolution, decay and extinction with its "higher morality" bravely

intact and flying in the breeze all the while. Foreign policy and international communications cannot, however, be carried on without objectives.

As our final suggestion, we think it fitting to offer, therefore, an *ideal* for both foreign policy and communication objectives, befitting the traditions and best achievements of the United States of America, that is both realistic and obtainable during the years left in the present century. We have suggested that the attention of our best researchers, philosophers, scientists and technologists be called to a number of matters. But none is more pressing than the formulation of a genuine "higher morality" in the matters of foreign relations and international communications policy that may serve our country as more than a temporizing instrument (or justification) for dramatic reactions to crises that seem momentarily expedient. Such a complex roster of "higher rights and wrongs," of course, requires more ingenious programs of implementations than merely "feeling the pulse of America" by half-baked public opinion polls, or than sifting from the rhetoric of our professional wise-men (difficult to sever from "wise-guys") a list of glittering platitudes. America's "higher morality" must deal with issues as difficult to face as those one may discover hidden in the rhetoric of Columbia Broadcasting's Frank Stanton, quoted in the previous chapter. They must take fair credence of the many legitimate discontents beating in the "third world," deal realistically with ideological confrontations as sharp as those that will occur when devout Maoists face clever Wall Street manipulators, accept both territorial arguments and the influence of man's religious convictions in the Near East, to say nothing of those of proponents and opponents of birth control at home and abroad, and deal directly, and sometimes cruelly, with hosts of other competing vectors that anthropologists so benignly call "cross-cultural conflicts." Can the United States—or its best minds, freed from the shackles of Ford-type Foundation servitude, Rand Corporation-style data worship, committee buck-passing, the pathetic quackery of "Presi-

dential Investigation Commissions" and think-tank stultifica-
tion—hew out for our nation the necessarily complex (but
viable) moral themes upon which her foreign policy and her
international communications posture may be rooted for
longer than a mere handful of years, without having to jig like
a fakir on hot coals—given twenty-seven (or so) years to accomplish the job? We think she can. We damn well *hope* she
can! Although we probably shall not live to indulge in its
ultimate benefit—a world where fear of the Armageddon is
no longer the undercurrent of every move we make in the international arena—the present writers, as Americans, will be
content to pass from this world to the next (the hot one or the
cold one, depending on factors having nothing to do with this
book) with infinite serenity. We hope, also, that nothing we
have written in the past pages will be construed by anyone—
today or tomorrow—in such a way as to impede this next phase
of progress in the maturing of the country we love. Let us, therefore, step, with both caution and hope, into the coming era of
the mute swan.

NOTES TO CHAPTER 10

[1] See the report of a Presidential study commission headed by Milton S. Eisenhower that was set up to review international broadcasting.
The report completed in February 1973 was released in May of the same
year. This 91-page report recommends continued Congressional financing
of Radio Free Europe and Radio Liberty for ten years," . . . since it is
unlikely that the free movement of information in the Soviet sphere will
become a reality any time soon." The report is titled: *The Right To Know*
(PR 37–8: R 11/44) and can be ordered from the United States Government Printing Office, Public Documents Department, Washington, D.C.,
20402.

Selected Bibliography

The following books have been selected mainly from those mentioned in this text and in the footnotes to each chapter in this volume. In general, the authors have limited this list to current publications that have been published within the past fifteen years. A few exceptions have been made for volumes, which in the authors' opinions, have had unusual significance and bearing upon the ideas, themes and recommendations developed in this this book.

Arendt, Hannah, *Crises of the Republic*. New York: Harcourt, Brace, Jovanovich, 1972.
———, *On Revolution*. New York: Viking Press Compass Edition, 1965.
———, *Eichman in Jerusalem: A Report on the Banality of Evil*. New York: Viking Press, 1963.

——, *The Human Condition.* New York: Doubleday, 1959.

Aronson, James, *The Press and the Cold War.* New York: Bobbs-Merril, 1970.

Bagdikian, Ben H., *The Information Machines, Their Impact on Men and the Media.* New York: Harper and Row, 1971.

Barber, Theodore X., *LSD, Yoga and Hypnosis.* Chicago: Aldine Publishing Co., 1970.

Beaton, Leonard, *The Reform of Power.* New York: Viking, 1973.

Berle, Adolph A., *Power.* New York: Harcourt, Brace and World, 1969.

Boelcke, Willi A. (ed.), *The Secret Conferences of Dr. Goebbels.* New York: E. P. Dutton and Co., 1970.

Boorstin, Daniel J. (ed.), *American Civilization: A Portrait from the Twentieth Century.* New York: McGraw-Hill, 1973.

——, *The Image.* New York: Harpers, 1961.

Bramstead, Ernst K., *Goebbels and National Socialist Propaganda 1925–1945.* Michigan: State University Press, 1965.

Brinton, Crane, *The Anatomy of Revolution* (revised and expanded edition). New York: Vintage Books, 1965.

Brown, J. A. C., *Techniques of Persuasion, From Propaganda to Brainwashing.* Baltimore: Penguin Books, 1963.

Cantril, Albert H. and Charles W. Roll, Jr., *Hopes and Fears of the American People.* New York: Universe Books, 1971.

Casty, Allan (ed.), *Mass Media and Mass Man.* New York: Holt, Rinehart and Winston, 1968.

Choukas, Michael, *Propaganda Comes of Age.* Washington, D.C.: Public Affairs Press, 1965.

Clews, John C., *Communist Propaganda Techniques.* New York: Frederick A. Praeger, 1964.

Crozier, Brian (ed.), *Annual of Power and Conflict 1971.* New York: National Strategy Information Center, 1972.

Daugherty, William E. and Morris Janowitz (eds.), *A Psychological Warfare Casebook.* Baltimore: Johns Hopkins Press, 1958.

Delgado, M. R. José, *Physical Control of the Mind.* New York: Harper and Row, 1969.

Ellul, Jacques, *The Technological Society.* New York: Alfred A. Knopf, 1965.

——, *Propaganda,* New York: Alfred A. Knopf, 1965.

Emery, Walter B., *National and International Systems of Broadcasting—Their History, Operation and Control.* East Lansing, Michigan: Michigan State University Press, 1969.

Ferkis, Victor E., *Technological Man*. New York: George Braziller, 1969.

Fischer, Heinz-Dietrich and John Calhoun Merrill (eds.), *International Communication* (part of the series: "Studies in Public Communications"). New York: Hastings House, 1970.

Fulbright, Senator J. William, *The Arrogance of Power*. New York: Vintage Books, 1966.

Gordon, George N., *Persuasion: The Theory and Practice of Manipulative Communication*. New York: Hastings House, 1971.

——, *The Languages of Communication*. New York: Hastings House, 1969.

——, Irving A. Falk and William Hodapp, *The Idea Invaders*. New York: Hastings House, 1963.

Grunberger, Richard, *The 12-Year Reich, A Social History of Nazi Germany: 1933–1945*. New York: Ballantine Books, 1971.

Hollander, Gayle Durham, *Soviet Political Indoctrination, Developments in Mass Media and Propaganda Since Stalin*. New York: Praeger, 1972.

Hovland, Carl, Irving Janis and Harold Kelley, *Communication and Persuasion*. New Haven, Connecticut: Yale University Press, 1961.

Hull, David Stewart, *Film In the Third Reich*. Berkeley and Los Angeles: University of California Press, 1969.

Jacobs, Lewis (ed.), *The Documentary Tradition*. New York: Hopkinson and Blake, 1971.

Johnson, Chalmers, *Revolutionary Change*. Boston: Little, Brown, 1966.

Joy, Admiral C. Turner, *How Communists Negotiate*. Santa Monica, California: Fidelis Publishers, 1970.

Joyce, Walter, *The Propaganda Gap*. New York: Harper and Row, 1963.

Kennan, George F., *Memoirs 1925–1950*, (2 vols.) New York: Atlantic—Little Brown, 1967.

——, *American Diplomacy*. New York: The New American Library, 1952.

Kiesler, Charles A., Barry E. Collins and Norman Miller, *Attitude Change*. New York: John Wiley, 1969.

Laswell, Harold, *Propaganda and Promotional Activities*. Chicago: University of Chicago Press, 1969.

Lerbinger, Otto, *Designs for Persuasive Communication*. Englewood Cliffs, New Jersey: Prentice-Hall, 1972.

Lévi-Strauss, Claude, *Structural Anthropology*. New York: Doubleday, 1967.

London, Perry, *Behavior Control*. New York: Harpers, 1969.

Maddox, John, *The Doomsday Syndrome: An Attack on Pessimism*. New York: McGraw-Hill, 1972.

MacCann, Richard Dyer, *The People's Films: A Political History of U.S. Government Motion Pictures*. New York: Hastings House, 1973.

Mead, Margaret, *Culture and Commitment*. New York: Doubleday, 1970.

Merrill, John C. and Ralph L. Lowenstein, *Media, Messages and Men*. New York: David McKay, 1971.

Merrit, Richard L. (ed.), *Communication in International Politics*. Urbana, Illinois: University of Illinois Press, 1972.

Merton, Robert, *Social Theory and Social Structure*, (enlarged edition). New York: Free Press, 1968.

Michael, Franz and Gaston J. Sigur, *The Asian Alliance: Japan and United States Policy*. New York: National Strategy Information Center, 1972.

Mortensen, C. David (ed.), *Basic Readings in Communication Theory*. New York: Harper and Row, 1973.

O'Neill, William, *Coming Apart*. Chicago: Quadrangle Books, 1971.

Ortega y Gasset, José, *The Revolt of the Masses*. New York: Norton, 1932.

Packard, Vance, *The Hidden Persuaders*. New York: David McKay, 1957.

Passell, Peter and Leonard Ross, *The Retreat From Riches: Affluence and Its Enemies*, forward by Paul A. Samuelson. New York: Viking, 1973.

Proffer, Carl R. (ed. and trans.), *Soviet Criticism of American Literature In the Sixties—An Anthology*. Ann Arbor, Michigan: Ardis, 1973.

Qualter, Terence H., *Propaganda and Psychological Warfare*. New York: Random House, 1962.

Rossiter, Clinton, and Jamers Lare (eds.), *The Essential Lippman*. New York: Random House, 1963.

Rostow, Eugene V., *Peace in the Balance: The Future of U.S. Foreign Policy*. New York: Simon and Schuster, 1973.

Rostow, Walter W., *The Diffusion of Power*. New York: Macmillan, 1973.

Sargant, William, *Battle for the Mind.* New York: Doubleday, 1957.

Schramm, Wilbur and Donald F. Roberts (eds.), *The Process and Effects of Mass Communication,* (revised edition). Urbana, Illinois: University of Illinois Press, 1971.

Shibutani, Tamotsu, *Improvised News: A Study of Rumor.* New York: Bobbs-Merril, 1966.

Smith, M. Brewster, *Social Psychology and Human Values.* Chicago: Aldine, 1969.

——, Jerome S. Bruner and Robert W. White, *Opinions and Personality.* New York: John Wiley, 1956.

Steibel, Gerald L., *How Can We Negotiate With The Communists?* New York: National Strategy Information Center, 1972.

Tarde, Gabriel, *On Communication and Social Influence.* Chicago: University of Chicago Press, 1969. (Originally published in various journals between the years 1890 through 1904.)

Vetter, Harold, *Language, Behavior and Psychopathology.* Chicago: Rand McNally, 1970.

Wells, Alan, *Picture-Tube Imperialism, The Impact of US Television on Latin America.* Maryknoll, New York: Orbis Books, 1972.

White, David Manning and Richard Averson, *The Celluloid Weapon.* Boston: Beacon Press, 1972.

Wiener, Norbert, *Cybernetics.* Cambridge: The MIT Press, 1965.

Yearly Statistical Yearbook of U.N.E.S.C.O. New York: United Nations Educational Scientific and Cultural Organization. (published annually).

Yost, Charles, *The Conduct and Misconduct of Foreign Affairs.* New York: Random House, 1973.

Zimbardo, Philip and Ebbe B. Ebbesen, *Influencing Attitudes and Changing Behavior.* Reading, Mass.: Addison-Wesley, 1969.

Index

献给

毛沢东阁下
及
中华人民共和国人民

尼克松总统
及
美利坚共和国人民赠

For the story of the Mute Swans of Peace see pages 45—46 and 50.